THE

GOSPEL OF
LUKE AND
ACTS OF THE
APOSTLES

INTERPRETING
I·B·T
BIBLICAL TEXTS

THE
GOSPEL OF
LUKE AND
ACTS OF THE
APOSTLES

F. Scott Spencer

ABINGDON PRESS
Nashville

THE GOSPEL OF LUKE AND ACTS

Library of Congress Cataloging-in-Publication Data

Spencer, F. Scott (Franklin Scott)
  The gospel of Luke and Acts of the apostles/ F. Scott Spencer.
    p. cm.
  Includes bibliographical references.
  ISBN 978-0-687-00850-6 (binding: pbk., adhesive perfect : alk. paper)
  1. Bible. N.T. Luke—Criticism, interpretation, etc. 2. Bible. N.T. Acts—Criticism, interpretation, etc. I. Title.

  BS2589.S64 2007
  226.4'077—dc22

                                                    2007021917

08 09 10 11 12 13 14 15 16 17—10 9 8 7 6 5 4 3 2 1
MANUFACTURED IN THE UNITED STATES OF AMERICA

To

J. M., L. M., and M. L.

*Pollē chara kai eirēnē hymin
nyn kai pantote*

CONTENTS

PART TWO
IMPLEMENTATION: PROCEEDING TO INTERPRET THE LUKAN NARRATIVES

CHAPTER 3
PREPARING GOD'S MISSION IN JUDEA AND GALILEE (LUKE 1:1–4:13)

CHAPTER 4
ESTABLISHING GOD'S MISSION IN GALILEE AND SURROUNDING AREAS (LUKE 4:14–9:50)

CHAPTER 5
EXPANDING AND INTERPRETING GOD'S MISSION ON THE WAY TO JERUSALEM (LUKE 9:51–19:44)

CHAPTER 6

DEFENDING GOD'S MISSION IN JERUSALEM AND JUDEA (LUKE 19:45–24:53)

CHAPTER 7

HIGHLIGHTING GOD'S MISSION FROM JERUSALEM TO THE "ENDS OF THE EARTH" (ACTS 1–28)

ACKNOWLEDGMENTS

After writing a good bit about the book of Acts over the years, I have enjoyed this opportunity to reflect more widely on Luke's literary and theological project, including his initial Gospel volume. Special thanks goes to Charlie Cousar for recruiting me for this work and for providing gracious support and expert advice throughout its production. The success of the Interpreting Biblical Texts (IBT) series owes in large measure to his superb editorial oversight.

Working with the staff of Abingdon Press has been equally rewarding. Kathy Armistead has been the primary point person and a model of professionalism and encouragement (not least with deadlines!) in steering this study to completion. I have also enjoyed getting to know other members of Abingdon's crack academic team a little better, especially Marianne Blickenstaff, John Kutsko, and Bob Ratcliff.

Thanks, too, to the wonderful community at the Baptist Theological Seminary at Richmond (BTSR), where I am privileged to serve with engaging and affirming staff, students, and faculty colleagues. I'm also grateful for the developing relationship with our partner schools in the Richmond Theological Consortium (RTC), Union-PSCE and STVU. I look forward to strengthening our academic and ecumenical ties.

Finally, the customary tip of the hat to one's family is much more than that in my case. I simply couldn't have done this (or much of anything else) without my beloved wife and two daughters. Abundant joy and peace to you "girls," now and always.

FOREWORD

Biblical texts create worlds of meaning, and invite readers to enter them. When readers enter such textual worlds, which are often strange and complex, they are confronted with theological claims. With this in mind, the purpose of this series is to help serious readers in their experience of reading and interpreting, to provide guides for their journeys into textual worlds. The controlling perspective is expressed in the operative word of the title—*interpreting*. The primary focus of the series is not so much on the world *behind* the texts or out of which the texts have arisen (though these worlds are not irrelevant) as on the world *created by* the texts in their engagement with readers.

Each volume addresses two questions. First, what are the critical issues of interpretation that have emerged in the recent history of scholarship and to which serious readers of the texts need to be sensitive? Some of the concerns of scholars are interesting and significant but, frankly, peripheral to the interpretative task. Others are more central. How they are addressed influences decisions readers make in the process of interpretation. Thus the authors call attention to these basic issues and indicate their significance for interpretation.

Second, in struggling with particular passages or sections of material, how can readers be kept aware of the larger world created by the text as a whole? How can they both see the forest and examine the individual trees? How can students encountering the story of David and Bathsheba in 2 Samuel 11 read it in light of its context in the larger story, the Deuteronomistic History that includes the books of Deuteronomy through 2 Kings? How can readers of Galatians fit what they learn into the theological coherence and polarities of the larger perspective drawn from all the letters of Paul? Thus each volume provides an overview of the literature as a whole.

The aim of the series is clearly pedagogical. The authors offer their own understanding of the issues and texts, but are more concerned about guiding the reader than engaging in debates with other scholars. The series is meant to serve as a resource, alongside other resources such as commentaries and specialized studies, to aid students in the exciting and often risky venture of interpreting biblical texts.

Gene M. Tucker
General Editor, *Old Testament*

Charles B. Cousar
General Editor, *New Testament*

PART ONE

ORIENTATION:

PREPARING TO INTERPRET THE LUKAN NARRATIVES

PREFACE

From the outset, intrepid interpreters of Luke and Acts confront a couple of thorny challenges. First is their sheer size. Individually, the two roughly equivalent narratives constitute the largest works in the New Testament, and together, they represent about a quarter of the canon and the largest corpus by a single author (dubbed "Luke" by convention).[1] Frankly, these two volumes are a lot to handle. Despite my best intentions, I have never satisfactorily covered all of Luke and Acts in full-semester courses devoted to them.

To complicate matters further, the New Testament's order splices the fourth Gospel between Luke and Acts. Such an arrangement has its merits: Luke's story of Jesus' career fits nicely with Matthew's, Mark's, and John's Gospels; and Acts' account of the apostles' witness to Jesus serves as an apt introduction to Paul, James, Peter, and John's letters. But obscured in this demarcation between "Gospel" and "Apostle" are linguistic and thematic connections between *Luke's* "Gospel" and the *Acts* of the "Apostles." Of course, nothing keeps us from jumping over the fourth Gospel, going directly from Luke 24:53 to Acts 1:1, like one might flip from the lectionary's "Gospel" reading to the "Epistle" text. But literary gaps can be frustrating to negotiate (we prefer one-stop reading), and canonical gaps can be forbidding (no trespassing sacred territory). We might be more inclined to examine Luke's two-volume work if it had come to us as 1-2 Theophilus, named after the addressee in both volumes, similar to 1-2 Corinthians or 1-2 Timothy.[2]

These obstacles, although far from insurmountable, highlight the importance of some orientation to the landscape of Luke and Acts, including borders and bridges between these two works, before traversing this vast territory. A basic interpretive guide to these writings, as they have survived through history, approaches

17

them as first and foremost *religious literature* or *scriptural narratives*. Hence, the ensuing introductory chapters explore Luke and Acts' (1) *literary framework* (how these books were composed in their final form) and (2) *theological focus* (why these books were written as narratives unfolding God's purposes for God's people and the world).[3] Exploring these "background" topics requires a number of strategic probes into Luke and Acts, but such preparatory work in no way substitutes for sustained immersion in their complex narratives; hopefully it stokes the desire for close reading and analysis.

CHAPTER 1

LITERARY FRAMEWORK:

How Were Luke and Acts Composed?

Newsflash—Luke and Acts are works of literature! Seems more like a flicker than a flash, but being reminded that Luke's contributions to early Christianity come to us as *literature* establishes key parameters for interpretation. Fundamentally, we read, hear, and process Luke and Acts as *literary* works, similar in some, but not all, respects to how we "read" other art forms. Although Luke's scenes have inspired artistic masterpieces,[1] Luke and Acts are not paintings. Although portions of Luke's birth narrative, like the *Magnificat* (Luke 1:46-55), resemble the psalter and have inspired Christian hymns, Luke and Acts are not musical scores. Although they may borrow popular conventions from Greek or Roman epic poets (Homer; Virgil) or comic playwrights (Terence; Plautus), Luke and Acts are neither poetic sagas nor dramatic comedies.[2] And although they feature numerous cities, regions, and other territories organized around various "journey" schemes, Luke and Acts are neither geographical textbooks (Strabo), nor cartographical sketches (Rand McNally), nor travel guides (Fodor's).

So we need to appreciate Luke and Acts as literature. But accepting that desideratum raises a host of attendant questions about Luke's literary project: How did Luke go about writing it? What structural and stylistic elements does it display? What kind of literature is it? Starting with a broad answer to this last question and stating the obvious (but not always the most observed by scholars),

Luke and Acts are principally works of *religious* or *sacred* literature. Luke probably had no clue his writings would wind up in a canon of Christian Scripture, alongside the Old Testament; but the fact that they did, and have been so preserved in the Church for centuries, demonstrates their dominant religious tenor. I will make much of this religious (theological) dimension throughout this study.

But the ultimate fate of Luke and Acts as Holy Writ does not demand that these books were originally penned within a hermetically sealed chamber in an esoteric dialect of "Holy Ghost Greek," as some older scholars quaintly opined. Luke's Greek is quite good, but not that good. Like all New Testament books, Luke and Acts reflect the common (*koinē*) Greek vernacular of the first century, even as they betray their own peculiar styles and patterns. Accounting, as we may, for a measure of spiritual guidance and prayerful insight (Luke makes much of both the Spirit and prayer), Luke's writings still emerged, like any other publications, out of creative human processes of gathering and forging thoughts and materials into a coherent literary composition. Understanding something of this scribal procedure promises to enhance our understanding of the final product.

Fortunately, we find a few hints of Luke's literary method in the prefaces to each volume.

Since many have undertaken to set down an orderly account of the events that have been fulfilled among us, just as they were handed on to us by those who from the beginning were eyewitnesses and servants of the word, I too decided, after investigating everything carefully from the very first, to write an orderly account for you, most excellent Theophilus, so that you may know the truth concerning the things about which you have been instructed. (Luke 1:1-4)

In the first book, Theophilus, I wrote about all that Jesus did and taught from the beginning until the day when he was taken up to heaven, after giving instructions through the Holy Spirit to the apostles whom he had chosen. (Acts 1:1-2)

These personal disclosures—the only "I" references from the Lukan author or narrator—introduce four issues concerning the composition of Luke and Acts:

- **Two Volumes.** Acts' reference to "the first book" (or "first word," *prōton logon*) addressed to Theophilus about Jesus' ministry points back to Luke's Gospel as the preceding work of a two-volume "set." But how is this "set" configured? Should we view Acts as a seamless continuation of Luke's story; a supplemental appendix, update, or revision of Luke; or a different book altogether?
- **Many Sources.** As any good writer in antiquity, Luke depends upon "many" (*polloi*) preceding documents and eyewitness reports. Although Luke "decided" (lit. "it seemed good to me") to offer his own account, he began by "investigating everything carefully" that others had reported and written. Accurate accounts of the past must be grounded in rigorous research. So what were Luke's primary sources, and how did he use them? Unfortunately, we have no footnotes or bibliography to check. We have similar, "Synoptic" Gospels, Mark and Matthew, that Luke might have examined for his first volume and possible parallels from Paul's letters informing Acts. But theories of literary dependence must be "carefully" sifted on a case-by-case basis.
- **Broad Patterns.** The NRSV designates both his predecessors' projects and Luke's own as "orderly," rendering two different Greek terms. The first, a verbal form of *anatassomai* used only here in the New Testament, generally means, "to organize a series of items," and, more specifically in Luke, "to organize (a report), to arrange, to compile, to put together."[3] The second term, the adverb *kathexēs* used five times in the New Testament (all in Luke and Acts), denotes "successively" or "sequentially" in relation to time (chronology, Acts 3:24), place (itinerary, Luke 8:1; Acts 18:23), or plot (narrating "step by step," Acts 11:4). Following Luke's cue, we seek to discover the main "orderly" sequences and patterns structuring his writings.
- **Various Genres.** Literary works, ancient and modern, typically appropriate one or more established generic templates, not as straitjackets stifling new developments, but as starter kits stimulating imaginative thought. The closest we come to a genre designation in the Lukan prefaces is *diēgēsis*, denoting "account" or, better, "narrated account"

or just "narrative" (Luke 1:1). As a literary *narrative*, Luke's Gospel is distinguished from other written discourses, such as a public inscription, personal diary, business letter, philosophical essay, technical manual, or medical journal. But the wide "narrative" classification still begs several questions. What specific type(s) of narrative(s) did Luke produce? Do Luke and Acts share the same *diēgēsis* genre or subgenre (the term is not repeated in the Acts preface)? What particular narrative forms or models do they follow? Has Luke composed, singly or as a set, a succession narrative, biographical narrative, historical narrative, fictional narrative, or a mixture of these (and other) genres?

TWO VOLUMES

In 1927 Henry Cadbury launched a new nomenclature for Luke's two-volume work: Luke-Acts. Acknowledging that the hyphenated label was "not typographically beautiful or altogether congenial to the English language," Cadbury suggested that the sacrifice in English style was worth gaining a convenient handle highlighting the "historic unity" of the two books.[4] However, in literature, no less than religion or politics, unity is a multifaceted ideal difficult, if not impossible, to achieve. Without selling our souls to a full-blown postmodern or deconstructive agenda, we can still acknowledge that no text exhibits perfect coherence; that awkward gaps, loose threads, and nagging inconsistencies complicate any narrative; and that readers' perceptions of unity and tension vary greatly across time, culture, and ideology.[5]

Concerning the unity of Luke and Acts in particular, apart from likely disjunctions and digressions within each book (counterpointing order and design), the fact that both volumes never circulated together or appeared adjacently in any canonical list, as far as we know, should give us pause. If Theophilus shelved the original Luke and Acts side by side in his library, he may have been the only one to keep them together! They were likely never copied and sold as a double-set (with or without a box). Moreover, as Mikeal Parsons and Richard Pervo have observed, Luke's Gospel nicely wraps up Jesus' career with his ascension and discloses no plans for a sequel, as we find at the end of first installments of two-volume treatises by Josephus (*Against Apion*) and

Philo (*Life of Moses*).[6] Finally, even a cursory comparison of the lengthy "travel narratives" in Luke 9–19 and Acts 13–28—the former, a loosely connected, vaguely situated string of episodes; the latter, a tightly linked, precisely mapped series of expeditions—demonstrates that Luke and Acts vary at points in their modes of presentation. More than grammatical infelicity strains the Cadbury hyphen.

But despite disruptions in the stylistic, canonical, and generic unity of Luke and Acts, the two works still enjoy authorial (though anonymous) unity and a close (not cloned) association in other areas: though free to shift styles between writings, Luke shows a preference for select vocabulary ("repentance," "salvation"), characters (Jesus, Peter), sources (Old Testament), and patterns (male/female pairings) in both volumes; though not directly paired in the New Testament, Luke and Acts still made the same scriptural canon (a rather exclusive club), separated by only one book (John); and although not identical generic twins, they bear more than a passing family resemblance as extended "narratives." Such observations (discussed further below) suggest that we may profitably interpret Luke and Acts as a "double work" by appreciating intertextual links between the two narratives while respecting the integrity and individuality of each. We may expect to find numerous unifying elements, even as we take care not to force them.

Although Luke may not have anticipated a companion volume to his Gospel, he clearly built upon it when composing Acts. Casting more than a perfunctory glance back to his "first book" for Theophilus, Luke picks up several strands from that work for further development in Acts 1. First, he succinctly summarizes the Gospel's contents: "I wrote about all that Jesus did and taught from the beginning until the day when he was taken up to heaven" (Acts 1:1b-2a). Excepting the birth narratives in Luke 1–2, this statement epitomizes Jesus' entire career from the beginning of his public ministry—in deed and word—to his heavenly ascension. (Chris-Gant--Youth Ministrytian belief in Jesus' ascension [cf. Apostles' Creed] derives almost exclusively from Luke and Acts.) The NRSV translation, "all that Jesus did and taught from the beginning," may also be rendered, "all that Jesus *began* (*ērxato*) to do and teach." This reading may offer a subtle clue to the contents of Acts: as the Gospel (Volume 1) tracked what Jesus *began* to accomplish on

(Volume 2) will track what the living Jesus *continues* to do and teach from his heavenly post. Indeed, Acts repeatedly shows Jesus' continued involvement in earthly affairs, albeit in Spirit and epiphany rather than body and ministry (2:33; 7:55-56; 9:3-6; 16:17; 18:9-10; 22:17-21). The ascended Lord is no absentee Lord. Comparing Jesus' words and works in Luke's two volumes opens up fruitful avenues for interpretation.

Second, Acts 1 flashes back to Jesus' post-resurrection appearances in Luke: "After his suffering (*paschō*) he presented himself alive to them by many convincing proofs, appearing to them during forty days and speaking about the kingdom of God" (Acts 1:3). Luke's last chapter features two "convincing" (eventually) appearances of the risen Jesus to his followers (24:13-32, 36-53; cf. v. 34), in which he affirms the necessity of his "suffering" or "passion" (*paschō*) in God's plan (24:26, 46). Acts adds extra temporal (forty days) and topical (kingdom of God) items to the Gospel appearance scenes, but such accoutrements coordinate well with other material in Luke: a forty-day period of instruction recalls Jesus' forty-day ordeal of "temptation" (Luke 4:2), and announcing the kingdom of God follows the prime directive of Jesus' mission: "I must (*dei*) proclaim the good news of the kingdom of God . . . for I was sent for this purpose" (4:43).

Third, the risen Lord's parting mandate in Acts 1:4-5, 8 that his apostles wait to "be baptized with the Holy Spirit" and empowered for witness echoes both the commencement and denouement of Jesus' mission in Luke.

	Luke	**Acts**
Resonating with John's Baptism	John answered . . . "I baptize you with water; but one who is more powerful than I is coming. . . . He will baptize you with the Holy Spirit and fire" (3:16).	"This," [Jesus] said, "is what you have heard from me; for John baptized with water, but you will be baptized with the Holy Spirit not many days from now" (1:4b-5).

Waiting in Jerusalem	"And see, I am sending upon you what my Father promised; so stay here in the city [Jerusalem] until you have been clothed with power from on high" (24:49).	While staying with them, he ordered them not to leave Jerusalem, but to wait there for the promise of the Father (1:4a).
Witnessing to Nations	"Repentance and forgiveness of sins is to be proclaimed in his name to all nations, beginning from Jerusalem. You are witnesses of these things" (24:47-48).	"But you will receive power when the Holy Spirit has come upon you; and you will be my witnesses in Jerusalem, in all Judea and Samaria, and to the ends of the earth" (1:8).

Acts' close dependence on Luke's Gospel in characterizing the Spirit's activity is hard to miss. Tracking the constants and developments of the Spirit's role across Luke and Acts opens ups further lines of interpretation.[7]

Fourth, in addition to maintaining the Gospel's starring roles for Jesus and the Spirit, Acts also brings back the apostles for a second run with fresh opportunities. Not merely recapping Luke's final episode, Acts expands upon the apostles' reaction to Jesus' ascension. Before returning to Jerusalem, they are confronted by two white-clad messengers: "Men of Galilee, why do you stand looking up toward heaven? This Jesus, who has been taken up from you into heaven, will come in the same way as you saw him go into heaven" (Acts 1: 11). The apostles seem frozen in their tracks, fixated with wide eyes and dropped jaws on their heaven-bound Lord. But just before departing, Jesus had commissioned them to be his witnesses across the earth (1:8). No time to stand still gawking up at heaven. Jesus' apostles have an urgent assignment to fulfill before he returns. How will they respond to this challenge? Stay tuned for more exciting adventures of "The Acts of the Apostles."

Lest we have forgotten, Luke reprises the names of the apostolic cast in Acts 1:13. They match the original list in Luke 6:13, except for one abbreviated name, a few changes in order, and the conspicuous absence of Judas Iscariot.

Luke 6:13	Acts 1:13
1. Simon called Peter	1. Peter
2. Andrew	2. John
3. James	3. James
4. John	4. Andrew
5. Philip	5. Philip
6. Bartholomew	6. Thomas
7. Matthew	7. Bartholomew
8. Thomas	8. Matthew
9. James son of Alphaeus	9. James son of Alphaeus
10. Simon the Zealot	10. Simon the Zealot
11. Judas son of James	11. Judas son of James
12. Judas Iscariot	12. ———————

Eliminating Judas Iscariot is scarcely surprising, given his original entry in the last position with the ominous qualifier, "who became a traitor" (Luke 6:16). He played out his villainous part at the end of Luke, betraying Jesus to the authorities (22:3-6, 47-53); and to complete the tragic story, Acts soon reports Judas's gruesome death and prompt replacement among the Twelve (1:15-26). Excepting Judas, the other apostles remain in the same clusters of four. The same figures head the subgroups (#1—Peter; #5—Philip; #9—James the son of Alphaeus), with some reshuffling underneath. In the top group John swaps places with Andrew. As it happens, the apostles from Andrew on down make no further appearances in Acts (they are effectively written out of the story).[8] Peter and John pair off for a while as early church leaders (Acts 3:1–4:22; 8:14-17), and James (John's brother) gets a brief, but noble, obituary as a martyr (12:1-2).

But the main apostolic spotlight in Acts trains on Peter. From the start, he "stands up" and superintends the first order of business— filling Judas' vacant post (1:15-22). Peter's leadership in this matter reflects as much irony as authority. The threefold *denier* of the arrested Jesus overseeing the replacement of the initial *betrayer*: what is wrong with this picture? Nothing, actually, from the perspective of Luke's Gospel, which set the stage not only for Peter's crushing denials of Jesus but also for his restoration of faith and strength:

> "Simon, Simon [Peter], listen! Satan has demanded to sift all of you like wheat, but I have prayed for you that your own faith may not fail; and you, when once you have turned back, strengthen your brothers." And he said to him, "Lord, I am ready to go with you to prison and to death!" Jesus said, "I tell you, Peter, the cock will not crow this day, until you have denied three times that you know me." (Luke 22:31-34)

Acts picks up the Gospel's cue and charts the remarkable recovery— and at times, regression—of the volatile Peter after Jesus' ascension. Tracking Peter's progress presents another banner case of "orderly" Lukan interpretation, following the story's plot and characters "step by step" (cf. Acts 11:4). A certain narrative unity between the two volumes coheres around common characters, but not in flat, static dimensions. Protagonists like Jesus, the Spirit, and Peter grow, develop, change, and "build character"[9] in Luke's narratives, and not always in predictable and positive (Peter) directions. The Peter of Acts both is and is not the Peter of Luke. Alertly navigating the story's dynamic ebbs and flows, breakers and detours, marks a basic, indispensable method for interpreting Luke's double work.

MANY SOURCES

Luke's methods and aims would have been more transparent if he had provided annotations and bibliography, as research projects require today. But such was not the literary practice in antiquity. Ancient writers freely borrowed from predecessors without attribution. This is not to say they practiced wholesale plagiarism or forgery.[10] Authors were expected to alter and amalgamate others' works into their own; then as now, literary artists (composers) were distinguished from technical copyists (scribes). The best composers, like Luke, deftly wove both traditional sources and original ideas into their own fresh tapestry. Still, critics persist in attempting to disentangle source from product, tradition from redaction, knowing full well the dubiousness of the enterprise, not only in terms of identifying uncited sources but also of discerning how and why a writer adapted other materials (authorial "tendencies" and "intention"). But the critical payoff of engaging an *ancient* text, as best we can, in its *ancient* context, in comparison with other *ancient* texts, makes the probe of sources worth the risk of uncertainty.

Fortunately, in Luke's case we are not completely in the dark. One source is explicit and pervasive throughout Luke's narratives: the scriptures of ancient Israel in Greek (Septuagint, or LXX). Luke ranges far and wide across the main sections of the Old Testament, following Jesus' pronouncement at the end of the Gospel: "These are my words that I spoke to you while I was still with you—that *everything* written about me in *the law of Moses, the prophets, and the psalms* must be fulfilled" (Luke 24:44, emphasis added). As Jesus concludes his ministry on a scriptural note, so he begins with a personal appropriation of an Isaiah lection: "Today this scripture has been fulfilled in your hearing" (Luke 4:16-21; Isa 58:6; 61:1-2); likewise Peter kick-starts the early church's mission in Acts with proof-texts from the prophet Joel and Davidic psalms (Acts 2:16-21, 25-28, 31, 34-35; Joel 2:28-32; Ps 16:8-11; 110:1), and Paul wraps it up with another Isaiah citation (Acts 28:25-27; Isa 6:9-10). Such evidence sparks Jacob Jervell's provocative assessment:

> [Luke] actually intends to omit nothing that Scripture offers. Everything in the Old Testament is Scripture, everything is important, everything is binding. Luke is the fundamentalist within the New

28

Testament. There is in Luke-Acts no criticism whatsoever of Scripture, such as we find in Matthew and Mark, not to mention Paul.[11]

Although Jervell might overplay the "fundamentalist" angle (Luke makes some strategic changes when quoting the Old Testament and also exploits biblical narratives in highly allusive as well as verbatim fashion), he correctly stresses the broad and thick scriptural foundation of Luke's writings. Interpreting Luke and Acts with a pocket New Testament will not do. To mine the riches of Luke's work, readers must regularly sound its vast Old Testament depths.

Given Luke's claim that he "carefully investigated" many accounts of events recently "fulfilled among us," we should also probe contemporary Gospel materials. Luke does not name these sources, but the Gospels of Matthew and Mark stand ready to hand for comparative investigation (John's Gospel provides some interesting character connections—Samaritans, Martha, Mary, and maybe Lazarus—but overall blazes its own narrative trail). But the situation is much sketchier with Acts. Its preface does not acknowledge literary predecessors (except for Luke's "first volume"), and it lacks true "synoptic" partners. The canonical Acts predates apocryphal "Acts" from the late second century and beyond, some of which build on Luke's work and embellish it with more "romantic" and "novelistic" elements.[12] However, beyond continued Old Testament usage, Luke may also have appropriated available apostolic speeches, Pauline traditions, and popular epics in composing Acts.

Mark

The dominant theory of Gospel origins posits "Markan priority" and Matthew and Luke's literary dependence on Mark's work. The main evidence derives from close comparative analysis of synoptic (parallel) stories. The following juxtaposition of "widow's mite" accounts, appearing only in Mark and Luke, illustrates why many scholars hypothesize Luke's use of Mark and how they assess Luke's editorial tendencies.[13] Single underlines represent identical language in both Greek and English (NRSV); double underlines indicate the same English translations of different Greek terms; italics emphasize distinct word choices in both Greek and English; and bold print signals redundancy of words or ideas.

29

Mark 12:41-44	Luke 21:1-4
[41]He sat down opposite the **treasury**, and watched the crowd putting *money* into the **treasury**. Many rich people put in large sums. [42]A poor widow came and put in two small copper coins, **which are worth a penny**. [43]Then he called his disciples and said to them, "<u>Truly I tell you, this poor widow has put in more than all</u> those who are contributing to the **treasury**. [44]<u>For all of them have contributed out of their abundance</u>; but she out of her poverty has put in **everything** she had, **all** she had to live on."	[1]He looked up and saw rich people putting their *gifts* into the **treasury**; [2]he also saw a <u>poor</u> widow put in two small copper coins. [3]He said, "<u>Truly I tell you, this poor widow has put in more than all</u> of them; [4]<u>for all of them have contributed out of their abundance</u>, but she out of her poverty has put in **all** she had to live on."

- The close similarities (verbatim in some cases) between accounts suggest literary dependence; the greater conciseness of Luke's text commends it as the secondary, edited (redacted) version.
- For better Greek style, Luke tends to eliminate Mark's cumbersome and simplistic repetitions ("treasury"; two coppers = penny; "everything/all"). Although the NRSV repeats "poor widow" in Luke 21:2-3 (as in Mark 12:42-43), Luke uses two distinct terms denoting her poverty (*penichran* ["penurious," 21:2]; *ptōchē* ["poor," 21:3]) where Mark keeps the same one (*ptōchē*).
- Luke shows further sophistication by replacing the archaic *Amēn*, transliterated from Aramaic, in Mark 12:43 with the more "proper" Greek *Alēthōs* ("Truly," Luke 21:3; the NRSV's "truly" in both Mark and Luke obscures this distinction).
- Another move toward more polished Greek emerges in Luke's changing Mark's colloquial *chalcon* ("money," "brass," "copper," Mark 12:41) to the more elegant *dōra* ("gifts" [given

by the rich], Luke 21:1). The difference is something like "greenbacks," "C-notes," or "plastic" versus "contributions" or "donations."

This brief sample reflects a general pattern of Luke's editing Mark in the interests of greater succinctness and sophistication. But Luke is not only about good form. Content matters, too, and Luke sometimes *expands* upon Mark in order to press key ideas. For example, Luke *adds* a significant "Isaiah" reading to the Nazareth synagogue service (Luke 4:16-30; cf. Mark 6:1-6), an "exodus" topic to the glorious transfiguration exchange (Luke 9:28-36; cf. Mark 8:34–9:1), and a "grief" explanation to the disciples' soporific prayer meeting (Luke 22:45; cf. Mark 14:37). Moreover, after following the thread of Mark's narrative at some length, Luke can suddenly shift gears and insert large blocks of his own material (e.g., Luke 9:51–19:27).

Matthew and Q

Surveying a collation (synopsis) of Gospel parallels quickly reveals several passages, mostly concerning Jesus' teaching, common to

Matthew 6:9-13	Luke 11:2-4
[9] "Pray then in this way:	[2] "When you pray, say:
Our Father *in heaven*, hallowed be your name.	Father, hallowed be your name.
[10] Your kingdom come. *Your will be done, on earth as it is in heaven.*	Your kingdom come.
[11] Give us *this day* our daily bread.	[3] Give us *each day* our daily bread.
[12] And forgive us our *debts*, as we also have forgiven our **debtors**.	[4] And forgive us our *sins*, for we *ourselves* forgive *everyone* indebted to us.
[13] And do not bring us to the time of trial, *but rescue us from the evil one."*	And do not bring us to the time of trial."

31

Matthew and Luke *but not Mark*.[14] This pattern has sparked the theory that Matthew and Luke shared a source *independent of Mark*. In the absence of ancient witnesses to such a document, it has been designated as "Q" (from the German *Quelle*, "source"). Much debate swirls around Q's nature and even existence.[15] But however we resolve these issues, we may still profit from comparing Luke and Matthew's respective reports of Jesus' instruction. The Lord's Prayer represents a key case in point.[16]

Accustomed to reciting Matthew's version of the Lord's Prayer in worship, Christian readers may be surprised to discover that Luke has another version in a different context. Whereas Matthew embeds the Lord's Prayer in Jesus' sermon about doing righteous acts (almsgiving, praying, fasting) for right reasons (Matt 6:1-18), Luke presents it as an example of Jesus' personal piety (Luke 11:1) followed by an explanatory parable (11:5-8). As for the prayer itself, Luke's account is notably briefer. Following Luke's use of Mark sketched above, we might assume that Luke has abbreviated Matthew's version, redlining redundancies ("in heaven," "debts/debtors") and other unnecessary phrases and substituting his characteristic "each day" (*kath' hēmeran*, 11:3; cf. 9:23; 16:19; 19:47; 22:53)[17] for Matthew's "this day/today" (*sēmeron*, 6:11). But other factors complicate this judgment: Luke's forgiveness petition (11:4) is *longer* than Matthew's and includes Luke's characteristic uses of intensive pronouns ("we ourselves [*autoi*]") and inclusive subjects and objects ("everyone/all [*pas*]");[18] the fact that elsewhere Luke also favors "this day/today" (*sēmeron*, 2:11; 4:21; 5:26; 19:5, 9; 23:43) lessens the likelihood that he altered Matthew's terminology; and for Matthew's part, his fuller version of the Lord's Prayer—far from a rough draft begging for editorial refinement—reflects a poetic liturgy suitable for public recitation.

These observations confirm the difficulty of solving the chicken-and-egg conundrum concerning Gospel origins. Which came first—the hypothetical Q, Matthew, or Luke? Did Matthew and Luke appropriate Q independently, and if so, which Gospel stands closer to the original Q? Or did Matthew and Luke have access to each other's Gospel, and if so, how did the editorial process work? Assured answers elude us. Even Luke's use of Mark, which seems more likely, must be judiciously assessed case by case; we cannot be certain that every distinction represents a purposeful adjustment by Luke. The final form of Luke's text, however it came to be, commands the interpreter's primary attention. But fine points of that form often come into sharper relief in close communication with other similar texts. Along with their copy of the Old Testament, interpreters of Luke do well to have a Gospel synopsis at their elbows.

Speeches

If a modern writer cites the text of Lincoln's "Gettysburg Address," Kennedy's "Ask Not" inaugural, King's "I Have a Dream" speech, or any other famous oration, we expect a verbatim transcript and would recognize, and probably wince at, a paraphrase or bowdlerization. Likewise, when we encounter orations in Luke's narratives, set in quotation marks and attributed to heroic figures like Jesus and Paul, we might assume they represent "the very words" originally delivered. That is, we trust that Luke either memorized these speeches (I remember reciting the Gettysburg address as a schoolboy) or faithfully transcribed copies he had at hand.

But such were not the rhetorical conventions of Luke's day. Just as our earliest Greek manuscripts lack footnotes and bibliographies, so they have no quotation marks. But punctuation aside, standards of ancient historiography from Thucydides on encouraged free renderings of renowned speeches, suiting the author's style and purpose. This freedom did not grant total license: historians should respect the character of the famous speaker and basic gist of what he said—or might say—in a suitable situation. But beyond these concessions to verisimilitude, writers were expected, as Lucian of Samosata advised, "to play the orator and to exhibit your rhetorical skill."[19] And Luke does just that. The major public addresses of Jesus (Luke 4:18-27), Peter (Acts 2:14-36; 3:12-26; 4:8-12; 11:5-18; 15:7-11), Stephen (7:2-53), James (15:13-21), and Paul (13:16-41; 17:22-31; 20:18-35; 21:40–22:41; 24:10-20; 26:1-23), while delivered "in character," all reflect characteristic Lukan language and interests.[20] In modern political parlance, Luke was the main speechwriter for all the candidates; or, in the case of several Acts speeches cast as forensic defenses, Luke functions as the apostles' lead attorney, adept in persuasive legal rhetoric.

Given Luke's heavy hand in shaping speeches, it's best to interpret them primarily in their internal narrative and rhetorical contexts rather than against external constructs of early Christian leaders' personalities and viewpoints. With the apostle Paul, for example, the personal, unfiltered voice of his letters—although accented, like Luke's writings, with Jewish and Greco-Roman rhetorical techniques—carries its own distinctive content, which may or may not cohere with the message of Luke's Paul.

Paul and "We"

The question of Luke's relationship to Paul merits further consideration. The traditional ascription of Luke and Acts to the historical "Luke, the beloved physician" (Col 4:14), an occasional companion of Paul (cf. 2 Tim 4:11), goes beyond our earliest manuscript evidence. We have no title page identifying author, date, ISBN, or other copyright information, and internally, the writer of Luke and Acts never discloses his name or occupation. As for his connection with Paul, the Lukan author gives considerable attention to Paul's career and periodically adopts a first-person viewpoint ("we") in narrating segments of Paul's journeys (mostly sea voyages; Acts 16:10-18; 20:5-16; 21:1-18; 27:2–28:16). But these features do not require direct partnership with Paul or participation in his travels. The Gospel preface seems to derive from a third stage following that of pioneering writers/evangelists (second stage) and eyewitnesses to Jesus' mission (first stage). Since Paul's writings and mission stem from the second phase, the author of Luke and Acts appears to be a later Pauline enthusiast and annalist. The "we"-references undoubtedly create a dramatic *sense* of being on board with Paul for both narrator and reader (the narrator pulls "us" readers into the "we" experience), but they may be nothing more than that—an engaging literary device rather than historical marker.[21]

We simply don't know whether Luke (the author) knew the historical Paul. But that does not preclude knowing Paul's letters. Indeed, given his investigative claims and keen interest in Paul, we might expect Luke to sift carefully Paul's writings. But curiously, we have scant textual evidence that Luke had any idea about Paul's letters. Acts includes two letters dealing with Pauline issues but not written *by Paul* (Acts 15:22-29; 23:25-30). Moreover, Luke never directly cites a Pauline document. Paul's parting address to the Ephesian elders—the only Acts speech delivered to an exclusively Christian audience (20:17-35)—comes closest to echoing Paul's epistolary language, but still falls short of citing any particular letter.[22]

As for events in Paul's life, his dramatic escape from Damascus represents one of the few "synoptic" incidents recounted in both Paul and Luke's writings.

2 Corinthians 11:32-33	Acts 9:23-25
[32] In Damascus, the governor under King Aretas guarded the city of Damascus in order to seize me, [33] but <u>I was let down</u> in a basket <u>through</u> a window in <u>the wall</u>, and escaped from his hands.	[23]After some time had passed, the Jews [of Damascus] plotted to kill him, [24] but their plot became known to Saul. They were watching the gates day and night so that they might kill him; [25] but his disciples took him by night and <u>let him down through</u> an opening in <u>the wall</u>, lowering him in a basket.

Both agree that Paul was "let down (*chalaō*) through the wall (*dia tou teichous*)" in Damascus (cf. Acts 9:22). But that's about all:

- Although obviously referring to the same "basket" case, they do not use the same word for "basket": *sarganē* ("rope-basket," 2 Cor 11:33); and *spyris* ("basket, hamper," Acts 9:25).
- They vary in describing the escape route: Paul recalls a "window" in the wall; Luke leaves the "opening" more ambiguous (actually no Greek term underlies "opening" in the NRSV).
- Most significantly, they identify different causes for Paul's flight: an arrest warrant issued by King Aretas (2 Cor 11:32), and a murderous plot hatched by "the Jews" (Acts 9:23-24).

Although the comparison demonstrates that Luke knew about this event in Paul's life, it does not prove that he *derived* this datum from reading 2 Corinthians 11. It does, however, intimate that Luke promotes an *image of Paul* distinct from the apostle's self-understanding. Having Paul run out of town by an angry Jewish mob rather than by a wary Arab-Nabatean ruler assumes a different social and political context for Paul's Damascus mission. Likewise,

35

comparing Luke and Paul's respective accounts of Paul's conversion and early ministry (Gal 1:11-23; Acts 9:1-31) and the so-called Jerusalem Conference (Gal 2:1-10; Acts 15:1-35) suggests alternative, if not competitive, agendas. Luke develops a complex portrait of Paul's identity and ideology in Acts 7–28 that cautions interpreters against either forcing a perfect bond between Luke and Paul or driving a sharp wedge between them. Overall I recommend a broad-based, mutually informing dialogue between Acts and Paul's letters, focused more on issues and ideas than sources and wrangles over historicity. As for who got it "right," we must admit that Paul's self-testimony, often in the heat of conflict, is as subject to rhetorical bias and manipulation as much as Luke's secondary report.

Israel's Bible and other "Classic" Inter-texts

We have already emphasized Luke's engagement with an array of Old Testament passages. The precise echoes and wider resonances of these texts-in-contexts offer rich opportunities for comparative analysis and interpretation. But beyond formal citations, a more extensive and allusive appropriation of scriptural images and patterns follows from Luke's pervasive knowledge of Israel's Bible and the ancient practice of imitating (*mimēsis*) and internalizing (not simply reproducing) classic literary works. For example, by casting Jesus in the messianic mold of David and Solomon and the prophetic pattern of Moses and Elijah, Luke invites reflection, not merely on this or that quoted text, but on these figures' overall biblical portraits.[23] The Moses-Elijah tandem—well known for their similar experiences of heavenly assumption, their associations with apocalyptic expectation, and their cameo at Jesus' transfiguration (Luke 9:29-33)—have attracted the most attention in Lukan scholarship.

Outside the transfiguration scene, Luke and Acts use Moses' name several times as a shorthand for God's covenantal law or Torah from Genesis to Deuteronomy (including, but not limited to, the Ten Commandments).[24] But two major Acts speeches invoke Moses' active role as Israel's prophet-leader as well as his representative function as legal mediator. After recounting Jesus' rejection by Israel and resurrection by God, Peter announces from Deut 18:15-20: "Moses said, 'The Lord your God will raise up for you from your own people a prophet like me. You must listen to whatever he tells you. And it will be that everyone who does not listen to that prophet will be utterly rooted out of the people'" (Acts 3:22-23). Stephen recalls the same text in shorter form: "This is the Moses who said to the Israelites, 'God will raise up a prophet for you from your own people as he raised me up'" (7:37). But this citation is embedded in a lengthy reflection on Moses' career, high-lighting Israel's rejection of his leadership (7:20-44; see especially 7:24-28, 35, 39-42); such obduracy persists in Israel's history of per-secuting God's prophets up to the recent betrayal and slaying of the "Righteous One," Jesus (7:51-52). According to Acts, then, Jesus fulfills the expectation of a faithful prophet-like-Moses, repudiated by God's people but vindicated by God's power. In retrospect, this image informs Jesus' ministry in Luke, beginning with his Moses-like, forty-day test in the wilderness. Although not using Moses' name, Jesus overcomes Satan's three tests by citing Moses' exhor-tation from Deuteronomy each time (Luke 4:4, 8, 12; Deut 8:3; 6:13, 16). The stage is set for Jesus' vocation as a Moses-style, Deuteronomy-shaped prophet.

Spurred by these clear Mosaic signals, David Moessner and Craig Evans have detected strong echoes of Moses' story and Deuteron-omy's outlook throughout Luke's major "Central Section," or "Travel Narrative" (Luke 9–19), even though Moses is rarely men-tioned (9:30, 33; 16:29, 31) and Deuteronomy quoted but once (Luke 10:27; Deut 6:5). Moessner reads this section as "The Story of the Deuteronomistic Journey Guest Prophet" fulfilled in Jesus.[25] This mouthful title attempts to capture the rich portraiture of Jesus as a "wilderness" wandering prophet like Moses, embodying and advo-cating Deuteronomic principles, often in hospitality or banquet set-tings (a "guest prophet," Luke 9:10-17; 11:5-8; 11:37-54; 12:35-48; 14:1-24; 15:1-2, 22-32; 17:7-10; 19:1-10). As intimated in mountain-top conversation with Moses, Jesus is launching a new, redemptive "exodus" (*exodos*, 9:31) for God's people. But as with Moses, not all welcome Jesus' prophetic leadership and mediation of God's covenant. For Moessner, "Deuteronomistic" encompasses not just the book of Deuteronomy but also an overarching "conceptual canopy" of Israel's history, featuring recurrent rejection of God's prophets and consequent incurring of divine judgment.[26]

Craig Evans focuses more pointedly on textual connections between Deuteronomy 1–26 and Luke 9:51–18:14.[27] Although cau-tioning against elaborate schemes that delineate Luke's Central Sec-tion as a systematic rewriting of Deuteronomy 1–26, Evans remains convinced of Deuteronomy's formative influence on this material. The parallels are not close enough to suggest Luke's *primary* dependence on Deuteronomy (as on Mark): he does not simply spin Jesus tales out of Deuteronomy's cloth. But Luke does appear to correlate Jesus' journey with Deuteronomy. In particular, the Travel Narrative's somewhat random order of events (atypical for Luke) may owe to Deuteronomy's sequence of ideas. The placement of Jesus' parables, for example, may follow Deuteronomy's "plot" line:

- **Parable of the Good Samaritan (Luke 10:25-37/ Deuteronomy 6–7)**. The narrative introducing the parable cites Deut 6:5 ("You shall love the Lord your God . . .") in Luke 10:27, and then the parable itself, featuring a merciful Samaritan "foreigner" (10:30-35, 37; cf. 17:18), challenges the ethnic cleansing policy of Deut 7:2 ("You must utterly destroy them [foreign peoples]. Make no covenant with them and show them no mercy").
- **Parable of the Great Banquet (Luke 14:15-24/Deut 20:1- 9)**. Excuses, pertaining to fiscal and marital obligations, for not attending the messianic feast in Jesus' parable (Luke 14:15-20) recall certain exemptions from holy war allowed in Deut 20:5-8. However, distinct from Deuteronomy, Jesus does not regard pressing personal business as a legitimate reason for skipping the banquet; those who make excuses forfeit their places to the poor, crippled, blind, and lame— those with nothing to manage (Luke 14:13, 21-24).[28]
- **Parables of the Lost Sheep and Son (Luke 15:3-7, 11- 32/Deut 21:15–22:4)**. Jesus' story of recovering the lone lost sheep (Luke 15:3-7) resembles Deuteronomy's injunction to return a stray sheep to its rightful owner as well as "anything else that your neighbor loses and you find" (Deut 22:1-4); and concerns over inheritance rights and paternal love link the parable of the prodigal son with Deut 21:15-17. But butchering the fatted calf and throwing a party for a returning rebellious son (Luke 15:22-24) strikes a sharp counternote to stoning a stubborn son and treating him as a "glutton and a drunkard" (Deut 21:18-21).

These cases illustrate Luke's critical engagement with the book of Deuteronomy in both sympathetic and antithetic directions and justify Evans' interpretive assessment: "Luke wishes his readers to study the materials of the central section in the light of the parallel passages and themes from Deuteronomy. Thus, the central section and Deuteronomy, set side by side, are mutually illuminating."[29]

As Moses and Deuteronomy seem to be salient on Luke's radar, so are Elijah/Elisha and the narratives in 1 Kings 17–2 Kings 9. As well as appearing with Moses at Jesus' transfiguration (Luke 9:30, 33), Elijah surfaces four times in Luke's Gospel: once as a model for John the Baptist (Luke 1:17), twice as a reflection of Jesus' prophetic identity (9:9, 19), and once as the subject of Jesus' proclamation (4:25-26). In this last case, Jesus specifically recalls Elijah's feeding of a destitute Sidonian widow and also Elisha's healing of the leprous Syrian, Naaman (4:25-27). Jesus invokes these prophetic ministries to *non*-Israelites as precedents for his conflict at Nazareth ("no prophet is accepted in the prophet's hometown" [4:24]) and outreach to needy foreigners, like a Roman centurion ("not even in Israel have I found such faith" [7:10]) and Gerasene demoniac (8:26-39). Even in the face of opposition, however, Jesus persists in working mostly among his own people; but here too he follows Elijah and Elisha by curing lepers (5:12-16; 17:11-19), supporting widows (7:11-17; cf. 18:1-8), and nourishing the hungry throng (9:10-17). Moses also miraculously feeds God's people, but healing lepers and restoring life to a widow's deceased son better fit the Elijah/Elisha profile (1 Kgs 17:8-24; 2 Kgs 4:1-37).[30] Moreover, although both Moses and Elijah partially prefigure Jesus' ascension, Elijah's biblical ascent (Moses' "assumption" is extracanonical)—involving the transfer of his mighty prophetic "spirit" to successor Elisha—more closely matches Jesus' Spirit-promising farewell to his disciples (although Elijah's fiery chariot outshines Jesus' cloudy elevator) (Acts 1:4-5, 8-11; 2 Kgs 2:1-16).[31]

With Luke's multifaceted portrait of Jesus as both prophet-like-Elijah/Elisha and prophet-like–Moses, it has suddenly gotten rather crowded on the interpreter's desk. In addition to the target texts of Luke and Acts, we need to investigate Luke's deep Old Testament (LXX) roots (Deuteronomy, Kings, Psalms, Isaiah, and more), parallels with Matthew and Mark (using a Gospel synopsis), and resonances with Paul's letters. But should we make yet more room (or get a larger desk) for Homer's hefty tomes of the *Iliad* and *Odyssey*—the "Bible" of the ancient Greeks?

Dennis MacDonald argues that just as Luke rewrote Jewish scriptural narratives, he also heavily "imitated" Homer's Greek epic poems.[32] No need to cramp Luke's style with a single literary model. Writers and rhetoricians in antiquity were "equal-opportunity imitators," lavishly "eclectic" in their mimetic endeavors.[33] Since Homer's works were fundamental to ancient Greco-Roman education, they offered a rich imaginative fund for Greek and Latin writers across a variety of genres (not just poetry)—including, in MacDonald's view, Christian storytellers like Mark and Luke. But there is a critical twist. Striving for the rhetorical goal of not merely parroting a mimetic text but "emulating," "transvaluing," or improving upon it, Mark and Luke's protagonists "trump" Homer's heroes. Mark's Jesus, for example, trumps Odysseus by waking up in a storm-tossed boat and *calming the tempest* rather than despairing of survival (Mark 4:35-41; *Odyssey* 10.1-69);[34] and Luke's Paul, in a farewell address to the Ephesian elders, morally betters the dying Hector by commissioning the elders to follow his humble servant's vocation ("it is more blessed to give than to receive") rather than a mighty warrior's campaign crusade, as Hector charged his son (Acts 20:18-35; *Iliad* 6.472-81; 7.1-3).[35]

This literary game of one-upmanship deliberately stretches the gap between revised (Mark/Acts) and standard (*Iliad/Odyssey*) versions and consequently blurs the mimetic process. MacDonald widens the gap further: "Mark *hid his dependence* by avoiding Homeric vocabulary, transforming characterizations, motifs, and episodes, placing the episodes out of sequence, and employing multiple literary models, especially from Jewish scriptures."[36] Luke is similarly adept at such a camouflage operation, although he does have Paul briefly allude to Greek poets (but not Homer) at Athens (Acts 17:28) and travel to familiar Homeric places (e.g. Troas/Troy, 16:8; 20:5-6). Still, this supposed aim of ancient authors to cover their mimetic tracks as much as possible represents the "Achilles heel," as Karl Sandnes wryly suggests, of modern quests for proto-types.[37] But not to worry: MacDonald spies "scores of flags" that dot Mark and Acts' neatly manicured narratives, "signaling the reader to compare these stories with their [Homeric] models."[38]

It's hard to miss an array of flags in the middle of the road—yet that's exactly what interpreters have done for two millennia with respect to Homeric flags in Mark and Acts. Of course, ignorance is not justified by longevity; the world was no flatter during the many centuries when everyone thought it was. But the novelty of Mac-Donald's theory gives one pause (as Luke might agree [Acts 17:21]). More to the point, however, is that Mark and Luke are in fact ardent flag wavers—*but not to signal Homer's poetry*. Although some Homeric language may seep into Luke's more sophisticated work, he, no less than Mark, never cites Homer's texts, names Homer's characters, or offers any "metatextual preparation for Homer's poems"[39]—as he does repeatedly, in spades, *with the Greek Old Testament*. Although MacDonald concedes Mark and Luke's use of the Old Testament, he does not take seriously enough the overwhelming majority of "pop-up" advertisements for Jewish scriptural texts and characters compared to an all but total "block-out" of Homeric materials. As Sandnes concludes, "[MacDonald's] reading is fascinating. . . . But he fails to demonstrate authorial intention while he, in fact, neglects the OT intertextuality that is broadcast in this literature."[40]

BROAD PATTERNS

Having explored various "inter-texts" Luke may have appropriated and that, in any case, interpreters may bring into illuminating dialogue with Luke's narratives, we turn now to focus on the interplay between "co-texts" *within* these volumes.[41] Talking, musing, even arguing with oneself is a common part of intelligent human experience. Likewise, thoughtful authors' personal struggles for meaning inevitably bleed into their writings, and complex narratives detonate an explosive internal combustion of voices beyond writers' control. Part II will chart twists and turns through the Lukan minefield in some detail. But before embarking on such an adventure, it's useful to know something about the grid of pathways we will traverse. Though by no means covering all the terrain, we survey four broad "architectural" patterns shaping Luke's landscape:[42] (1) paired stories and examples involving male and female characters, (2) parallel actions and experiences between Jesus and his followers, (3) previews of coming attractions and reviews of previous episodes, and (4) circular or chiastic structures.

Male-Female Pairing

Luke often juxtaposes a pair of stories or statements involving male and female figures, mostly in material unique to his narratives.[43]

41

The following chart displays the principal examples; (M)ale and (F)emale are so designated.

Common Experience	Male Figure	Female Figure	Texts
Angelic Birth Announcement	Zechariah	Mary	Luke 1:5-23 (M) Luke 1:26-38 (F)
Hymn of Praise	Zechariah (Benedictus)	Mary (Magnificat)	Luke 1:46-55 (F) Luke 1:67-79 (M)
Elderly Prophets at Temple	Simeon	Anna	Luke 2:25-35 (M) Luke 2:36-38 (F)
Foreigners Aided by Elijah/Elisha	Naaman the Leprous Syrian Officer	Anonymous, Destitute Sidonian Widow	Luke 4:25-26 (F) Luke 4:27 (M)
Forgiven by Jesus in Pharisees' Presence	Paralytic	Anointing Woman	Luke 5:17-26 (M) Luke 7:36-50 (F)
Household Member Restored by Jesus	Centurion's Valued Servant Healed in Capernaum	Widow's Only Son Resuscitated in Nain	Luke 7:1-10 (M) Luke 7:11-17 (F)
Afflicted Victims Healed by Jesus	Gerasene Demoniac	Hemorrhaging Woman and Deceased Daughter	Luke 8:26-39 (M) Luke 8:40-56 (F)
Contrasting Helpers	Active Good Samaritan; Passive Priest/Levite	Active Martha; Passive Mary	Luke 10:30-37 (M) Luke 10:38-42 (F)
Determined Hosts	Male Host Seeking Aid from Resistant Neighbor	Hostess Martha Seeking Help from Resistant Sister	Luke 10:38-42 (F) Luke 11:5-8 (M)
Infirm Healed by Jesus on Sabbath	Man with Dropsy	Woman with Bent Back	Luke 13:10-17 (F) Luke 14:1-6 (M)
Little Makes Much Parables	Mustard Seed Planted by Farmer Becomes Tree	Little Yeast Used by Baker Woman Permeates Flour	Luke 13:19 (M) Luke 13:20 (F)
Seeking and Finding the Lost	Shepherd Finding Lost Sheep out of One Hundred	Housekeeper Finding Lost Coin out of Ten	Luke 15:3-7 (M) Luke 15:8-10 (F)

Common Experience	Male Figure	Female Figure	Texts
Seeking and Finding the Lost	Father Finding Lost Son out of Two	Housekeeper Finding Lost Coin out of Ten	Luke 15:8-10 (F) Luke 15:11-32 (M)
Public Piety	Scribes Display False Piety while "Devouring Widows' Houses"	Poor Widow Displays True Piety	Luke 20:45-47 (M) Luke 21:1-4 (F)
Spirit-Filled Prophets	Sons and Male Slaves	Daughters and Female Slaves	Acts 2:17-18 (M) Acts 2:17-18 (F)
Dishonest Contributors	Ananias	Sapphira	Acts 5:3-6 (M) Acts 5:7-10 (F)
Afflicted Victims Restored by Peter	Paralyzed Aeneas in Lydda	Deceased Tabitha in Joppa	Acts 9:32-35 (M) Acts 9:36-43 (F)
Generous Contributors Encountered by Peter	Cornelius "Devout Man" who "Gave Alms Generously" in Caesarea	Tabitha "Devoted to Good Works and Acts of Charity" in Joppa	Acts 9:36-39 (F) Acts 10:1-4 (M)
Hosts of Pauline Group in Philippi	Purple-Dealer, Lydia; Household Belief/Baptism	Philippian Jailer; Household Belief/Baptism	Acts 16:13-15 (F) Acts 16:25-34 (M)
Employees whose Job Security Is Threatened by Paul	Jailer Despairs of Life when Paul is Freed from Prison	Slave-Girl Freed by Paul from Divination Spirit; Useless to Owners	Acts 21:9 (F) Acts 21:10-11(M)
Prophets in Caesarean Home of Philip the Evangelist	Visiting Judean Prophet, Agabus	Philip's Four Virgin Daughters with "Gift of Prophecy"	Acts 21:9 (F) Acts 21:10-11(M)

Such prevalent pairings of male-female characters obviously invite comparative analysis. But interpreters must beware drawing facile conclusions from this pattern, such as Luke's unequivocal support for women's equality and opportunity for ministry. *Pairing does not guarantee parity*. Order and length of linked reports may vary. Simeon's Spirit-inspired prophecies, for example, regarding Mary and the Christ Child (Luke 2:25-35) both precede and exceed Anna's brief announcement (2:36-38), and Philip's four prophetic daughters, though in their father's house before Agabus arrives (21:9), remain still and silent while the visiting male prophet dramatically predicts Paul's impending arrest (21:10-11). On the other hand, though appearing *after* their male counterparts, Mary outshines the dubious Zechariah as a believer in God's word (Luke 1:5-23, 26-38), and a poor, pious widow upstages hypocritical scribes (20:45–21:4). Thus, women can take the spotlight in Luke's narratives, although generally they stand out for their humble service, not their dynamic speech.[44] Even in Acts, which hints at gender equality in several passing references to "both men and women" (5:14; 8:3; 9:2; 13:50; 17:4, 12; 22:4) and named married couples (Ananias/Sapphira [5:1-2], Priscilla/Aquila [18:2, 18, 26], Felix/Drusilla [24:24], Agrippa/Bernice [25:23]),[45] men remain the chief preachers, teachers, and authorities. Still, we should not overplay generalizations: each male-female "couple" begs for careful analysis on its own merits.

Jesus-Followers Parallels

In Jesus' "Sermon on the Plain," he sets forth a guiding principle about teacher-student relations: "A disciple is not above the teacher, but everyone who is fully qualified will be like the teacher" (Luke 6:40). Bona fide disciples of Jesus, therefore, follow his example in word and deed. And that is precisely what we find in Acts. Jesus' emissaries do not merely bear witness to him but often sound and act just like him. They perpetuate "all that Jesus did and taught from the beginning" (Acts 1:1).

- **Healing Miracles**. As Jesus restored a paralyzed man early in his ministry (Luke 5:17-26), so Peter and Paul's first public miracles feature healings of congenitally lame men in Jerusalem (Acts 3:1-10) and Lystra (14:8-10), respectively. Philip the evangelist also cures "many others who were paralyzed or lame" in Samaria (8:7). Further, as Jesus raised a widow's son and Jairus's daughter from the dead (Luke 7:10-17; 8:49-56), so Peter resuscitates the deceased, widow-aiding Tabitha (Acts 9:36-43) and Paul revives the lifeless youth Eutychus (20:7-12).
- **Dying Petitions**. Gazing heavenward at the exalted Lord, the dying Stephen echoes the earthly Jesus' final prayers from the

cross: "Lord Jesus, receive my spirit" (Acts 7:59); "Father, into your hands I commend my spirit" (Luke 23:46); "Lord, do not hold this sin again them" (Acts 7:60); "Father, forgive them; for they do not know what they are doing" (Luke 23:34). Although stoned rather than crucified, the martyred Stephen dies like his Lord.

- **Escapes from Death**. As Jesus escaped his burial wrappings and tomb (Luke 24:1-12), so Peter is twice supernaturally freed from prison in Jerusalem (the second time on death row) (Acts 5:17-21; 12:1-17); Paul also experiences a miraculous jailbreak (Acts 16:25-34) and (perhaps) resuscitation after being stoned to death (14:19-20).
- **Satanic and Demonic Conflicts**. As Jesus exposed and expelled the devil and his malevolent minions (Luke 4:1-13, 31-37; 8:26-39; 9:37-43; 10:17-18; 13:10-17), so do Peter (Acts 5:3, 16), Philip (8:7), and Paul (13:9-11; 16:16-18; 19:11-19; 26:18).
- **Temple and Synagogue Conflicts**. As Jesus provoked opposition within local synagogues and the Jerusalem temple (Luke 4:16-30; 6:6-11; 13:10-17; 19:45–21:37), ultimately leading to his arrest, so Peter, Stephen, and Paul are seized for disruptive activities in the temple and synagogues of Jerusalem and the Diaspora (Acts 3–5, 6–7, 9:19-25; 13:44–14:7; 17:1-15; 18:4-17; 21:27-36).

This network of common experiences between Jesus and his followers in Luke and Acts creates a strong sense of divinely orchestrated character and plot development. But again, we must appreciate Luke and Acts as dynamic narratives, not formulaic catalogues, and we must not mistake resemblance for replica, similarity for sameness. Spotlighting characters side by side in similar situations also exposes subtle differences between them. As Peter, Paul, and company carry Jesus' torch throughout Acts, their shortcomings and separate identities from Jesus also come to light. The risen-ascended Jesus remains an active, independent character in Acts, intervening at will in human affairs. The apostles may preach and heal in Jesus' name, but they do not replace or replicate Jesus. In Peter's case, for all his remarkable progress in Acts, he still balks at following Jesus' examples of table-service to hungry clients (Acts 6:1-3)[46] and table-fellowship with "unclean" strangers (10:9-29;

11:1-17); in the latter situation, nothing less than a dramatic heavenly vision changes Peter's mind.

With respect to Paul, we must not forget his former campaign of religious terrorism that Jesus challenges head-on (9:1-18); and even after his conversion to Jesus Messiah, Paul's volatile temperament continues to flare up now and then. Striking the false prophet Elymas with a curse of blindness (13:6-11), refusing to give the deserter John Mark a second chance at missionary duty (15:36-41), and vilifying Jewish opponents in Corinth with a menacing threat ("Your blood be on your own heads!" [18:6]): such actions do not readily recall the weeping, forgiving Jesus of Luke's Gospel, who does not even curse a fig tree to make a point (Luke drops this scene from Mark 11:12-14). Further, for all the parallels we may draw between Jesus and Paul's "trials," Paul's multiple defenses before Jewish and Roman authorities, his appeal to Caesar as a Roman citizen, his turbulent sea voyage to Rome, and his two-year sojourn there in a private dwelling, stretch miles beyond Jesus' shotgun trial and crucifixion in Jerusalem.

Previews-Reviews

Few have analyzed Luke's literary patterns more astutely than Robert Tannehill. His many essays and monumental two-volume commentary on the Lukan narratives are must-reads for the serious interpreter of Luke and Acts.[47] Tannehill pays close attention to both linear and circular movements under the headings of "narrative development" and "echo effect." "Good reading," he avers of Luke's writings, "will engage in two activities simultaneously: tracing the forward movement of the plot through a series of causally connected events [narrative development] and listening for the enriching echoes of similar events in other parts of the narrative [echo effect]."[48] These reading strategies correlate with our previous discussion concerning the paths Jesus blazes for his disciples to follow (narrative developments) and the consequent parallels that emerge in their missions (echo effects). While Tannehill emphasizes how these literary links contribute to the narrative unity of Luke's work, he also remains alert to shifts and gaps that disrupt the flow and adjust readers' expectations.

In addition to parallels in characters' activities, Tannehill highlights four internal keys to the plots and purpose of Luke's story:

(1) previews of anticipated actions and reviews of past events, (2) scriptural citations at strategic junctures, (3) commission statements from authoritative figures, and (4) interpretive comments from reliable voices.[49] Previews and reviews (often combined with other elements) are especially influential in shaping and sharpening readers' responses over the course of the narrative. Prime examples include

- **Natal Prophecies (Luke 1–2)**. The hymns of Mary (*Magnificat*), Zechariah (*Benedictus*), and Simeon (*Nunc Dimittis*) in Luke's birth narratives praise God for the blessings that will attend Jesus' advent as Lord and Messiah. Simeon, for example, inspired by the Holy Spirit and Isaiah's prophecy, *previews* God's "salvation . . . of all peoples" that will radiate as "a light for revelation to the Gentiles and for glory to your people Israel" (Luke 2:30-32; Isa 40:3-6; 49:6). Luke thus raises high hopes for the Messiah's universal acceptance by both Jews and Gentiles. Too good to be true? Too much to hope for? We are spurred to read on and find out, risking the chance that the story might take a tragic turn and not deliver as promised.[50]
- **Nazareth Sermon (Luke 4:16-30)**. In his first public act, set in his hometown synagogue at Nazareth, Jesus personally identifies with key messianic texts from Isaiah 61:1-2 and 58:6: "Today this scripture has been fulfilled in your hearing." Via Isaiah, Jesus thus *previews* his mission agenda: "to bring good news to the poor . . . to proclaim release to the captives . . . sight to the blind, to let the oppressed go free" (Luke 4:16-21). From this point on, the reader is poised to evaluate how and to what extent Jesus carries out this redemptive program.
- **Post-Resurrection Retrospect (Luke 24:6-7, 18-24, 44)**. In Luke's final chapter, the two dazzling messengers at Jesus' empty tomb (24:6-7), the two perplexed travelers on the Emmaus road (24:18-24), and Jesus himself (Luke 24:44) all *review* aspects of Jesus' ministry prior to his death ("Remember how he told you, while he was still in Galilee"; "These are my words that I spoke to you while I was still with you"). Readers are thus encouraged to "remember" Luke's preceding narrative and to reflect on its movement toward this astounding climax.

47

- **Farewell Commissions (Luke 24:44-49; Acts 1:4-8).** Combining review/preview, scriptural emphasis, commission statement, and the authoritative voice of the risen Jesus, Luke 24:44-49 emits a strong signal of narrative purpose. Before ascending to heaven, Jesus not only *reminds* the disciples of his scripture-saturated teaching (24:44) but also *previews* their appointed mission "in his name to all nations, beginning from Jerusalem" in the power of the Spirit. The opening chapter of Acts reinforces this vocation and projects the gospel's movement beyond Jerusalem to "all Judea and Samaria, and to the ends of the earth" (Acts 1:8). A bold plan for global outreach: the rest of Acts will monitor its successes and failures.

- **Pentecost Speech (Acts 2:14-36).** Another programmatic *preview* emerges in Peter's Pentecost appeal to the prophet Joel. In Peter's view, the outpouring of the Holy Spirit fulfills Joel's eschatological ("last days") promise and anticipates an eruption of dreams and visions, signs and wonders, prophetic utterances and salvific experiences for all God's people, female and male, young and old (Acts 2:17-21; Joel 2:28-32). But as Peter sets the stage for Acts, he also *reviews* key moments in the preceding story. The Lukan Jesus laid the foundation for the church's Spirit-filled mission through his own signs and wonders, death and resurrection, Lordship and Messiahship (Acts 2:22-36).

- **Miletus Speech (Acts 20:17-35).** As Paul takes his final leave of the Ephesian elders, he both *reviews* his three-year mission in Asia (Acts 20:17-21, 26-27, 34-35), providing a self-evaluation that the reader may test against the preceding narrative (18:18–20:16), and *previews* the difficult course that lies ahead for him (20:22-25) and his churches (20:25-33), creating suspense for the final chapters of Acts.

Chiastic Patterns

The popular ancient literary technique of *chiasmus*, named after the Greek letter *chi* (shaped like the English X), features a structural framework of parallel materials flanking a central hub. It may organize a brief text in a simple A-B-A' pattern or, more elaborately, a longer passage or entire section. In an earlier study, I laid out the story of Philip's encounter with the Ethiopian eunuch in a chiastic format with eighteen parallel elements surrounding the citation of Isa 53:7-8 in Acts 8:32-35 as the centerpiece of the episode.[51] Of course, this scriptural focal point is fairly obvious without the chiastic package, some aspects of which are admittedly more convincing than others. I continue to regard Isa 53:7-8 as a major key to understanding the eunuch incident[52] but am less enamored with the intricate chiastic scheme. The method is susceptible to overplay, speculation, and forced parallels. As someone has quipped: "anyone can fake a chiasm."

The problem becomes more acute with larger literary blocks. The more material, the harder it is to fit all the pieces on a chiastic grid. Various scholars have endeavored to impose some chiastic order on Jesus' meandering journey to Jerusalem in Luke's Central Section. Loose ends, however, complicate each of the proposed arrangements, and there is little agreement concerning the precise center of the chiasm (Luke 13:31-35? 13:22-35? or 14:1-24?).[53] Although some parallels are patent—such as two stories commencing with identical questions to Jesus, "Teacher, what must I do to inherit eternal life?" (10:25-37; 18:18-30), and twin parables about persistent prayer (11:5-8; 18:1-8) and dying rich men (12:13-21; 16:19-31)—others are murkier. Careful readers of Luke and Acts do well to keep *chiasmus* on their interpretive radars, but not allow it to control the entire screen.

VARIOUS GENRES

Investigations of genre or literary type branch out beyond questions of source materials and internal patterns to pursue architectural templates in the wider literary environment. Did Luke closely follow an overarching generic model in constructing his work or strike out in new directions? Few issues of Lukan scholarship have generated more confusion and less consensus.

From the start, determining *the* genre(s) of Luke and Acts, or any sophisticated literary work, is vexed by creative authors' tendencies to mix models. Neat categories of Shakespeare's history plays, tragedies, and comedies unravel with numerous acts and scenes best described as tragicomic, comic-historical, tragic-historical, or all three. In Luke and Acts, the rich mix of poems/hymns, scriptural citations, aphorisms, parables, speeches, letters, miracle stories, martyr accounts, sea voyages, and other literary forms, complicates any single generic label. Moreover, the unity question rears its head again. However else they may be linked, must Luke and Acts represent the same genre? Could the first volume's historic association with the four gospels, apart from Acts, represent a generic as well as canonical distinction? Both books can safely be called "narratives" in the broad sense. But how far does that get us? Richard Pervo rightly notes, "'Narrative' is something of a weasel word," allowing perhaps a tad too much wiggle room to be useful. On the other hand, Pervo concedes that "narrative" provides "an invaluable refuge" when other, narrower categories fail to fit and remains helpful in defining "the intention to make a case by telling a story (or stories), rather than by means of a treatise or dialogue."[54]

Biography

Those who insist on keeping Luke and Acts within the same generic camp often opt for some kind of ancient *biographical* narrative.[55] Charles Talbert argues that Luke's two-volume work bears closest resemblance to ancient cultic biographies, like Diogenes Laertes's *Lives of Eminent Philosophers*, which recount the career of a spiritual or intellectual figure (as opposed to a political or military leader) who founded a religious-philosophical movement and passed on his authoritative tradition to faithful successors. Such composite biographies of ideological pioneers and disciples served chiefly to legitimate their tenets and practices. In Talbert's view, the Lukan narratives vindicate the new Christian faith and community by tracking the Spirit-inspired succession from (1) Jesus to the twelve apostles, (2) the twelve apostles to the seven "deacons" (Acts 6:1-7), and (3) Paul to church elders (14:23; 20:17-38).[56]

Loveday Alexander agrees that Luke's literary roots reach into the ancient tradition of intellectual, rather than political, biography. But seeing too many disjunctions between Luke's work and Diogenes's *Lives*, Alexander gravitates more toward a "Socratic paradigm." Comprising more of a popular portrait than a formal genre, several well-known defenses of Socrates as the prototypical philosopher-hero—recounting his divine call (Delphic oracle), teaching mission, and series of unjust trials leading to imprisonment and martyrdom—provide a "template" for Luke's depiction of Israel's latest heroic prophet-sages, chiefly Jesus and Paul.[57]

The biographical model has much to commend it with general reference to legitimating controversial figures and their movements and with particular relevance to Luke's portrait of Jesus from birth to death. But it works less well with Acts for various reasons: (1) succession theories break down because Jesus remains a "live" and leading character in Acts, sharing his mission with the apostles but not transferring it to them; (2) whereas Stephen may qualify as a genuine martyr-hero, the major figures, Peter and Paul, are not so heroic, not only because they don't actually die in the narrative but also because they don't always readily follow their Lord's will; (3) and as Beverly Gaventa has persuasively argued, however much Peter, Paul, and other human leaders do and say in Acts, they remain wholly subordinate to Israel's *God*—the main "hero" or protagonist propelling the plot and controlling the characters.[58] If we classify Luke's work as biography, we might best crib Jack Miles's Pulitzer-winning work and call it a "biography of God."[59]

Historiography

Interpreters who distinguish the genres of Luke's two volumes typically accept the Gospel's biographical classification but view Acts in broader *historiographical* terms. And some scholars who maintain a closer link between Luke and Acts prefer designating both volumes as *historical narratives*. But the broad enterprise of "history writing" could take a variety of forms in antiquity, ranging from annalistic chronicle to novelistic entertainment (historical fiction). The *diēgēsis* or "narrative" label in the Lukan preface does not narrow the field much. The Greek rhetorician Theon, for example, defined *diēgēsis* in general terms as "an expository treatise of events which happened or could have happened" (*Progymnasmata* 4).[60]

Options for classifying Acts as a separate genre from Luke's Gospel (biography) include

- **Historical Monograph**. Pegging Acts as a concise overview of early Christian origins over a three-decade span, Darryl Palmer associates it with ancient Greek, Roman, and Hellenistic-Jewish historical monographs, such as Thucydides'

51

classic treatment of the Peloponnesian War, Sallust's survey of Roman history with special interest in the military conspiracy of Catiline (*Bellum Catilinae*), and accounts of the Jewish revolt against Greco-Syrian rule (1-2 Maccabees)—all of which represent a relatively short "particular history" of a people/nation over a limited period.[61] However, the lack of war stories in Acts (it is not military history), which predominate in the examples, poses a glaring challenge to this thesis.

- **Historical Fiction**. Richard Pervo slots Acts into the historical fiction category of Greek romance novels, such as the *Alexander Romance*, Chariton's *Chaereas and Callirhoe*, and Hellenistic Jewish tales like Esther (LXX), Judith, Tobit, and *Joseph and Asenath*. However, as with war and fighting, so with love and wooing: the interests of Acts lay elsewhere, well apart from battlefield and bedroom. The four married couples in Acts have small roles with no romantic bits. Still, in Pervo's view, what Acts lacks in amorousness and titillation, it makes up in adventure and edification—driving home key moral lessons through entertaining anecdotes.[62] But though he has aptly challenged interpreters to take more "seriously" the swashbuckling and humorous elements of several Acts episodes, the evidence does not demand a total generic identification with historical fiction. Many subtypes of ancient Greek history writing valued a tale well told, with rhetorical flourish and creative license adorning "events which happened or could have happened."

Historical models treating Luke-Acts as a generic unit include

- **Biblical History**. Robert Maddox and Brian Rosner regard Luke's two volumes as dependent on the Old Testament not merely for discrete ideas, motifs, character models, and proof-texts, but also for a comprehensive framework of proclaiming God's purposes for Israel and the world *through the writing of history*. Like the books of Samuel-Kings, 1-2 Chronicles, Ezra-Nehemiah (and Maccabees), Luke-Acts does theology via history. Rather than a *Summa Theologica* or *Institutes of the Christian Religion*, Luke writes a narrative theological history of God's mission, "meant to instruct in the character of God, to appeal for allegiance to [God], and to inspire in [God's] service."[63]

- **Apologetic History**. Although also perceiving a close connection with biblical forebears, Gregory Sterling classifies Luke's double work more specifically as *apologetic historiography*, representing an insider's "story of a subgroup of people in an extended prose narrative . . . in an effort to establish the identity of the group within the setting of the larger world."[64] For Jews in the Greco-Roman world Josephus' *Jewish Antiquities* represents the banner example of this genre, (1) offering a positive, native perspective on Judaism correcting the prejudicial, naïve assessments of Greek observers; (2) certifying and bolstering Roman tolerance of Jewish faith and practice; and (3) commending to the Jews themselves a particular (Pharisaic) way of being faithful to their history and traditions.[65] In Sterling's view, Luke tackled a similar project, aiming to define and defend the "Christian" community—an upstart, messianic Jewish sect attracting numerous Gentile converts—within a dominant pagan environment, among non-Christ-believing Jews, and to Christians themselves. Although using Hellenistic techniques, Luke and Josephus derived their basic "understanding of what history is" from biblical predecessors, like the Deuteronomic historian, with whom they shared a "confessional stance towards the activity of God in human activities."[66]

- **Historical Epic**. Marianne Palmer Bonz expands the scope of Luke's project beyond that of a parochial, ethnic apology toward a more universal, cosmic mythology, after the fashion of grand epics, like the Babylonian *Gilgamesh*, Homer's *Iliad* and *Odyssey*, and Virgil's *Aeneid*. Whereas, on the surface, these poetic sagas seem generically unrelated to Luke's prose narratives, on a deeper structural level, they share a common pattern and purpose. Bonz especially advocates "the *Aeneid* as a paradigm and inspiration for Luke-Acts."[67] As Virgil's work aimed "to celebrate Rome's divine election and elevate *Romanitas* (the Roman way) as the universal human ideal for the new millennium of Roman power,"[68] so Luke's narrative promoted "the Way of the Lord" advanced by Jesus Christ as the ultimate path to salvation for *all* who follow him. Both authors conveyed their sweeping ideologies through heroic odysseys linked by symmetrical patterns and controlled by divine prophecies, visions, and oracles; and they constructed their "foundational" histories of the Roman state and Christian church, respectively, on the foundations of established epics: Homer's poetic sagas (Virgil) and the Bible's historical narratives (Luke).[69] In particular, Luke fashioned his work as a two-volume "continuation of the story line of Israel's scriptural past," culminating in Jesus Christ and the early church.[70]

Although the quest for the precise historical genre of Luke and Acts, considered together or separately, has branched out in various specialized directions and yielded little consensus, affirming Luke's fundamental "appropriation and transformation"[71] of Old Testament themes, trajectories, and templates remains a refreshing constant among Lukan scholars, though not always a dominant factor in their interpretation. Our investigation of the literary sources, patterns, and genres of Luke and Acts has repeatedly confirmed the formative function of Israel's scriptures. Close inter-textual dialogue with this rich biblical heritage—law, prophets, and psalms (Luke 24:44)—commands priority attention in interpreting Luke's "sacred narratives."[72]

CHAPTER 2

THEOLOGICAL FOCUS:
Why Were Luke and Acts Written?

Meaningful discourse, whether oral or written, does not materialize out of thin air, but rather answers or responds to some other pressing discourses or situations in the "rhetorical environment." In Bakhtin's terms, all communication is dynamically inter-textual or "dialogic" within an "elastic" or "agitated and tension-filled environment of alien words, value judgments and accents."[1] In a sense, every word is "called out" (think Wild West) by another word with which it fights for meaning and persuasive effect. As Patricia Tull summarizes Bakhtin's argument, a text's "rhetorical environment . . . involves competing answers to the same question, competing constructions of the same event, competing views of the same world, differing characterizations and valuations of the same idea, and a profusion of other voices already speaking before the text adds its voice."[2]

Of course, a text may "answer" its rhetorical environment in a variety of ways, not necessarily profound or philosophical. A dime-store romance or mystery may serve little purpose beyond providing escapist entertainment, but even that represents a kind of response to the cultural milieu. But in the case of Luke's narratives, however much they offer a "good read," their primary purpose is not diversionary or escapist. Rather, they aim to assess the significance of key "events that have been fulfilled among us" and to provide Theophilus and other readers with *asphaleia*—rock solid confidence, assurance, or certainty—"concerning the things about which you have been instructed" (Luke 1:1-4). This goal implies a contested rhetorical environment where doubts and questions are being raised about important events and issues. On some level, then, Luke mounts a defense or apology (*pace* Sterling) for his view of "the truth" (Luke 1:4).

So what are the main debating points Luke seeks to score? What thorny matters are Theophilus and company struggling to understand? What are the questions and concerns in Luke's milieu that "call out" Luke's narratives, and what answers and responses do these narratives fire back? Sorting out these problems would get us a long way toward ascertaining *why* Luke and Acts were written. But that is no easy task, given both our remote location from Luke's original situation and the narrative form of Luke's literary project. We are equally distant from the cultural contexts of Paul's writings and hampered by direct access to only Paul's side of the conversation, but Paul's letters at least provide some hard evidence about the audiences and problems he addresses. With Luke's work, however, we are more in the dark, since he gives us a network of stories, not a set of arguments, targeted to no particular place or people, except "most excellent Theophilus" (Luke 1:3; Acts 1:1).

Although the "Theophilus" reference may seem promising, it falls well short of the informative value of "Corinthians" or "Thessalonians" or "Timothy" or "Philemon" addressed in Paul's correspondence. The form of Theophilus's name suggests a Greek background, possibly with ties to Judaism, and the "most excellent" (*kratiste*) appellation may hint at some kind of official position, perhaps in Roman administration (cf. Acts 23:26; 24:3; 26:25). But we know nothing more about him from Luke's work or any external materials. We do not know where he resided or what Christian community he might have supported or joined. Hypotheses regarding the provenance of Theophilus (and Luke) in Ephesus or Antioch are informed guesses but nothing more. And finally, we can't even be sure that Luke's Theophilus was a real person instead of a cipher for any "Theo-philus" or "God-lover" anywhere.

Ultimately, we have only Luke's narratives themselves from which to infer Luke's purposes. It's like the popular game show *Jeopardy*: we must derive the fundamental "questions" from the narrative "answers" Luke gives us. It's a fun game to play but fraught with risk (jeopardy). With a little imagination, we can devise a list of *possible* issues or problems in Luke's historical ("real") world that various elements in Luke's story ("fictive") world *might* address or explain, but we cannot be certain Luke had these connections in mind when composing his works. Authorial intention is notoriously difficult to uncover, especially for ancient writers, like Luke, who engage in precious little self-revelation. Luke leaks his desire to explicate certain "events" that have occurred and certain "things" his readers have been taught, but he does not spell out what those events or things are. They obviously revolve around the complex of "events" in Jesus' life and "things" Jesus said, but why Luke selected particular Jesus incidents and sayings and shaped them the way he did is never made explicit.

Given these complications, why bother at all with trying to decode the voices in Luke's head and world that his writings addressed? Why wager good interpretive capital on the hazardous category of "Lukan aims," attempting to match a list of hypothetical questions with narrative answers? Why not just immerse oneself in Luke's story world, as narrative critics often advocate, and leave it at that?[3] Readers may indeed reap great enjoyment and profit from reading Luke and Acts as self-contained narratives.[4] The rich interplay of literary parallels, images, and allusions suggested in the previous chapter afford an inexhaustible trove of interpretive insights. But no one enters any story world with a *tabula rasa*; there is no such thing as a truly "naïve" reading (superficial readings, yes, but not naïve). We inevitably bring a slew of questions from our own rhetorical environments, whether we acknowledge them or not. Given my context as an American seminary professor and father of two daughters in the twenty-first century, for example, I bring an array of personal and pastoral, social and political, "male"-stream and feminist questions (among others) to my reading of Luke's writings—questions that Luke may not have intended and might scarcely recognize. Although such contemporary "reader responses" are a legitimate and vital part of biblical interpretation in the modern world, they run the risk of producing myopic, solipsistic readings if not balanced and challenged by others' questions and responses, not least those from the original environment that generated the text. Before we shape Luke too thoroughly in our own images, we do well to expand our horizons and give Luke a sympathetic hearing in his own setting.

So we are back to our quest for problematic questions, issues, and events that precipitated Luke's work—with all the difficulties attending that quest suggested above. But we can mitigate the jeopardy in a couple of ways. First, we might test issues implicitly hinted in Luke's narratives against more direct disclosures in Pauline discourse. Of course, just because Paul dealt with a particular problem in one of his letters does not certify that Luke confronted the same problem or handled it the same way. But Paul's correspondence does provide a pool of live, documented controversies within the wider early Christian rhetorical environment encompassing Luke's work. Second, we are on safer ground if we explore a broad range of questions that Luke might be answering (if not Tull's "profusion of other voices," at least a healthy sample) instead of betting the farm on a single, overarching purpose driving Luke's entire project.[5] So in this chapter, we will canvass *seven* possible issues that Luke's narratives might be negotiating. By investigating Luke's aims, my aim is not to constrict our reading of Luke and Acts, but to expand our interpretive horizons and prepare us to grapple with the complex "answers" these narratives offer.

Before working through the list, I preview one of the seven issues, for the sake of both illustrating the method and exposing a major unifying factor—the closest thing to a dominant perspective Luke's narratives share amid their rich diversity. Note the climactic statement of Peter's Pentecost sermon: "Therefore let the entire house of Israel know with certainty that God has made him both Lord and Messiah, this Jesus whom you crucified" (Acts 2:36). The concern for knowing "with certainty" (*asphalōs*) recalls Luke's prefatory purpose to bolster Theophilus' "certainty" or "assurance" (*asphaleia*) concerning Christian "truth." The Lukan Peter pinpoints one key perplexing "event" that "the entire house of Israel" must apprehend "assuredly," namely, *the crucifixion of Jesus Messiah.* Modern Christians may become so accustomed to the cross as an attractive symbol of the faith, adorning our buildings and bodies, that we forget how very odd, if not offensive, the notion of a *crucified Savior* would have been to many ancients. The apostle Paul was under no illusions about society's first impression of his Gospel: "we proclaim Christ crucified, a stumbling block (*skandalon*) to Jews and foolishness (*mōrian*) to [Greeks]" (1 Cor 1:23). Far from good news, the idea that human salvation somehow depended on a brutally executed figure seemed more like a "scandalous" tragedy or "moronic" joke than evangelical truth. Salvation and crucifixion did not naturally compute; if Paul or Luke thought otherwise, they had some serious explaining to do.

Additional signs of struggling with Jesus' crucifixion in Luke and Acts will be presented below. But at this preparatory stage, it is important to underscore a critical *theological* component of Luke's response to this and other issues in his environment. Here I use "theological" in its strictest sense of "God"-centered. The "certainty" for Luke that troubling events, like Jesus' crucifixion, have ultimate meaning and purpose springs from the root conviction that the God of Israel is behind them, that God's plan (*boulē*) is being forwarded through them, that God's scriptural story is being fulfilled, that God is making happen what ought to happen for the good of all God's people: "Let the entire house of Israel know with certainty that *God has made him* both Lord and Messiah, this Jesus whom you crucified" (Acts 2:36, emphasis added).

Emphasizing the pivotal role that God plays in religious narratives like Luke and Acts may seem like overplaying the obvious, but in fact God routinely gets lost in the mad scramble of literary, historical, and ideological interests that drive biblical scholarship. From time to time, however, prominent scholars dare to call the guild back to "God," so to speak, and currently a number of leading commentators have promoted such a theological revival in Lukan studies. For example, Jacob Jervell argues frankly that "the girder in Luke's theological thinking is the notion of God";[6] Joel Green concurs: "To a degree not fully appreciated in many earlier studies of the Third Gospel, Luke's narrative is *theo*logical in substance and focus; that is, it is centered on God";[7] and focusing on Luke's second volume, Beverly Gaventa contends: "If readers of Acts find themselves in a journey, the major sights are not those created by human hands; they result from the actions of God alone."[8]

Simply put, for Luke, *God is the answer* to any question that might arise concerning the recent explosion of strange and wonderful Christ-events. God is the answer that any "God-lover" (*Theophilus*) might desire. Luke conveys this answer not in some neat package of metaphysical propositions about the divine nature, but in a pulsating story about the biblical God of Israel's continuing work in history on behalf of God's people and all creation. And Luke tells this story of God not primarily to humor his audience, but to help them cope with their lives and find meaning in their experiences. Jervell suggests that the "purpose and content" of Luke's narratives "show that he is more of a pragmatic historian in the sense that he writes history to solve problems in his own church(es)."[9] In today's seminary parlance, "pragmatic historian" might be better rendered "practical theologian" or even "pastoral theologian." We now explore several pastoral problems that Luke's writings seek to "solve" from a theocentric perspective.

SHALLOW ROOTS

Our hyper-technological Western culture affords an optimal environment for new ideas and inventions. We pump billions of dollars into discovering more effective cures for disease, faster means of communication, and more efficient sources of energy. We expect tomorrow to be different and better than yesterday—and certainly than the "good old days," which are only "good" for fossils and fogies. Quite the opposite of our "new"-world mentality, however, dominant worldviews of ancient peoples were rooted in even more ancient soil. In antiquity, older was better, beginnings were best, and novelty was scorned. There was nothing new of value under the sun or around the sun (until Copernicus). Consequently, it was incumbent on any ruling people or nation to legitimate their power by demonstrating their noble heritage as far back as possible.

This was no easy task for the first Greeks and Romans. For all their distance from our world and cultural and military prowess in their own world, early Greeks and Romans were relatively new kids on the block compared to ancient Egyptians, Babylonians, and even Israelites. Antiquity was not their strong suit. They still played the game, of course: on the Roman side, for example, Dionysius of Halicarnassus wrote his *Roman Antiquities*, Virgil composed his *Aeneid* (tracing Roman roots back to Trojan times), and Cicero claimed that Roman "religious rites . . . were handed down to us by the gods themselves, since ancient times were closest to the gods" (*Leg.* 2.10.27).[10] But such efforts smacked of special pleading, and many in Greco-Roman society were attracted to the greater antiquity of other religions and cultures. Louis Feldman has demonstrated that, even amid rampant anti-Judaic prejudice in the Hellenistic world, many Gentiles admired the Jews' long and venerable history.[11] Perhaps the Jews' most effective apologetic tool was their antiquity, as evidenced most prolifically in Josephus' twenty volumes of *Jewish Antiquities*. In a later work, *Against Apion*, Josephus further pressed his case for the "very great antiquity" of his Jewish nation (*Ag. Ap.* 1.1-4), contending that "in the Greek world," in dramatic contrast to Jewish history, "everything will be found to be modern and dating, so to speak, from yesterday or the day before" (1.7). Before the hoary Israelite lawgiver Moses, even the greatest Greek jurists appear as but infants (2.154-56).

In this rhetorical environment assuming "nothing can be both new and true,"[12] if Greek, Roman, and Jewish religions had to fight for antiquarian legitimacy, where did that leave an upstart sect like Christianity that followed a maverick Teacher and Lord who died within the last generation? And where did that leave the Christian apostle-come-lately Paul, who proclaimed some "*new* covenant" ratified in the blood of Jesus, whom Paul never knew in the flesh (1 Cor 11:25, emphasis added)? What it left Paul was a heavy chip on his shoulder and a pressing challenge to vindicate his message. He met this challenge in part by claiming immediate revelation from the living Jesus (cf. 1 Cor 11:23-26; Gal 1:11-12) but also by plugging into established tradition. He may not have been with Jesus from the beginning; he may be the "last" and "least of the apostles"; but what he knew and proclaimed about Christ was firmly grounded in preceding apostolic and longstanding scriptural authority: "For I handed on to you as of first importance what I in turn had received: that Christ died for our sins *in accordance with the scriptures*, and that he was buried, and that he was raised on the third day *in accordance with the scriptures*, and that he appeared to Cephas, then to the twelve [apostles]" (1 Cor 15:3-5, emphasis added). This double scriptural appeal to the "Old" Testament, multiplied many times over in Paul's writings, anchors his bold "new" testimony in the venerable depths of Israel's antiquity. And behind Israel's old, old story lay the most ancient power and wisdom of the eternal God "decreed before the ages" (1 Cor 2:7). It doesn't get any older than that.

Luke's accounts of Paul's mission hint at similar concerns with justifying the fledgling Christian faith. In Athens, for example, the seat of classical Greek thought, some philosophers press Paul to explain further his novel message: "May we know what this *new teaching* (*kainē didachē*) is that you are presenting? It sounds rather strange to us, so we would like to know what it means" (Acts 17:19-20, emphasis added). This interest in Paul's "new" ideas is sincere as far as it goes, since "all the Athenians and the foreigners living there," the narrator comments, "would spend their time in nothing but telling or hearing something *new* (*kainoteron*)" (17:21, emphasis added). But Luke's sarcastic tone in reporting this well-known Athenian obsession with novelty seeps through. Sitting around all day discussing "nothing but" newfangled notions would not have appealed to wider Greco-Roman society. And when Paul answers the curious philosophers, he does not promote his gospel as the hottest new thing, but quite the opposite, as the word of the one true "God who made the world and everything in it, he who is Lord of heaven and earth" (17:24)—in other words, the Ancient of Days, the Creator and Ruler of all. In a later incident, when Paul defends himself against Roman and Jewish accusations that he is a "pestilent fellow, an agitator . . . and a ringleader of the sect of the Nazarenes"—that is, of a breakaway, new religious faction—he staunchly insists that this so-called "sect" is in fact deeply rooted in the exalted God and sacred scriptures of Israel: "But this I admit to you, that according to the Way, which they call a sect, I worship the God of our ancestors, believing everything laid down according to the law or written in the prophets" (24:1-9, 14).

Other evidence of Luke's appeals to ancient roots of God's eternal purpose and scriptural plan for Israel may be briefly cited. Peter's Pentecost sermon claims that Jesus' career was "attested to you by God" and unfolded "according to the definite [determined] plan (*boulē*) and foreknowledge (*prognōsei*) of God" (Acts 2:22-23); and the early Jerusalem church prayerfully lives out its communal life before the Creator God "who made the heaven and the earth, the sea, and everything in them," who spoke in Spirit-inspired Scripture "through our ancestor David," and who accomplished through "your holy servant Jesus . . . whatever your hand and your plan (*boulē*) had predestined to take place" (4:23-28). The Lukan Jesus and Philip the evangelist both comfort and counsel perplexed people by "beginning" (*arxamenos*) with scriptural foundations (Luke 24:27; Acts 8:35). And perhaps the most dramatic sign of Luke's deepening Christianity's roots is the extended birth narrative added to Mark's Gospel, demonstrating Jesus' divinely purposed origins in thick Old Testament (Septuagintal) accents.

CRUCIFIED MESSIAH

We suggested above that, given the stigma of crucifixion, promoting the crucified Jesus as Lord and Messiah was a particularly hard sell for the early Christians. The stalwart faithful might believe, with the writer of Hebrews, that Jesus "endured the cross, disregarding its shame" (Heb 12:2), but most ancient observers would have found the cross too abhorrent to disregard, especially for a messianic figure. Modern modes of execution may be less public and bloody than crucifixion but are no less chilling and shameful in their own ways, and the image of a death row criminal as a spiritual leader is as ludicrous now as then.

Of course, justice is not always served, and innocent people suffer unfairly—even to the point of wrongful execution. Luke presses this travesty of justice with respect to Jesus' death, such that even a Roman centurion supervising his crucifixion ultimately concludes, "Certainly this man was innocent" (Luke 23:47). But this officer was an exception. Mob mentality typically rules at public executions, and, as Luke's narrative concedes, most of the audience probably felt Jesus got what he deserved.

Jewish biblical tradition—represented by Job, lament Psalms, Servant Songs of Isaiah 40–55, and martyr accounts of 4 Maccabees—honors the poignant figure of the *righteous sufferer* vindicated by God. Luke especially identifies Jesus with Isaiah's suffering servant, including direct citations of Isaiah 53:7-8, 12 (Acts 8:32-33; Luke 22:37).[13] But nothing in Isaiah or elsewhere in the Old Testament quite prepared for a *crucified* righteous one, still less a crucified *Messiah*. The cross of Jesus remained a tough image to swallow. Paul's fancy exegetical footwork—correlating Deuteronomy's curse on "everyone who hangs on a tree" with Jesus' redemptive act of "becoming a curse for us" by hanging on a cross (Gal 3:13-14)—finds no match in Luke's scriptural repertoire, although he does associate Jesus' crucifixion with tree-hanging (Acts 5:30; 10:39; 13:29).

However much the early Christians mined the Old Testament for insights concerning the crucified Jesus, their trump card in coping with Jesus' ignominious death was *God's mighty act of raising him from the dead*, attested by his followers:

- "But *God raised him up*, having freed him from death" (Acts 2:24, emphasis added).

63

- "This Jesus *God raised up*, and of that all of us are witnesses" (Acts 2:32, emphasis added).
- "Let it be known to all of you . . . that this man is standing before you in good health by the name of Jesus Christ of Nazareth, whom you crucified, whom *God raised from the dead*" (Acts 4:10, emphasis added).
- "The *God* of our ancestors *raised up Jesus*, whom you had killed by hanging him on a tree" (Acts 5:30, emphasis added).
- "They put him to death by hanging him on a tree; but *God raised him* on the third day and allowed him to appear" (Acts 10:39b-40, emphasis added).
- "They took him down from the tree and laid him in a tomb. But *God raised him from the dead*. . . . what *God* promised to our ancestors he has fulfilled for us . . . by *raising Jesus*" (Acts 13:29-30, 32-33, emphasis added).
- "He [*God*] has given assurance to all by *raising him* [*Jesus*] *from the dead*" (Acts 17:31, emphasis added).

But for all this testimony to God's vindicating Jesus through resurrection (and exaltation to God's right hand; Acts 2:33; 5:31; 7:55-56), the enigma of Jesus' crucifixion still nagged. Why did God's plan involve *this particular kind of painful, shameful death* for Jesus? Could God not have vindicated Jesus just as effectively by raising him from some other mode of death? God might overcome the lethal sting of crucifixion, but the social stigma of such vicious capital punishment dies hard.

Various internal clues suggest that Luke's narratives were written in part to "answer" persisting questions within the Christian community and wider rhetorical environment concerning Christ's crucifixion. Simeon's revelation that the infant Jesus is destined "to be a sign that will be opposed," although not specifying that he will be killed by crucifixion or any other means, stirs up a bevy of perplexing "inner thoughts" about Jesus' tragic fate, not only for Mary but also for generations of pondering believers (Luke 2:34-35). When through a series of Jesus' self-predictions, it becomes clear—or should have become clear—that Jesus will "take up his cross," his disciples "understood nothing about all these things" and "were afraid to ask him" for clarification (Luke 9:44-45; 18:31-34; cf. 9:21-24; 13:33-34; 17:24-25). Talk about Jesus' crucifixion and (especially) *taking up one's cross with Jesus* was scary and confusing business for Jesus' early—and later—followers. The resurrection did not change the costly demands of Christian discipleship (cf. Luke 9:23-27; 14:25-33).

Finally, on the third day after Jesus' death, two disciples trudge along the road from Jerusalem to Emmaus, skeptical about rumors of Jesus' resurrection and crestfallen that this one destined "to redeem Israel" had been tragically "condemned to death" by the religious authorities (Luke 24:19-24). Although the risen Jesus soon reveals himself to this troubled couple and suggests a scriptural basis for a suffering Messiah, he quickly disappears without pinpointing particular proof-texts (24:25-31). The two disciples are left with a "burning" memory of Jesus' presence and teaching (24:32), which would doubtless spark more questions and concerns. The truth about a crucified and resurrected Messiah did not fully dawn in a momentary flash of insight: it needed telling and retelling, mulling and re-mulling. To such ends Luke composed his two-volume work.

DELAYED LORD

While many Christians today still anticipate Jesus' "soon" return to earth and final establishment of God's kingdom, other believers, including some who yet long for a restorative "second coming," have little confidence in urgent timetables. After a yawning bimillennial delay, it hardly seems worth pleading, "How long O Lord?" anymore.

As for the early Christians, many, if not most, in the first generation following Jesus' resurrection shared a lively expectation of his near *parousia,* or coming (again). Jesus' immediate and periodic post-resurrection appearances were widely regarded as apocalyptic signs of an imminent and permanent reappearance at the end of the age, "when," as Paul avers, "[Christ] hands over the kingdom to God the Father, after he has destroyed every ruler and every authority and power" (1 Cor 15:23-24). "The appointed time has grown short" (1 Cor 7:29). Yet, even with this first Christian generation—and certainly by the second and third—doubts and questions began to surface. The young congregation at Thessalonica, for example, became anxious about loved ones who had died *since* Jesus' resurrection. Had the delay of Jesus' *parousia* left these departed souls out in the cold, with no hope? And if God keeps postponing Jesus' return indefinitely, might not all present believers miss out on God's kingdom as well? In response to this crisis of faith, Paul assures the Thessalonian church that God has not forgotten them or their deceased kinfolk. When Jesus returns, "God will bring with him those who have died" for a glorious reunion "in the air" with the faithful who remain alive (1 Thess 4:13-18). And though Paul refrains from setting dates and times, he maintains a vigorous hope in the Lord's soon and "sudden" (like a thief in the night) return (5:1-11). He keeps the Thessalonians on high alert and implies that he and many of them will indeed live to witness Jesus' coming (4:15). In the meantime, as Paul's closing benediction suggests, they need not feel abandoned by or apart from Jesus: even now, "the grace of our Lord Jesus Christ be with you" (5:28).

If, as most scholars contend, Luke's narratives were written a generation after Paul's letters, then the "practical theological" problems associated with Jesus' apparent absence and delayed return would only have become more acute. Notable signs of Luke's pastoral concern with these issues include the following.

- **Jesus' Parables in Luke**. Three parables feature an absentee landlord who finally returns to his estate and reckons with workers who have been tending to his interests (Luke 12:35-48; 19:11-27; 20:9-19). In comparison with Matthew and Mark, Luke accentuates both *how far* and *how long* the landlord was away from his household. The parable of the pounds presents a "nobleman [who] went to a *distant country* to get royal power for himself and then return" (19:12, emphasis added), and the parable of the wicked tenants focuses on a vineyard owner who "went to another country *for a long time*" (20:9, emphasis added) before sending various servants—and his "beloved son" (20:13)—to the vineyard, and finally coming himself. Tenants' varied responses to these distant, delayed lords (and son) evoke early Christians' struggles with a seemingly distant God and delayed Jesus.
- **Post-resurrection Appearances in Luke**. The risen Jesus' unpredictable, now-you-see-him-now-you-don't manifestations in the days before his ascension create as much anxiety as excitement among his followers. While the Emmaus couple tells the Jerusalem disciples about their recent surprise encounter with Jesus, he suddenly pops again into their midst; and despite his "peace" offering, the group becomes "startled and terrified, and thought that they were

seeing a ghost" (Luke 24:36-37). After Jesus' departure to heaven, the potential for disciples' doubts and fears regarding Jesus' presence could only have increased.

- **Ascension Scene in Acts**. The ascension scene in Acts 1:6-11 exposes the apostles' preoccupation with Jesus' immediate establishment of God's reign: "Lord is this the time when you will restore the kingdom to Israel?" (1:6). Before transferring to heaven, Jesus shifts their focus away from eschatology ("it is not for you to know the times or periods") to missiology ("you will be my witnesses . . . to the ends of the earth") (1:7-8). Messengers announce that Jesus will come again "in the same way as you saw him go into heaven," but they set no schedule (1:10-11). The apostles must quit gawking up to heaven and get on with their assignment until Jesus returns—whenever that might be. The longer Jesus delays, the more his followers need strength and encouragement to fulfill their mission.

- **Special Visions and Healings in Acts**. Although between his ascension and anticipated second advent, Jesus is officially posted, so to speak, at God's right hand in heaven, he remains vitally interested in earthly affairs and even makes intermittent "advance" visits. In short, his absence should not be interpreted as abandonment. In the interim before his *parousia*, Jesus (1) pours out the gift of the Holy Spirit upon his followers (Acts 2:33); (2) stands up at God's right hand and reveals himself to the dying Stephen (7:55-56); (3) appears in various visions to Peter and Paul, alternately challenging and comforting them (9:3-8; 10:9-16; 11:5-10; 18:9-10; 21:17-21; 23:11); and (4) lends the authority of his name for healing miracles (3:6-7, 16; 4:10; 9:34).[14] But along with these signs of Jesus' continued spiritual presence are plenty of reminders that God has not yet fully subdued evil and restored all things under Christ's feet. Judas, Ananias/Sapphira, Stephen, and James all die violent deaths (for different reasons), and Peter, Paul, and associated missionaries suffer multiple unjust imprisonments, beatings, and other hardships. Paul and companions' terrifying ordeal at sea—threatened by storm and starvation "for a long time" *before* God's angel "stood by" Paul and assured their survival (27:18-26)—mirrors the *long* suffering of Christians in

Luke's environment *before* Jesus' return. As the delay of the *parousia* stretched on for decades, many believers might have been tempted to sink into the seafarers' despair: "all hope of our being saved was at last abandoned" (27:19).

EVIL POWERS

In our tumultuous twenty-first-century world, rulers of various nations and organizations continue to target other authorities and peoples as wicked powers ("axis of evil") that must be eliminated in "God's" name, with "God's" strength and blessing, in the interest of domestic security. Eerie echoes of the Hebrew prophets' fiery "oracles against the nations" may be heard, though all too often without the prophets' corresponding judgment against evil and injustice *within their own nation*. In any case, fear of devastating attack from "godless" powers pervades international politics across the ages.

Sometimes, however, the perceived threat of evil forces extends beyond national and political interests into more personal and cosmic spheres. In the ancient Hellenistic era, whereas some people viewed Greece or Rome as "evil empires" jeopardizing indigenous cultures, many others—including many Greeks and Romans—felt extremely vulnerable to personal (physical, psychological, financial) attacks from a colossal army of diabolical spirit-powers (devils, demons, volatile deities). As Clinton Arnold comments, the Hellenistic world was permeated by a "cognizance of a spirit world exercising influence over virtually every aspect of life."[15]

Although first-century Jews and Christians confessed the ultimate authority of the one true God over all powers, they also acknowledged a host of good (angelic) and evil (demonic) spirit-forces affecting the human environment until the apocalyptic "Day of the Lord" (D-Day). Rarely mentioned in the Hebrew Bible, the devil, or Satan, and his wicked minions regularly harass God's people in Hellenistic Jewish and early Christian literature.[16] While anticipating God's final defeat of the Evil One, in the meantime the fourth evangelist refers to the devil as "the ruler (*archōn*) of this world" (John 12:31; 14:30; 16:11). Paul speaks of God's enemies as "the rulers (*archontes*) of this age, who are doomed to perish" (1 Cor 2:6) and "every ruler (*archē*) and every authority (*exousia*) and power (*dynamis*)" destined to be crushed under Christ's feet (15:24-25). The language suggests a vast network of evil powers—

earthly and cosmic, human and supernatural, political and spiritual—arrayed against God's good purposes. Although their "doom is sure," as Luther's great hymn extols, these diabolical forces must still be resisted by the faithful until the Day of Judgment. The Pauline writer of Ephesians (roughly contemporary with Luke and Acts) envisions the current struggle of God's people as nothing less than lethal warfare "against the rulers (*archas*), against the authorities (*exousias*), against the cosmic powers (*kosmokratoras*) of this present darkness, against the spiritual forces (*pneumatika*) of evil in the heavenly places" (Eph 6:12).

How, then, did anxious first-century folk wage war against these virulent "spiritual forces of evil?" On a basic level, they sought the protective and restorative aid of the good God or gods ("A mighty fortress is our God," to cite Luther again). But what, if anything, can besieged humans do to court the favor of the beneficent spirits, to get the good gods on their side? In addition to calling for trust "in the Lord and in the strength of his power," the Ephesians author encourages "put[ting] on the whole armor of God, so that you may be able to stand against the wiles of the devil." The prescribed pieces of this armor represent what we might call spiritual disciplines—righteousness, proclaiming peace, faith, salvation, and prayer (Eph 6:10-20). Beyond this practice of personal spirituality, however, many in the Hellenistic world (including some Jews and Christians) endeavored to insure their security through a range of magical formulas and procedures.

The favor of God and other gods was up for sale, and "magic" was its currency.[17] "Magic" was big business in this society, and "magicians" were in hot demand, not so much for entertainment and diversion as for health and welfare. And with hot demand came heavy competition: Who were the true and false "magicians?" Who genuinely mediated salutary spiritual power, and who was an impotent charlatan or, worse, a secret agent of malevolent forces? Actually, given the rampant fraud associated with the magic trade, the "magician" label tended to be slung as a pejorative slur against rivals; if you wanted to promote a "good" practitioner, you might call him "healer," "savior," "prophet" (Acts 13:6), "savior" or "Great Power of God" (8:10)—not "magician." In any case, when talk of "magic" was in the air, one could assume a tense, contested environment. As Susan Garrett summarizes: "In the Greco-Roman world, accusations of magic typically occurred in situations of social conflict. Because the use of magic was regarded as socially unacceptable, labeling someone a 'magician' was an effective way to squelch, avenge, or discredit undesirable behavior."[18]

Whether or not Luke's target readers were actively consulting putative wonder-workers, Luke's narrative clearly assumes an embattled milieu threatened by an evil devil, demons, and other diabolical powers. Such nefarious supernatural forces may be in league from time to time with dangerous earthly rulers—like certain Roman officers and Jewish leaders—but are not coterminous with them. Put another way, all Roman and Jewish authorities are not evil. In keeping with Luke's theocentric focus, the ultimate battles in Luke and Acts are not "against enemies of blood and flesh, but against . . . the cosmic powers of this present darkness, against the spiritual forces of evil in the heavenly places" (Eph 6:12).

Using this "dark" imagery, equated with "the realm of Satan, the ruler of this world," Garrett observes that "darkness lies like a shroud over much of the world in which the reader of Luke-Acts is drawn."[19] The devil makes an early appearance in Luke's Gospel, tempting Jesus for forty days at the outset of his public ministry (Luke 4:1-12). Although Jesus successfully passes this test, the devil's wicked campaign is far from over: "When the devil had finished every test, he departed from him [Jesus] *until an opportune time*" (4:13, emphasis added). Jesus goes on the offensive, liberating afflicted persons from malevolent spirits (4:31-37; 8:26-39; 9:37-43) and giving his followers authority to expel demons in his name (9:1-2, 6; 10:17). He deals a heavy blow to the evil powers, "watch[ing] Satan fall from heaven like a flash of lightning" (10:18). But while Satan may be down, he is not out. Toward the end of the story, "Satan enter[s] into Judas called Iscariot," prompting him to hand Jesus over to hostile authorities (22:3), and Jesus acknowledges that Satan has "demanded to sift all of you [disciples] like wheat" (22:31). Peter will especially find himself strained in Satan's sifter, to the point of denying he ever knew Jesus. All is not lost, however, since Jesus prays for Peter's personal restoration and pastoral nurture of other sorely tested disciples (22:31-32). But the situation remains critical: this side of the full realization of God's kingdom, God's people must remain vigilant against the attacks of evil powers that will surely persist.

Acts confirms the ongoing struggle. Peter bounces back from his failure with remarkable Holy Spirit-power generated in the name of the risen Jesus. But Jesus' early followers are still dogged by stiff competition from evil cosmic forces, often channeled through sinister "magicians."[20] Simon Magus—the self-styled "Great One" who claimed to embody the "power of God" in Samaria—seeks to co-opt the apostles' ability to impart the Holy Spirit for his own un-holy, selfish ends (Acts 8:9-24); Bar-Jesus, also known as Elymas— "a certain magician (*magos*) [and] Jewish false prophet"—opposes the mission of Paul and Barnabas in Cyprus (13:4-12); and seven sons of a Jewish high priest named Sceva, who fancied themselves as exorcists in Ephesus, attempt to exploit "the name of the Lord Jesus" in their magical formulas, without knowing the true identity or message of Jesus (19:13-16).

While agents of the bona fide, beneficent power of God through Jesus Christ expose and best all these "magicians," the conflict between good and evil "power"-brokers remains open. Terrified by Peter's curse and condemnation of his "chains of wickedness," Simon Magus pleads for Peter to "pray for me to the Lord, that nothing of what you have said may happen to me" (8:20-24). But that's where the story ends, leaving us wondering whether Peter ever prays for Simon's restoration (as Jesus prayed for his), whether Simon repents of his wicked ways, and whether Simon regains any of his influence with the Samaritan people. In Cyprus, Paul curses Elymas with blindness "for a while" (13:11), but we know nothing of what happens when Paul leaves the island and Elymas can see again. In Ephesus, Sceva's seven sons are humiliated by frustrated attempts to exorcise in Jesus' name (the evil spirit jumps on them and strips them), and as a result, many other area "magicians" renounce their professions and burn their manuals, valued at some "*fifty thousand* silver coins" (emphasis added) (that's a *lot* of magic supporting the Ephesian economy). Still more, we learn that "many *believers* [in Christ]" (emphasis added) come out of the closet to confess their continued participation in magical practices (19:15-19). Apparently, turning to the one God revealed in Jesus Christ did not fully relieve people's anxieties about evil spirits. Many still felt compelled to hedge their bets with various magical goods and services. And, accordingly, Luke felt compelled to offer a practical-theological "answer," in narrative form, to the "fifty thousand silver question" in Luke's Hellenistic world: "what must I do to be saved?" (Acts 16:31).

DISPLACED EXILES

In the wake of Hurricane Katrina—the costliest natural disaster in U.S. history—modern Americans experienced firsthand the tragedy of *exile* within its borders. Suddenly thousands of Gulf Coast residents became refugees from their devastated homes and cities, forced to find shelter in other sectors of the country and faced with dim prospects of returning home again. This crisis shook the prevailing political ethos: such disastrous displacement is not supposed to happen here; this is the land of opportunity, after all, where beleaguered exiles from *other nations* come and find a new paradise. American jingoism aside, it is true that other parts of the world are more familiar with the hardships of exile. As I write these words, thousands of Lebanese are fleeing their war-torn country, which is nothing new, sadly, in the Middle East. The intertwined plots of *exodus* and *exile* comprise one of the grand "macro-stories" spanning the horizon of biblical history.[21] The displacement of Adam and Eve from Eden (Gen 3:22-24), the flight of Cain to Nod ("Wandering," 4:16), the scattering of Babel-builders "over the face of all the earth" (11:8-9), and the abrupt transfer of Abraham "to the land that I will show you" (12:1) set a pattern of dispersion that snakes through the gamut of ancient Israel's experience, spiking at the "Exodus" from Egyptian slavery, the subsequent "Wilderness Wandering" in the Sinai desert, and the later "Exile" in Babylonian captivity.

In the New Testament period, Paul's itinerant missionary career—following his apocalyptic encounter with the living Christ (*apocalypsis*, Gal 1:12)—bears the marks of exilic displacement and distress. He may have viewed his immediate retreat to the Arabian desert (Gal 1:17), perhaps extending for three years, as something of a self-imposed exile. At any rate, when his gospel-proclaiming and church-planting mission got into full swing throughout Syria, Asia Minor, and Greece, he put down few roots and drifted from place to place, sometimes fleeing from hostile authorities, at other times landing in prison, and almost always suffering a string of hardships along the way. At one point, Paul speaks "like a mad-man" on the run, rattling off a list of adversities:

> more imprisonments, with countless floggings, and often near death.
> Five times I have received from the Jews the forty lashes minus one.

> Three times I was beaten with rods. Once I received a stoning. Three times I was shipwrecked; for a night and a day I was adrift at sea; on frequent journeys, in danger from rivers, danger from bandits, danger from my own people, danger from Gentiles, danger in the city, danger in the wilderness, danger at sea, danger from false brothers and sisters; in toil and hardship, through many a sleepless night, hungry and thirsty, often without food, cold and naked. (2 Cor 11:23-27)

Whereas Paul regarded these "exilic" sufferings as signs of a true apostle, in whom Christ's "power is made perfect in [Paul's] weakness" (12:9), other Christian leaders were not so sure. Is constantly being on the lam, fighting for respect and survival, a gauge of God's favor? Is this the kind of résumé we're looking for in our ministers? As an imperiled refugee, Paul had to struggle for legitimacy even in his own churches.

At times, however, congregations suffered *with* Paul as fellow aliens on the margins of society. Encouraging the Philippian believers to pull together during persecution, Paul writes, "For [God] has graciously granted you the privilege not only of believing in Christ, but of suffering for him as well—since you are having *the same struggle that you saw I had and now hear that I still have*" (Phil 1:29-30, emphasis added). In his letter to the Roman church, Paul raises questions that imply the community's "separation" anxiety fueled by disruptive experiences of hardship, distress, persecution, famine, nakedness, peril, and sword and ultimately answers that no crisis "will be able to separate us from the love of God in Christ Jesus our Lord" (Rom 8:35-39). The letter of 1 Peter, probably written a generation after Paul's death to several congregations in Asia Minor where Paul had labored, explicitly addresses these Christians' exilic identity:

- "To the *exiles of the Dispersion* (*parepidēmois diasporas*) in Pontus, Galatia, Cappadocia, Asia, and Bithynia . . ." (1:1).
- "Live in reverent fear *during the time of your exile* (*paroikos*)" (1:17).
- "Beloved, I urge you as *aliens* (*paroikous*) *and exiles* (*parepidēmous*) to abstain from the desires of the flesh that wage war against the soul" (2:11).

Whether a literal descriptor of dislocation from hearth and homeland, a metaphorical image of ostracism from the dominant culture,

73

or both, "exile" represents a core component of these believers' self-perception.

Even though the evidence doesn't support constant persecution and dispersion of Christians throughout the first century, as is sometimes supposed, the potential threat of forceful displacement still lurked in the environment of many Christian communities. At several points, Luke's narratives project such an insecure environment and offer some assurances for coping with it. Jesus' birth takes place in a doubly-displaced setting: an imperial census decree forces Joseph and his pregnant wife Mary southward from their residence in Galilean Nazareth to their ancestral roots in Judean Bethlehem; and here Mary bears Jesus not in a relative's home or hotel room, but in a feed trough, "because there was no place for them in the inn" (Luke 2:1-7). Jesus begins life as an exile in his own country. Little changes during the course of his public ministry. Though staying for the most part in familiar territory, he seldom settles long in any one place. Early on he is booted out of hometown Nazareth (4:29-30), and from that point he keeps on the move, roaming about Galilee, Samaria, and Judea with "nowhere to lay his head" (9:58). His longest and, arguably, most moving parable features an unfortunate runaway "to a distant country," isolated and impoverished by his own foolish choices, but finally restored to his gracious father (15:10-32). Exilic struggles—whether self-inflicted or caused by others' rejection, whether distant or more local—poignantly mark Luke's narrative world.

In Acts, the persecution-dispersion crisis heightens for the followers of Jesus (as he predicted in Luke 6:22; 21:12-19). Stephen's defense speech before the Jerusalem Council highlights Israel's checkered history of being mistreated slaves and "resident aliens (*paroikon*) in a country belonging to others" (Acts 7:6) and of initially spurning Moses' leadership so that he "fled and became a resident alien (*paroikos*) in the land of Midian" (7:29). These experiences of forced displacement in Israel's past prove prophetic of Stephen and the early church's fate. Stephen is dragged outside the city and stoned to death, and the young firebrand, Saul, who had attended (supervised?) Stephen's lynching, launches "a severe persecution . . . against the church in Jerusalem" (7:58–8:3). As a result, the Jerusalem congregation "scatters" or "disperses" (*diaspeirō*) throughout the regions of Judea, Samaria, Phoenicia, Syria, and Cyprus (8:4; 11:19). Later we learn that Jewish Christians at Rome, like Aquila and Priscilla, had to leave the city because of Claudius's edict expelling all Jews (Suetonius reports that persisting Jewish conflicts over "Chrestus" [Christ?] prompted the expulsion order). Through all of this disruption, however, Christ's movement survives and even thrives. As believers scatter, they disseminate the gospel and begin new congregations. Jesus himself soon stops the persecutor Saul/Paul in his tracks and commissions him to spread the gospel throughout the Gentile world. Ironically, as he had harassed many followers of Jesus, Paul would now "suffer [much] for the sake of my [Jesus'] name" (9:15), fleeing from town to town, facing imprisonment, mob violence, and sundry trials at every turn, much like Paul's letters report. But as the "exiled" Paul stays on the move in Acts, he also stays on mission, testifying to Christ wherever he goes, under Christ's watchful care.

However much disruptive events like Saul's terror campaign and Claudius' expulsion order still haunted Luke's environment a generation or two later (traumas have long shelf lives), they doubtless took a backseat to the more recent and more catastrophic *destruction of Jerusalem and its temple* by the Roman army in 70 C.E. It would be difficult to overplay the severity of the social, psychological, and spiritual effects of this disaster on the Jewish community, not only in Jerusalem, but also throughout the Diaspora, which looked to Jerusalem as the center ("navel") of the universe (9/11 or Hurricane Katrina are suggestive, but insufficient analogies). As Erich Gruen remarks

> For the Jews of antiquity, the loss of the Temple [in 70 C.E.] represented an enduring trauma. . . . Of course, prior catastrophes had marked Jewish history. But the fall of Jerusalem to Rome represented a wholly different order of magnitude. It must have been clear to most, and soon to all, that recovery of the Temple could no longer even be contemplated for the indefinite, perhaps the infinite, future. In the general view, the resounding reverberations of that event determined the diasporic consciousness of Jews throughout the centuries to follow. The eradication of the center, which had given meaning and definition to the nation's identity, obliged them to alter their sights, accommodate to a displaced existence, and rethink their own heritage in the context of strange surroundings.[22]

Babylon's battering of Jerusalem and the first (Solomonic) temple in 587 B.C.E., precipitating forced exile for those Jews who survived, represents the "prior catastrophe" most like Rome's razing of the second (Herodian) temple in 70 C.E. In some post-70 Diaspora circles, ancient Babylon became a thinly veiled cipher for present-day Rome (1 Pet 5:13; Rev 18:2-24). As the "strange surroundings" of the Babylonian Empire posed a formidable challenge to Jewish faith and identity, so now did the alien environs of the Roman Empire. Many who knew their biblical history must have wondered if the Jews could recover from another knockout blow against their holy city and religious foundations.

As we have seen, Luke knew his biblical history very well and demanded the same from his readers. "Babylon" appears only once in Luke's narratives, but this reference betrays Luke's editorial hand and comes at a strategic point in the story. The long review of Israel's past in Acts 7 includes a citation from Amos 5:25-27, recalling the nation's forty years of wilderness wandering and later exile to a foreign land (Acts 7:42-43). However, otherwise sticking close to his Septuagint source, Luke *changes* Amos' original destination from "beyond Damascus" to "beyond *Babylon*," thereby evoking memory of the temple's destruction and the Babylonian exile. By incorporating this citation into *Stephen's speech* (7:2-53), where he responds to charges of speaking against "this holy place" (temple) and predicting its demolition (6:13-14), Luke draws a subtle link between the Babylonian and Roman assaults on the Jerusalem temple in the sixth century B.C.E. and first century C.E., respectively.

In other places, Luke demonstrates not-so-subtle concerns over the terrible effects of Jerusalem's "crushing" and "trampling" by "the Gentiles," driving its citizens to "flee to the mountains" and to "be taken away as captives among all nations" (Luke 19:44; 21:21, 24; cf. 13:32-35; 19:41-44; 21:5-6, 20-24; 23:27-31). A few days before his crucifixion, Jesus—a faithful devotee of the temple since childhood (2:21-50)—shockingly illustrates the temple's demise (driving out merchants) and laments its sad condition as a "den of robbers," just as Jeremiah did during the Babylonian crisis (Luke 19:45-46; Jer 7:11). Rather than a haven for refugees, the temple has become a hideout for oppressors who turn away God's suffering people and scatter them abroad. Robert Tannehill, who focuses on the internal narrative world of Luke and Acts, nonetheless grants the significance of the "historical setting, in which memory of the temple's destruction was still painful for any who honored Israel's tradition and respected the devout men and women who worshiped in its temple," as a critical piece of "information shared by author and reader."[23] The early Jerusalem church perpetuates Jesus' practice of preaching, praying, and gathering in the temple precincts: "Day by day . . . they spent much time together in the temple" (Acts 2:46; cf. 3:1–4:22; 5:12-42). And lest there be any doubt that Paul's mission among the Gentiles dampens his commitment to Israel's traditions, he sponsors members of the Jerusalem congregation in completing vows of consecration in the temple (21:17-26).

Luke's story makes clear that Christ's church, wherever it extends, builds on the foundation of Israel's temple tradition and thus faces a shattering loss when that foundation is dismantled by Rome. The questions are predictable, but no less painful for that: Why did God let this happen? What purpose did it serve? Whose fault was it? How do we survive our "exile"? Can we ever go "home" again to the roots of our faith? Will the city and temple ever be rebuilt? What do we do if they can't? In part, Luke and Acts were written to provide some of the answers.

STRATIFIED SOCIETY

Romantic notions of the "New Testament Church" as an idyllic, egalitarian community still persist among some contemporary Christians. If we could just get back to the good old halcyon days of Paul and Acts, all would be well. Favorite texts that fuel this nostalgia include, from Paul: "There is no longer Jew or Greek . . . slave or free . . . male and female; for all of you are one in Christ Jesus" (Gal 3:28); and from Acts: "All who believed were together and had all things in common" (Acts 2:44; cf. 4:32-35). Whatever hierarchies and conflicts beset society at large appear neutralized in the one big, happy Christian family. But these utopian proof texts are conspicuous by their *contrast* with the prevailing picture of particular churches in the New Testament as struggling communities riddled with rivalry and strife.

One way or another, all of Paul's letters respond to congregational conflicts. The Galatians correspondence, for example, even with its ideal of Christ-centered unity (3:28), reflects the bitter reality of Pauline opponents preaching "a different gospel" (1:6-9) and of Galatian believers needing stern warnings against "enmities, strife, jealousy, anger, quarrels, dissensions, factions . . . competing against one another, envying one another" (5:20, 26). Whereas those belonging to the *same* ethnic group (Jew or Gentile), social status (slave or free), and gender (male or female) may fuss and fight among themselves, hostilities were just as likely, if not more so, to erupt between *different* strata of Greco-Roman society. Although we have limited evidence regarding the social composition of early Christian communities (no "church rolls" have surfaced), scholars such as Wayne Meeks and Gerd Theissen have made strong cases for the *mixed makeup* of Pauline congregations, reflecting a heterogeneous cross-section of urban society from relatively low to high ranks, with few, perhaps, on the extreme ends.[24] This picture challenges popular perceptions of early Christians as a monolithic group of low-class folk, whether imagined by pagan critics like Celsus, who mocked Christianity as the religion of "the most illiterate and bucolic yokels" (Origen, *Cels*. 3.44), or by liberal idealists, who paint primitive Christians as a quaint, happy band of simple peasants.[25] Paul and other missionaries may have advanced alternative visions of a more inclusive, egalitarian "body," but these ideals created considerable dissonance within and among members from diverse social stations. It could not have been easy, for example, for a wealthy Greek male businessman to live as "one in Christ" with a poor Jewish female slave (or vice versa) in a cosmopolitan center like Corinth.

Speaking of the church at Corinth, Paul's letters to the Corinthians and Romans (written from Corinth) offer interesting glimpses into its social dynamics. Paul writes 1 Corinthians in response to disturbing reports of schismatic "quarrels" in the congregation (1 Cor 1:10-11). Among several factors contributing to these conflicts, one related to members' diversity in status. The majority clustered near the bottom of the social ladder: "Not many of you were wise by human standards, not many were powerful, not many were of noble birth" (1:26). Of course, "not many were powerful, etc." implies that a minority *was* (e.g., Gaius, who hosted "the whole church" in his sizeable residence, and "Erastus, the city treasurer" [Rom 16:23]). Paul's audience knew full well how they rated in the social register. He brings up this profile in order to assure the "lower" folk that God blesses and honors them as much, if not more, than elites: "God chose what is weak in the world to shame the strong; God chose what is low and despised in the world, things that are not, to reduce to nothing things that are, so that no one might boast in the presence of God" (1 Cor 1:27-29). But Paul also sends a message here to the "strong" church members: whatever high positions they hold in society, they have no right to lord their authority over fellow believers of lesser status. Before God, all are lowly. The fact that Paul underscores this point suggests not everyone at Corinth had gotten it; status variables doubtless contributed to community tension. Later in 1 Corinthians, Paul addresses some specific sore spots such as (1) conflicts between "weak" and "strong" regarding meat-eating practices (apart from the theological problem of consuming meat dedicated to idols was the sociological factor that the poor could scarcely afford any meat; 1 Corinthians 8–10), (2) disparities in observing the Lord's Supper (a full feast at this time), such that some better-off members gorge themselves while "those who have nothing" get nothing to eat (11:17-22), and (3) controversies between male "heads" of households and subordinate female prophets (11:2-16; 14:33-35).[26]

By and large, Luke's narratives are embedded in the same agonistic, stratified environment that surrounds Paul's letters. Although Luke has often been touted as a champion of the poor, a friend of women, and an advocate of Christian unity, the society reflected in Luke and Acts is much more complex. Although Jesus and his followers reach out to the poor and needy and associate with women, the interests of more prominent and wealthy men are by no means shortchanged. As Jesus sharply criticizes self- indulgent rich folk (e.g. Luke 6:24-25; 13:13-21; 16:19-31; 18:18-25), he also honors the generosity of wealthy benefactors, like the centurion at Capernaum (7:1-10) and the tax collector Zacchaeus (19:1-10). Moreover, well-to-do female disciples, like Mary Magdalene and Joanna, help finance Jesus' movement (8:2-3), as house-holding women like Martha of Bethany, Mary of Jerusalem, and Lydia of Philippi host Jesus in Luke and local houses host churches in Acts (Luke 10:38-42; Acts 12:12-17; 16:11-15, 40). Counterpointing these supporting roles for women of means, however, are keynote speaking parts played exclusively by male authorities. For all the inclusiveness anticipated at Pentecost ("your daughters . . . and [female] slaves . . . shall prophesy" [Acts 2:17-18]), it doesn't work out that way as Acts unfolds: the prophetic daughters and slave-women are scarcely heard from again.[27] Also, for all the mutual care provided by the Jerusalem church such that "there was not a needy person among them" (Acts 4:34), mistrust and conflict still erupt over some wealthier members (Ananias/Sapphira) less inclined to fork over all their possessions to the community chest (5:1-11) and some poorer members (Hellenist widows) not getting their fair share of benefits (6:1-7).

Thus, all is not bliss in Luke's world—which is no great surprise given the diverse swath of people that inhabit this environment. Along with hierarchical gaps in economic (rich/poor) and gender (male/female) status, Meeks reminds us that many other status markers stratified ancient Greco-Roman society, such as "ethnic origins, *ordo*, citizenship, personal liberty, wealth, occupation, age, sex, and public offices or honors," which may characterize individuals in various low/high combinations.[28] For example, the purple-handling businesswoman, Lydia, may have combined relatively *low occupational* (artisan) and *gender* (female) status with relatively *high economic* status.[29] Numerous permutations are possible in a complex social system. The Lukan narratives may not feature every type of character in antiquity, but they do provide a thick sample. Concluding his trenchant study of *Community and Gospel in Luke-Acts*, Philip Esler sketches a broad outline of Luke's social setting and potential conflicts within it:

> [T]he community encompassed individuals both from the highest strata in the city—Roman officers, for example, and possibly even decurions—and also from the lowest levels, the beggars and the impoverished day-labourers. The presence within the same group of representatives from the glittering elite and from the squalid urban poor was very unusual in this society and created severe internal problems, especially since some of the traditions of Jesus' sayings known to the community counselled the rich to a generosity to the destitute quite at odds with Greco-Roman attitudes to gift-giving.[30]

Although there is no necessary one-to-one correspondence between the *dramatis personae* in Luke's *literary work* and the membership of Luke's *local church*, the range of characters in Luke and Acts represents a cross-section of first-century readers' social environment.[31] And it's likely that one major purpose of Luke's composition was to help believers from a variety of backgrounds and statuses negotiate complex relations with each other and the surrounding society and sort out what it means to love "your neighbor [whoever that might be!] as yourself" (Luke 10:27).

RELIGIOUS PLURALISM

Burgeoning globalization has heightened awareness, though not always understanding, of the many different religions practiced in our world. Even within so-called "Christian" America, many are waking up to the fact that a sizeable minority (millions) of our citizens devoutly worships non-Christian "gods" and practices non-Christian forms of spirituality. Such religious pluralism poses special challenges of *definition* (what fundamental issues distinguish one faith from another?) and *dialogue* (what do different faiths have in common, and how might they coexist with mutual respect?).

A lively mix of religious devotion also characterized the first-century Mediterranean world. With its vibrant pantheon of deities, ancient Greco-Roman society fostered and tolerated many expressions of faith and superstition, including local native religions like Judaism, provided they did not obtrusively disturb the peace (*pax Romana*). Paul—the Jewish apostle of Jesus Christ to the Gentiles—labored in this pluralistic environment and regularly struggled with interfaith issues. On the *definition* side, Paul cared little about fine distinctions between various Greco-Roman cults. In sharp contrast to Judaism's bedrock monotheism, he lumps all polytheistic pagan religions together as foolishly *idolatrous*. Anyone who worships other so-called gods and idols, that is, any figure other than Israel's one true God and God's Messiah Jesus, worships in vain:

> we know that "no idol in the world really exists," and that "there is no God but one" [cf. Deut 6:5]. Indeed, even though there may be so-called gods in heaven or on earth—as in fact there are many gods and many lords—yet for us there is one God, the Father, from whom are all things, and for whom we exist, and one Lord, Jesus Christ, through whom are all things and through whom we exist. (1 Cor 8:4-6)

Accordingly, the only hope for the pagan world, in Paul's judgment, is to "flee from the worship of idols" (1 Cor 10:14) and turn "to God from idols, to serve a living and true God, and to wait for his Son from heaven, whom he raised from the dead—Jesus, who rescues us from the wrath that is coming" (1 Thess 1:9-10). No budging here; no room for compromise: the only living and true religion is that devoted to the one "living and true God" of Israel revealed in God's Son, the one Lord, Jesus Christ.

Although many idols and temples dedicated to many gods thrived in the Roman Empire, overriding the related domains of religion and politics was the juggernaut of the *imperial cult*. Idolized in images and inscriptions on coins, statues, buildings, and gravestones across the Roman world, emperors like Caesar Augustus commanded utmost allegiance as almighty God (*theos*), Lord (*kyrios*), and Savior (*sōtēr*). Paul's staunch devotion to Israel's Sovereign God, who raised Jesus from death (on a Roman cross!) and exalted him as Lord and Savior of all, was bound to clash with imperial interests. Essentially branding all divine representations of Caesar as worthless idols was not the mark of good citizenship and contributed to Paul's frequent sojourns in Roman prisons (2 Cor 6:5; 11:23; Phil 1:12-13; Phlm 1:1, 10-13; cf. Eph 3:1; Col 4:3, 18). Crossan and Reed suggest that Paul's expectation of Jesus' imminent coming (*parousia*)—when, as noted above, Jesus "hands over the kingdom to God the Father, after he has destroyed every ruler [like Caesar!] and every authority and power" (1 Cor 15:23-24)—poses a head-on challenge to the emperor's grand entrances (*parousia*) into cities as conquering hero and gracious benefactor.[32] Caesar's "coming" to town is nothing compared with Jesus' "coming" to establish God's kingdom on earth.

With Paul's unwavering convictions about God's Sovereignty and Jesus' Lordship, we might not expect much from him in terms of interfaith *dialogue*. But Paul was no rigid fundamentalist. He absolutely insisted that Gentiles turn from idols to serve God and Christ alone, but once they did that, there was room to breathe. Inscriptional evidence from ancient Jewish synagogues confirms the presence of Gentile sympathizers with Judaism, who embraced the one God of Israel and the ethical ideals of Moses, but stopped short of becoming converts (proselytes) through circumcision and full observance of Jewish customs.[33] As an educated Hellenistic Jew who wrote in Greek and integrated Greek ideas into his faith, Paul was doubtless conversant with these Gentile patrons on the margins of Judaism. And after he accepted Jesus as God's Messiah, he actively incorporated these (and other) Gentile believers into the community of God's people *without insisting on their circumcision and conformity to the whole Mosaic Law*. In fact, Paul vigorously opposed hardliners who demanded that Gentiles become Jews in order to be saved (see Galatians). By the same token, however, as more and more Gentiles came to the faith, Paul did not for a moment compel Jews (like himself!) to give up their ethnic-religious identity and become Gentiles. Further, he firmly challenged any Gentile smugness and intolerance toward the minority of more scrupulous Jewish believers in Christ as well as the many more Jews who had not believed. Without the Creator God who made a faithful covenant with Israel, the Gentiles would be hopelessly trapped in their "degrading passions" and "debased minds" (Rom 1:18-32). Without being grafted into the solid root of God's promises to Abraham, the Gentile "wild shoots" would be utterly fruitless (11:11-24). They owe everything to the God of Israel and can bank on the fact that "all Israel will be saved" (11:26).[34]

So Paul's gospel—"to the Jew first and also to the Greek" (Rom 1:16)—allows for ongoing dialogue between Jews and Greeks, within the parameters of Jewish monotheism and messianism. But it also risks continuing conflict within mixed Jewish and Gentile congregations, often centered on fellowship meals. One time Paul "opposed" the Jew Cephas (Peter) "to his face" for withdrawing from Gentile members of the Antioch church and eating at a separate "circumcision table" (Gal 2:11-14). On other occasions, however, Paul exhorted freethinking Gentiles (and liberal Jews) at Rome and Corinth not to eat any meat offered to idols (even though they're worthless) if it causes offense to scrupulous Jews (and conservative Gentiles) or provokes them to violate their consciences (Rom 14–15; 1 Cor 8–10). Religious dialogue is precarious business, but worth the effort from Paul's perspective. Note his "winning" approach to the challenges of religious pluralism:

> For though I am free with respect to all, I have made myself a slave to all, so that I might win more of them. To the Jews I became as a Jew, in order to win Jews. . . . To those outside the law I became as one outside the law (though I am not free from God's law but am under Christ's law) so that I might win those outside the law. To the weak I became weak, so that I might win the weak. I have become all things to all people, that I might by all means save some. I do it all for the sake of the gospel. (1 Cor 9:19-23)

The bustling narrative worlds of Luke and Acts include a host of Jewish, Greek, and Roman people with different religious orientations. Whether or not Luke's "home church" had members from all these backgrounds, it doubtless interacted on some level with the wider Israelite and Greco-Roman spiritual environment. As a new messianic "sect" in a pluralistic society, believers in Jesus Christ faced critical challenges of self-definition and interfaith dialogue. As in Paul's letters, Luke's narratives draw a sharp line of distinction between Jewish and pagan notions of God/gods and worship. Jesus and his followers stand firm in their Jewish roots against the vapid cults of polytheism and idolatry. Even when engaged in some *intra*-Jewish ethical dispute, Jesus' exclusive devotion to Israel's One God is transparent: in a debate with a Jewish legal expert, Jesus happily affirms the Deuteronomic mandate to "love the Lord your God with all your heart" (Luke 10:27); and in a tense exchange with a wealthy Jewish ruler, Jesus unequivocally avers, "No one is good but God alone" (18:19).

In Acts, Peter, Paul, and Barnabas make similar confessions of monotheistic faith in the face of idolatrous challenges.

- When the God-fearing Roman centurion Cornelius, who should have known better, threw himself at Peter's feet and "worshiped him," the apostle promptly pulled Cornelius up, "saying, 'Stand up; I am only a mortal'" (10:25-26).
- When the pagan Lycaonians attempted to offer sacrifices to Barnabas and Paul as "the gods [Zeus and Hermes] have come down to us in human form," the missionary pair "tore their clothes" in disgust and pleaded with the crowd: "Friends, why are you doing this? We are mortals just like you, and we bring you good news, that you should *turn from these worthless things to the living God*, who made the heaven and the earth and the sea and all that is in them" (14:11, 14-15, emphasis added).
- In Athens, the heart of Greek religiosity and a city "full of idols"—even one dedicated to "an unknown god," just to cover all the bases—Paul became "deeply distressed" and, standing at the Hill of Ares, proclaimed in no uncertain terms "the God who made the world and everything in it . . . who is Lord of heaven and earth, [who] does not live in shrines made by human hands" (17:16, 22-24).

Luke concedes nothing to idolatry. Worshiping the one Invisible Creator God is a *sine qua non* of true faith. But Acts does disclose

Paul and Barnabas' attempts at monotheistic bridge-building with pagan audiences: they remind the Lycaonians at Lystra that the one Living God "has not left himself without a witness in doing good—giving you [unbelievers] rains from heaven and fruitful seasons, and filling you with food and your hearts with joy" (14:17); and before the Athenians, Paul shrewdly cites two "of your own poets" to support his point: "'In [God] we live and move and have our being'"; "'For we too are [God's] offspring'" (17:28). But these dialogic efforts have limited impact. At Lystra, "even with these words" from Paul and Barnabas about God's abundant grace, "they scarcely restrained the crowds from offering sacrifice to them" (14:18); and at Athens, while a few were persuaded by Paul's argument, many others either mocked him or put him off until another time (17:32-34). In Luke's rhetorical environment, interfaith dialogue remains a formidable challenge.

As for the Jesus movement's encounter with Roman religion, Luke's narratives shy away from explicit clashes with the emperor cult. But Luke's unique setting of Jesus' birth during Caesar Augustus' reign over "all (*pas*) the world" carries strong religio-political implications (Luke 2:1-2; cf. 3:1-2). The angel of the Lord announces "for all (*pas*) the people" the glorious arrival "this day in the city of [King] David, a Savior (*Sōtēr*), who is the Messiah (*Christos*), the Lord (*Kyrios*)" (2:10). In essence, Lord Jesus comes with an alternative imperial agenda: to establish the sovereign, salutary empire (kingdom) of God on earth.[35]

How Roman authorities respond to the aggressive mission of Jesus and his followers is a complicated and delicate matter in Luke and Acts. Bald assessments of Luke's theology as either apologetically pro-Roman or radically anti-Roman fail to grapple with Luke's multifaceted narrative presentation. Jesus' execution on a Roman cross between two convicted criminals surely fueled Roman suspicions concerning Jesus' movement and, conversely, Christian anxieties about Roman opposition to their faith. Luke negotiates these tensions, in part, by soft-pedaling Pontius Pilate's endorsement of the traitorous accusations against Jesus (23:1-5) and highlighting other Roman officers' affirmation of Jesus' authority (7:1-10) and innocence (23:47). On the other hand, however, Jesus elevates "the things that are God's" over the emperor's interests, such as taxation, represented by idolatrous coins bearing his "divine" title and image (20:20-26; cf. 23:1).[36] Moreover, the early Jerusalem church does not let Pilate off the hook for Jesus' death, considering him a full partner with those "gathered together against your [God's] holy servant Jesus, whom you anointed" (Acts 4:25-27). As for Paul, the book of Acts makes much of his Roman citizenship (never mentioned in Paul's letters) as a "get out of jail" free card and guarantee of protective custody so he can testify before Caesar. But all is not smooth sailing for Paul en route to Rome, and not all Roman officers prove to be friends in high places. For example, the Roman governor Felix, though affording Paul a measure of freedom, kept him imprisoned at Caesarea for two years in order to placate Paul's enemies and to ply Paul for bribe money (24:22-27). The centurion Julius, an Augustan officer charged with ferrying Paul and other prisoners to Rome, "treated Paul kindly and allowed him to go to his friends to be cared for" at one port of call and restrained other soldiers from killing him after a terrible shipwreck (27:1-3, 39-44). But Julius also refused to heed Paul's warnings about impending peril and put Paul's life, and everyone else's on board, in jeopardy (27:11).

As Jesus and his followers have a varied and volatile relationship with the Roman Empire in Luke's writings, so it is with the Jewish temple and its hierarchy. Again, extreme judgments concerning either Luke's thoroughgoing anti-Judaism[37] or his uncritical Jewish "fundamentalism"[38] skew a more mixed presentation. We may tot up verses on both sides:

- One minute Jesus accepts an invitation to dine with Pharisees (Luke 7:36; 11:37; 14:1); the next he criticizes their dining habits (11:39-41; 14:7-24).
- One minute Jesus amiably discusses theology with temple scholars (Luke 2:46-47); the next he drives out temple merchants and denounces temple leaders as a band of "robbers" (19:45-48).
- One minute the Pharisees criticize Jesus' eating practices (Luke 5:30; 15:1-2); the next they invite him to dinner as an honored guest (7:36; 11:37; 14:1).
- One minute the Pharisees are "filled with fury" at Jesus (Luke 6:11) or have "ridiculed" his teaching (16:14); the next they call him "Teacher" and encourage him to speak (7:40) or advise patient consideration of his movement (Acts 5:33-39).

- One minute Peter blasts his fellow Israelites as Christ killers "outside the law" (Acts 2:23); the next he promises them forgiveness and "times of refreshing" from God through Jesus Messiah "appointed *for you* [Israelites]" (3:19-20, emphasis added).
- One minute Paul curses an unreceptive synagogue audience ("Your blood be on your own heads!") and writes them off in favor of Gentiles (Acts 18:6); the next he is back in the synagogue, winning over as many fellow Jews as he can to Jesus Messiah (19:8-9; cf.17:10-11), but *not* at the expense of their (or his) Jewish identity, faith, and practice (16:1-3; 18:18; 21:17-26).

Jesus, Peter, Paul, and other leaders of Jesus' movement did not aim to establish a new religion called "Christianity." The term *Christianos* appears only twice in Luke's writings, both as a label assigned to Christ's followers by *outsiders*, not as a self-designation (Acts 11:26; 26:28).[39] In Luke's presentation, Jesus himself and the early believers in his messianic mission are all Jews seeking to renew their historic faith from within. They claim to know the right "Way" of salvation for God's people in Jesus' name (cf. Acts 4:12), but it is most certainly *not a way out* of Judaism.[40] Of course, not all Jews in Luke's day agreed that Jesus' "Way" was best, just as Jews, and every other religious group, today disagree *among themselves* on key matters of faith and practice. Ultimately, Luke's story wrestles with "a divided Israel" in which "some were convinced" by the Christ-centered gospel "while others refused to believe" (Acts 28:23-25). Whether Luke anticipates a continuing mission to "unbelieving" Jews in hopes that "all Israel will be saved" (cf. Rom 11:26) is likely, in my judgment, but not entirely clear. However, it is clear that Luke's narratives grapple with persisting issues of *intra-Jewish* dialogue—and heated disagreement—surrounding the messianic figure of Jesus.

Between the poles of Jewish and Greco-Roman religionists in Luke's world are two more ambiguous groups—Samaritans and "God-fearers." The *Samaritans* worshiped the biblical God of Abraham, Isaac, and Jacob but set themselves apart from most Jews, who, for all their differences, shared a common devotion to Jerusalem and Mt. Zion (temple site) as the sacred center of their faith. By contrast, Samaritans fixed on Shechem and Mount Gerizim as the true holy places and had little patience with Jews traipsing through their territory en route to Jerusalem. For their part, most Jews united in their prejudice against Samaritans, not only because of Samaritan anti-Jerusalem sentiments but also because of their supposed "half-breed" heritage rooted in the commingling of northern Israelites (Samarians) with idolatrous Assyrian conquerors in the eighth century B.C.E. (cf. 2 Kgs 17:24-41). In ancient Jewish circles, Samaritans might be variously regarded as apostate Jews, pagan Gentiles, or some strange hybrid, neither Jew nor Gentile. In any case, Jewish-Samaritan relations remained strained in the first century C.E. from both sides.

The first encounter between Jesus, his disciples, and the Samaritans in Luke's Gospel reflects this tense environment. Precisely "because his face was set toward Jerusalem," inhabitants of a Samaritan village refuse to allow Jesus and his followers into their borders. In response, two disciples, James and John, propose a plan "to command fire to come down from heaven and consume them"—not exactly a proportional response, but one apropos of the lethal hostilities between Jews and Samaritans. Jesus wants nothing to do with such fireworks, however, and whisks his hotheaded followers away "to another village" (Luke 9:51-56). Although bypassing Samaritans on this occasion, Jesus later passes through "the region between Samaria and Galilee" and cures a Samaritan along with nine Jews afflicted with leprosy. Jesus further commends this Samaritan as the only one from the group to thank Jesus and "give praise to God" (17:11-19); but he also distinguishes the man as "this foreigner (*allogenēs*)," confirming the Samaritans' alien status within Israel. In Acts, Philip evangelizes and baptizes a throng of Samaritans in the name of Jesus Christ, thus linking them with the messianic Jesus community in Jerusalem (Acts 8:4-13), but the odd delay in the Samaritan believers' reception of the Holy Spirit—until Jerusalem apostles Peter and John come and lay hands upon them (8:14-17)—suggests something of the Samaritans' marginal, even subordinate, position in the early church. Ethnic-religious tensions between Jews and Samaritans persist in Luke's world.

Acts identifies Gentiles attracted, but not wholly converted, to the Jewish faith and synagogue as "*God-fearers (phoboumenoi)*" (10:2, 22, 35; 13:16, 26) or "*God-worshipers*" (*sebomenoi*) (16:14; 18:7). The banner example is the devout—but uncircumcised and non-kosher—Roman centurion Cornelius (10:2, 22, 35, 45-46; 11:3). Other Gentile "God-fearers/worshipers" include attendees of the

Pisidian Antioch synagogue (13:16, 26), the purple-dealing Lydia at Philippi (16:14), and a man named Titius Justus, who lived next door to the synagogue at Corinth (18:7).[41] These Gentiles are distinguished from converts or "proselytes" to Judaism (*prosēlytoi*, 2:11; 6:5; 13:43), who presumably had submitted to circumcision and committed themselves to keeping the whole Mosaic law.

Leading witnesses to Jesus find a welcome audience for the gospel among these "God-fearers" and "proselytes"—as well as native Jews—in synagogues and houses throughout the Greco-Roman world. Moreover, Paul and associates also win a number of pagan Gentiles (with no previous attachment to Judaism) to faith in Christ. To state the obvious, such a mix of ethnic Jews and three groups of Gentiles—proselytes, God-fearers, and pagans, in varying relations with Judaism—creates a challenging social and religious situation for the early church. As we observed in Paul's letters, so in Acts, accepting Jesus as Lord and Messiah does not bring automatic harmony in the community. Two basic identity questions come to a head at two Jerusalem "conferences." First, in the wake of Paul and Barnabas' successful Gentile mission, apostles, elders, and "the whole church" (Acts 15:22) gather in Jerusalem to consider: Must all Gentile believers live like Jews (become proselytes)? Is it "necessary for them [Gentiles] to be circumcised and ordered to keep the law of Moses" (15:5)? Some Christ-believing Pharisees say, "Yes." But James's more conciliatory proposal carries the day: "[No], we should not trouble those Gentiles who are turning to God" by imposing circumcision and the entire Law upon them (15:19). *But we do ask them for some concessions to their Jewish brothers and sisters.* "Turning to [the One] God" who exalted Jesus as Lord and Messiah is the critical unifying element among God's people (15:19). Put negatively, the issue of *idolatry* again comes to the fore: Gentiles should abstain from anything associated with pagan temple worship, including eating foods offered to idols, having sex with temple prostitutes, as well as direct idol worship (15:20-29).[42]

The matter is not so easily settled, however. When Paul returns to Jerusalem in Acts 21, after many more Gentiles and "many thousands (*myriades*)" of additional Jews have come to faith in Christ, James again mediates Jewish concerns about Paul's handling of Jewish-Gentile relations. "They [Jews] have been told about you," Paul, "that you teach all the Jews living among the Gentiles to forsake Moses, and that you tell them not to circumcise their children or observe the customs" (21:21). If the leading question in Acts 15 was, "Must Gentiles become Jews in order to be saved?" the focus now flips: "Must Jews become Gentiles?" It's not clear whether James personally shares his compatriots' doubts about Paul's loyalty to Judaism, but he recalls the previously agreed prohibitions against idolatrous practices—as if Paul had forgotten them!—and presses Paul to "do what we tell you" in order to assuage persisting Jewish suspicions regarding his mission activity (21:22-25). On James's command, Paul sponsors four fellow Jews in completing their vows of consecration in the temple; but toward the end of the weeklong ritual, certain "Jews from Asia" falsely accuse him of defiling the temple by bringing "Greeks" into its holy precincts. These charges incite the temple crowd and "all Jerusalem" against Paul, forcing the Roman tribune to arrest Paul before the mob kills him (21:26-36)! Though overplaying the drama (Paul too readily obeys James's order, and his temple conduct scarcely captivated "all Jerusalem"), the narrative vividly demonstrates that religious dialogue between Jews and Gentiles remains precarious in Luke's rhetorical world.

SUMMARY

Luke's dense two-volume narrative evinces a complex thought-world and multiple possible purposes for its composition. I've suggested seven key practical-theological issues/questions addressed in Paul's letters that remained contested in Luke's rhetorical environment a generation later and in some measure "called out" his literary work. This is not to say that Luke inherited these issues from Paul or handled them the same way as Paul; or that I have captured a "perfect seven" constellation of Lukan (or Pauline) concerns. These matters are representative, not definitive, of struggles that Luke, Paul, and other first-century disciples of Jesus experienced in living out their new faith in a turbulent world.

In "answering" a variety of issues and questions, Luke's aims cohere around a central *theological* axis. One way or another, Luke's purposes in writing his two volumes grapple with *God's purposes* in the world. One way or another, Luke's many questions derive from one main question: *How do recent events involving Jesus Christ and his followers fulfill God's plan for God's people?* The following summary chart highlights this dominant *practical-theological focus* of Luke's narratives.

90

Practical Issues	Theological Questions
1. Shallow Roots	*How ancient and rooted in God's eternal purpose is this "new" Christ-centered faith? Is it old and solid enough to stake our lives on?*
2. Crucified Messiah	*Why did God let God's Anointed One (Messiah) die on a cross? What good purpose did Jesus' crucifixion serve?*
3. Delayed Lord	*When is Jesus coming back to restore fully God's gracious rule on earth? What are God and Christ doing in the meantime to help us?*
4. Evil Powers	*What must we do to insure God's salvation from evil cosmic powers that threaten our welfare? How can we cope with our anxious fears of demonic attacks?*
5. Displaced Exiles	*Why did God allow the catastrophic destruction of the temple in 70 C.E. and the dispersion of God's people? How can we rebuild our communities, our homes, and our lives?*
6. Stratified Society	*How should we as God's people love others from different backgrounds and statuses as our neighbors and as ourselves? How should we handle conflict among different genders, classes, and other social hierarchies both inside and outside God's household?*

Practical Issues	Theological Questions
7. Religious Pluralism	*How should we believers in Israel's One God and Messiah Jesus from various Jewish and pagan backgrounds define ourselves with respect to different forms of Judaism and Greco-Roman religions? How might we profitably dialogue with people from other faiths?*

As we make our way through Luke and Acts (see part 2), we will discover few "objective" answers to these critical questions, no fill-in-the blanks, no set of dogmatic propositions, no systematic theology. But we will encounter a thick tapestry of stories offering a rich, imaginative fund for practical-theological reflection. These are narratives written in the swirl of confusion and conflict, aiming to supply God's people much-needed "assurance" (*asphaleia*) that God faithfully works all things for good according to God's eternal purpose (cf. Rom 8:28-30).

PART TWO

IMPLEMENTATION:

PROCEEDING TO INTERPRET THE LUKAN NARRATIVES

PREFACE

At the seminary where I teach, our Master of Divinity curriculum requires a course called "Mission Immersion Experience" (M.I.E. for short). This "experience" includes classroom orientation to a particular cross-cultural environment but more importantly involves an intense, three-week "mission immersion" in that different culture. The premise is clear: one must live and work with a people *in their context* in order to know and understand them (of course, three weeks is just a start). Similar aims undergird "language immersion" programs: a semester's close encounters with Argentines in the bustling streets, subways, cafes, and tango halls (*milongas*) of Buenos Aires provide much more opportunity for understanding the Spanish language and Argentine culture than an equivalent period of study on a U.S. campus. And so it is with interpreting biblical narratives like Luke and Acts. In part one, we introduced several key literary and theological features of these writings, supported by selected citations and scene summaries. However, in order to know and understand Luke's narratives beyond an introductory level, we must delve into them more deeply and thoroughly: plotting their "orderly" development from start to finish, tracking the literary dimensions as they take shape, and uncovering the theological "answers" that emerge in response to various controversial issues (such as the seven sketched in chapter 2).

The analogy of a "mission immersion experience" is particularly apt, not only because of the interpreter's need to become "immersed" in the strange, cross-cultural worlds of Luke and Acts but also because of the "mission" impulse that drives the two-volume project.[1] For all the scholarly debates about the genre(s) of Luke and Acts sampled in chapter 2, in a very basic sense, these books present a grand *mission story*—that is, the story of *God's world-restoring*

95

mission advanced in word and deed through his Son Jesus Christ and Christ's emissaries. The main characters keep on the move, and the plot largely coheres around a series of journeys across the eastern Mediterranean world. And these characters are fundamentally *missionaries* undertaking *mission journeys*—not commercial trips, political junkets, scientific expeditions, tourist excursions, recreational getaways, or any other type of travel we might imagine. These treks proceed by divine commission for the sole purpose of carrying out God's will and extending God's rule on earth.

We may outline both Luke and Acts according to a broad four-part scheme of fulfilling God's mission:

I. Preparing God's Mission
　　Luke 1–4　　　Acts 1–7
II. Establishing God's Mission
　　Luke 4–9　　　Acts 8–12
III. Expanding and Interpreting God's Mission
　　Luke 9–19　　　Acts 13–21
IV. Defending God's Mission
　　Luke 20–24　　Acts 21–28

The headings are self-explanatory, charting a rapid, progressive growth in God's mission through Section III, and then slowing down in Section IV to solidify the movement and defend it against detractors. Although all the sections are vital to Luke's purposes, this outline places heaviest emphasis on Section III—"Expanding and Interpreting God's Mission"—as (1) the largest units in each book (Luke 9–19/Acts 13–21), (2) the central and most "expansive" segments in the respective mission plots, and (3) the most analytical, "interpretive" parts of the story. This last feature is especially evident in the thick concentration of Jesus' parables and other teachings in Luke 9–19 and the two critical "mission conferences" in Acts 15 and 21. These "interpretive" components *within* the Lukan narratives offer key perspectives and guidelines for subsequent interpreters of these biblical texts.

Partly because of space constraints in the present volume and partly because I have previously written an extended "travel guide" to the book of Acts,[2] I provide more detailed commentary on Luke's Gospel, reserving the last chapter for a fresh overview of Acts.

Apart from these utilitarian considerations, such an approach also suits the distinctive literary frameworks of the two books (see chapter 1). Whereas both present "orderly" narratives with a number of common themes, Luke's Gospel offers a looser, more episodic composition than the tighter-knit story of Acts. In travel terms, Luke allows more "free time" for unstructured activity within a broadly mapped itinerary, whereas Acts follows a more rigid schedule. Hence, in an introductory interpretive guide, Acts can be more easily surveyed in a brief compass than Luke. This is not to say Acts is any less rich or worthy of careful analysis than its Gospel companion; it's just somewhat more "user friendly" in its overall design.

CHAPTER 3

PREPARING GOD'S MISSION IN JUDEA AND GALILEE
(Luke 1:1–4:13)

In contrast to Mark's Gospel, which plunges into John's baptizing work and Jesus' mission of promoting God's kingdom with only a brief introduction (Mark 1:1-13), Luke's story proceeds much more deliberately, setting the stage or "preparing the way" (Luke 3:4) for Jesus' work over four chapters containing a preface (1:1-4), a birth (and childhood) narrative (1:5–2:52), a portrait of Jesus' advance man (John) (3:1-20), and accounts of Jesus' baptism, genealogy, and temptation (3:21–4:1-13). Concern to establish Jesus and John the Baptist's honorable roots drives much of this section: they must not be mistaken for maverick, wild-eyed upstarts who suddenly burst on the scene and fizzle out just as quickly (this is a harder sell with John than Jesus). These are solid "servants of the word" (1:2) in the mold of Israel's venerable prophets, predestined from their mothers' wombs to fulfill God's eternal will.

PREPARING READERS (1:1-4)

Readers who feel secure in their understanding of God's purposes "fulfilled" in the recent Christ-"events" and satisfied with other Gospel accounts of these events need not bother with Luke's narrative. Luke writes for "God-lovers" (*Theophiloi*), whose love for God spurs them to know God more fully and to gain a firmer grasp of God's ways in the world. Anselm's classic motto, "faith seeking understanding," aptly epitomizes the learning outcome Luke envisions for his God-loving readers: "so that you may know the truth concerning the things about which you have been instructed" (Luke 1:4). Luke assumes his faithful readers have not yet fit all the pieces together; hence he offers an "orderly" narrative to provide greater cohesion and to fill in some of the gaps. Likewise, appreciating the persisting anxieties and questions that percolate in his audience's environment, Luke weaves some vital theological "assurances" (*asphaleia*) and "answers" into his gripping stories. A basic prerequisite, then, for fruitful interpretation of Luke's Gospel is a passionate desire for and humble openness to fresh and fuller understandings of God's truth.

PREPARING PARENTS AND CHILDREN (1:5–2:52)

1. Zechariah and Mary (1:5-80)
2. Elizabeth and Mary (1:39-56)
3. Mary and Joseph (2:1-52)
4. John and Jesus (1:5–2:52)

Although, in contrast to Matthew, Luke does not begin with a formal genealogy of Jesus, the opening two chapters still track the noble family taproots of Jesus and his precursor John with two main foci:

- In terms of ancient roots, Luke explicitly links Jesus and John with Israel's priestly lines of Abijah and Aaron (1:5), prophetic mission of Elijah (1:17), royal house of David (1:27, 32; 2:11), and covenantal heritage of Abraham (1:55), and otherwise heavily exploits biblical language, style, and models throughout this section.
- In terms of immediate family roots, Luke profiles the parents of Jesus and John—Joseph/Mary and Zechariah/Elizabeth, respectively. All but Elizabeth bear biblical names; all but Joseph proclaim God's word inspired by the Holy Spirit ("filled with the Holy Spirit," 1:41, 67; cf. 1:35). Jesus' "supposed" (3:23) father, Joseph, remains the least

100

distinguished of the bunch, giving way to Jesus' true Divine Father (1:35; 2:49).

Make no mistake: despite their controversial lives and ignominious deaths (beheading; crucifixion [9:9; 23:33]), John and Jesus come from noble scriptural and spiritual stock.

Beyond the solidity of their roots, the *circumstances of their births* also commend Jesus and John as extraordinary agents of God. Beginnings as well as backgrounds set the course for one's identity in antiquity. How one came into the world determined the life one would lead. The greatest leaders—like Moses, Alexander, Augustus—were all known for their preternatural and precocious infancies.[1] Anyone could achieve a measure of honor at various stages of their lives, but the greatest heroes were anointed with divine power and favor from the womb. Accordingly, Luke presents the births of Jesus and John as nothing short of miraculous events, demonstrating that "nothing will be impossible with God" (1:37). The remarkable nativity stories actually begin just before conception with special announcements from the angel Gabriel, who "stand[s] in the presence of God" (1:19), to one of the parents-to-be: John's father, Zechariah, and Jesus' mother, Mary.

Zechariah and Mary (1:5-80)

The juxtaposition of angelic birth announcements to Zechariah and Mary fits the Lukan pattern of pairing male and female characters, but in a somewhat unusual way. The more natural pairing would feature either the two fathers or mothers or each parental couple; focusing on the father of one son and the mother of another strains normal kinship ties. Additional hints of family tension surface in Gabriel's forecast that Zechariah's son will "turn the hearts of the parents [fathers, *paterōn*] to their children" (Luke 1:17)[2] and in Mary and Joseph's frustration over young Jesus' separation from them in the temple (2:41-51). Stark statements regarding household divisions between parents and children (12:51-53) and mandates to "hate father and mother . . . and children" (14:25-26) later in the Gospel heighten the level of family conflict as part of a wider atmosphere of social disruption.[3]

Beyond their distinct gender and family roles, Zechariah and Mary prove to be an "odd couple" in several other respects.

	Zechariah	**Mary**
Age/Gender	Old man (1:7)	Young woman (1:27)
Marital Status	Married to Elizabeth, descendant of Aaron (1:5)	Engaged to Joseph, house of David (1:26-27)
Social Location	Judean priest (1:5, 39)	Galilean virgin (1:26-27)
Epiphany Location	Altar of incense in Jerusalem temple sanctuary (1:8-11)	Nondescript place (home?) in Galilean village of Nazareth (1:26)
Annunciation	"Your wife Elizabeth will bear you a son, and you will name him John" (1:13)	"You will conceive in your womb and bear a son, and you will name him Jesus" (1:31)
Interrogation	"How will I know that this is so? For I am an old man, and my wife is getting on in years" (1:18)	"How can this be, since I do not know a man?" (1:34)
Adjudication	"You will become mute, unable to speak, until the day these things occur" (1:20)	"The Holy Spirit will come upon you, and the power of the Most High will overshadow you" (1:35)
Celebration	Benedictus— "Blessed be the Lord God of Israel . . ." (1:67-79)	Magnificat—"My soul magnifies the Lord . . ." (1:46-55)

Both Zechariah and Mary receive announcements of naturally "impossible" births: Gabriel promises Zechariah that, although he and his "barren" wife (1:7) are well beyond child-producing years, they will soon have a son and likewise promises Mary that, although a betrothed virgin, she will soon have a son *before* she consummates her relationship with her fiancée (or anyone else). It's scarcely surprising, then, that both Zechariah and Mary immediately interrogate the angel concerning how "this thing (*houtos*)," this genetic absurdity, is supposed to occur. But how Gabriel responds to their questions is as shocking as the initial announcements: he strikes Zechariah mute—poor man won't be able to utter another word until his wife gives birth (as Elizabeth's womb is opened, his mouth is shut); by contrast, however, the angel happily answers Mary's question, and before long she is joyously comparing pregnancy notes with Elizabeth and bursting forth in jubilant praise to God (her speech as fruitful as her womb) (cf. 1:39-56).

Why such different answers to similar questions in similar circumstances? Why is Zechariah blasted whereas Mary is blessed? In Zechariah's case, he asks, "On what basis will I know this?" (*kata ti gnōsomai houtos*, 1:18). Ironically, even though the preface expresses Luke's intention that "you may know (*ginōskō*) the truth," the first time a character within the narrative asks "to know" (*ginōskō*) something, he is rebuffed and struck dumb. Readers might question how pastorally sensitive Luke really is. In fact, however, before posing his question, Zechariah had already been offered more assurances than most readers could expect to receive, namely—a personal appearance by "an angel of the Lord, standing at the right side of the altar of incense" and declaring in no uncertain terms that God had answered Zechariah's prayers and was going to give him a son to be named John (1:11-13). Such a dramatic announcement in the temple (where better to meet the Lord's angel?) is not enough for the Lord's priest (who better to accept the Lord's message?). Zechariah's problem is not that he lacks divine assurances, but rather that he does "*not believe*" the good news he's been given (1:19-20). Sure, the news is extraordinary, but it's not without precedent. A wise, elderly priest faithfully devoted "to all the commandments and regulations of the Lord" (1:6) should know that the ancient roots of God's covenant people first sprouted with God's gift of a son (Isaac) to a nonagenarian barren woman (Sarah) and her century-old husband (Abraham) (Gen

103

17:15-22; 21:1-17) and that at another critical juncture in Israel's history, God listened to the prayers of a desperate childless woman (Hannah) in the sanctuary and granted her a son as well (Samuel) (1 Sam 1:1-20; cf. Judg 13:2-25).

Unlike Zechariah's profile, Mary's introduction elicits little expectation of spiritual acumen. She appears as an unremarkable young engaged woman, with the most common Jewish female name of the period, from a small, no-account Galilean village called Nazareth ("Can anything good come out of Nazareth?" [John 1:46]). Her husband-to-be comes from a promising lineage ("the house of David"), but is otherwise undistinguished. Gabriel pays Mary a special visit in her home hamlet, not in the Jerusalem temple, and there is no indication that she had been praying or seeking divine guidance. The angel's appearance and annunciation are acts of pure grace: hence, Gabriel greets Mary as "a favored/graced woman (*kecharitōmene*)" (1:28) who has "found favor/grace (*charin*) with God" (1:30). Moreover, the bombshell "virgin birth" announcement that Gabriel drops on Mary has no biblical prototype for her to consider. Long-suffering barren women might miraculously conceive, but they still need a male sexual partner; virgins who do not "know a man" are, by definition, childless.[4]

More so than Zechariah, then, Mary might be forgiven for asking Gabriel for clarification. The thrust of her question is also subtly, but significantly, distinct from Zechariah's. Mary asks: "How can this be (*Pōs estai touto*), since I do not know (*ou ginōskō*) a man?" Whereas a skeptical Zechariah wants hard proof so he can "know" if the angel's word is true, Mary simply admits what, or rather whom, she does "*not* know" and honestly asks how the unusual birth "will be." Her query is about process, not proof. Unlike Zechariah, Mary believes the extraordinary event *somehow* "will be." After Gabriel briefly explains the spiritual mechanics ("the Holy Spirit will come upon you"), Mary confirms her faith with an astounding declaration: "Here am I, the servant of the Lord; let it be with me according to your word (*kata to rhēma sou*)" (1:38). Whereas Zechariah wonders "on what basis" (*kata ti*, "according to what") the angel's promise could be fulfilled, Mary accepts the divine word as sufficient basis for faith. Fuller knowledge and assurance spring from incipient faith ("faith seeking understanding"), not the other way around.

Mary's growth in understanding soon takes a quantum leap with her celebratory prophetic outburst (1:46-55). Whereas mute Zechariah struggles with written notes and hand gestures (1:62-63), Mary breaks out in powerful song. (After John's birth, Zechariah will regain his voice and echo much of Mary's song with his own [1:68-79].) Echoing the strains of Hannah's psalm (1 Sam 2:1-10), Mary's hymn exalts "God my Savior" and the "great things" this mighty and merciful God has done for her and her people. On the personal side, Mary is overwhelmed with God's regard for her "lowly" (*tapeinōsis*) status (1:48), which she interprets as representing God's wider mission of "lift[ing] up the lowly (*tapeinos*)" in Israel (1:52). Further good news for those on the lower rungs of a stratified society emerges in Mary's exclamation that God resists the proud and prosperous in favor of the humble and hungry (1:50-52). Displaced exiles will also find hope and comfort in Mary's affirming God's faithful remembrance of the ancient Abrahamic covenant (including a promised homeland) and announcing God's "scattering" of haughty rulers who threaten God's people (1:51-52, 54-55). In short, Mary's *Magnificat* sets the agenda for God's gracious work in the rest of Luke's narrative and beyond—"from generation to generation" (1:50).

Elizabeth and Mary (1:36-45)

Although John's mother, Elizabeth, does not receive an angelic annunciation, she and Mary still enjoy a maternal solidarity. Gabriel makes a point of linking Mary's wondrous impending pregnancy with that of her elderly "relative" Elizabeth, already in her sixth month (1:36). Following the angel's visit, Mary takes off "with haste" to visit Elizabeth in her Judean home and winds up staying three months (1:39, 56). This dash from Galilee to Judea is the first hint of a journey motif in Luke's Gospel and, more specifically, a north-south axis between the two regions. Where Zechariah and Mary are largely set in contrast to one another, Mary and Elizabeth are cast as spiritual, as well as maternal, partners. Though "she enter[s] the house of Zechariah" (the patriarchal head), Mary "greet[s] Elizabeth" (1:41; of course, if she had spoken to Zechariah, he couldn't have returned the favor!). In turn, at "the sound" (*phōnē*) of Mary's voice, Elizabeth's child "leaps for joy" in her womb (John can't wait, it seems, to get on with his mission), and she pronounces a "loud" benediction on Mary and her child, whom Elizabeth does not hesitate to call "my Lord" even in his fetal state (1:41-45). Buoyed by Elizabeth's blessing, Mary then launches into her marvelous *Magnificat* (1:46-55; see above). In the absence of patriarchal, priestly proclamation, the two Spirit-filled women take the lead in sharing and declaring the good news. And it is good news indeed: the "leaping," "lifting" environment of joy surrounding these erstwhile "barren" pregnant women signals the "dawning" (cf. 1:78) of a fresh era of revitalization and restoration from exile envisioned by the prophet Isaiah.[5] Compare:

Then the lame shall leap like a deer,
and the tongue of the speechless sing for joy.
For waters shall break forth in the wilderness,
and streams in the desert (Isa 35:6)

Sing, O barren one who did not bear;
burst into song and shout,
you who have not been in labor!
For the children of the desolate woman will be more
than the children of her that is married, says the LORD.
(Isa 54:1)

Mary and Joseph (2:1-52)

Jesus' birth, childhood, and adolescence are briskly described in Luke 2 in the context of three family trips from Nazareth to Bethlehem or Jerusalem involving Jesus and both parents, Mary and Joseph.

- Joseph and his pregnant wife travel from Nazareth to Joseph's ancestral home of Bethlehem (the "city of David"), where Mary gives birth to Jesus in an animal shelter containing a fodder trough ("manger") that serves as Jesus' first crib (2:1-20).
- Having circumcised the infant Jesus on his eighth day, according to Jewish custom, Mary and Joseph later consecrate their young "firstborn" son to the Lord in the Jerusalem temple, again following "the law of Moses" (2:21-40).
- As they did "every year," Mary and Joseph take the twelve-year-old Jesus to Jerusalem to celebrate the annual Passover festival; on this occasion, however, family tension develops when Jesus stays behind in the temple for three days, without his parents' knowledge or consent, before returning home to Nazareth (2:41-52).

Born in the "city of David" (2:4, 11) and raised in compliance with "everything required by the law of the Lord" (2:39; cf. 2:22-24, 27), Jesus betrays his core identity as a faithful Israelite from the beginning of his life. His roots run deep in Israel's history and piety. But another people and culture currently dominating the Mediterranean "world" (*oikoumenē*) also affect the life of Jesus and his compatriots. Luke 2:1 sets Jesus' early experiences against a backdrop of *Roman imperial rule* headed by Emperor Augustus and powerful deputies like the Syrian governor Quirinius. In fact, from one perspective, Jesus' birthplace is determined by an imperial census decree (a major instrument of sociopolitical control, compiling rosters for taxation, conscription, and inspection). No heavenly angel orders Joseph and Mary to Bethlehem; it's the Roman despot that dispatches them there for registration. And there Jesus is born, displaced from Joseph and Mary's current home in Nazareth and even, to some extent, from their ancestral home in Bethlehem: though in the city of David, they sojourn in no particular "house" of David, being forced instead into makeshift quarters with animals "because there was no place for them [even] in the [local] inn" (2:7). A yawning gap appears to separate Augustus' Roman throne from Jesus' Bethlehem manger.

Yet even in the baby Jesus' "exile," impelled by imperial edict, Luke sees the higher authority of God at work in inaugurating Jesus' messianic, David-like reign over God's people. Gabriel may not have directed Mary and Joseph to David's native Bethlehem, but he clearly told Mary that her child "will be called the Son of the Most High, and the Lord God will give to him the throne of his ancestor David" and establish an eternal kingdom, of which "there will be no end" (1:32-33). Further, after Jesus' Bethlehem birth, an angel of the Lord, backed up by a vast heavenly choir, announces: "a Savior (*Sōtēr*), who is the Messiah (*Christos*), the Lord (*Kyrios*)" has come "for all the people" in general and a group of nearby shepherds in particular ("to *you* [shepherds] is born this day in the city of David . . .") (2:10-11, emphasis added). Caesar Augustus and other emperors claimed titles of "Savior" and "Lord," and the "Messiah" ("Anointed One") designation and shepherd vocation were closely associated with David in Jewish thought (e.g., Ezek 34:23-24; 37:24-25; Mic 5:2-4). Aligning the newborn Jesus with Israel's greatest king and against Rome's mighty emperor gives a sharp political as well as theological edge to Luke's Christmas story and inspires hope for the liberation and restoration of God's oppressed and displaced people.[6] If wearing swaddling clothes and lying in a manger does not support typical regal images of "soft robes" and "royal palaces" (see 7:25), that is because God's messianic kingdom is anything but typical in its preferential attention to the poor, the hungry, and the lowly (cf. 1:51-54). And David's earliest roots, it must be remembered, were in the fields tending sheep (1 Sam 16:11-13) and then with a nomadic band of "everyone who was in distress . . . and . . . in debt . . . and . . . discontented" (1 Sam 22:1-2). As it happened, the more David later assumed conventional ruling powers, the less he exemplified "a man after God's heart" (cf. 1 Sam 13:14).

As angels and shepherds clarify the first phase of Mary and Joseph's experience with the Christ-child, so other character pairs help interpret successive phases. In the second segment, featuring Jesus' temple dedication (as firstborn son), a devout, elderly man called *Simeon* and a prophet "of a great age" named *Anna* proclaim the good news embodied in this special child. Cradling the baby in his arms, Simeon announces God's "salvation (*sōtērion*) . . . of all peoples"—Gentiles (*ethnē*) as well as "your [God's] people (*laos*) Israel"—destined to be fulfilled through Jesus' life and work; similarly Anna exults in the child's vocation as God's agent for the "redemption of Jerusalem" (2:25-38). The projected effects of Jesus' messianic mission radiate throughout the world—from Jerusalem to Israel to the Gentile nations (cf. Acts 1:8). The geriatric Simeon and Anna recall the elderly Zechariah and Elizabeth, and together, these old "couples" frame the Lukan birth stories and bridge the foundational "older" era of God's dealings with Israel (and the world) and the climactic "newer" phase realized in Jesus the Christ. But tension also surfaces: the two contrasting temple scenes displaying Zechariah's doubt and silence, on the one hand, and Simeon's faith and song of praise, on the other, portend the tragically divided responses of "righteous" (*dikaios*, Luke 1:6; 2:25) Israelite elders to the gospel throughout Luke's narratives.[7]

The third trip culminates in twelve-year-old Jesus' theological discussion with the *temple teachers* before a larger *temple assembly*. "All"—including teachers and audience—in attendance are "amazed" at Jesus' precocious questions and answers (2:45-47). Such reaction may reflect a mix of admiration (what a dedicated and gifted young man!) and indignation (how dare this upstart presume to instruct our elder-scholars!) within the episode. But the narrator's bracketing statements unequivocally affirm Jesus' exceptional, God-given wisdom:

> The child grew and became strong, filled with wisdom; and the favor of God was upon him (2:40).

> And Jesus increased in wisdom and in years, and in divine and human favor (2:52).

Readers are thus poised to pay close attention to Jesus' teaching throughout Luke's Gospel. If he shows such astonishing wisdom at such an early age, imagine the deeper understanding of God's purposes he will reveal as he matures.

While appreciating the interpretive roles of characters outside Jesus' family, we must not overlook key parts played by Jesus' parents in these scenes. In particular, Mary again takes the lead (Joseph is little more than a bit player)—this time in a moving *contemplative* role. In each segment, Mary personally receives and reflects upon stunning revelations about Jesus "in her heart" (*kardia*, (2:19, 51) or "soul" (*psychē*, 2:35).

- When the shepherds come to the manger and convey "good news of great joy" about the Christ Child disclosed by the Lord's angel, Mary "treasures" (*syntēreō*) this message and "ponders" (*symballō*) it in her heart (2:11, 19). Where others are merely "amazed" (*thaumazō*) at the shepherds' report and leave it there (2:18), Mary takes it in and mulls it over, seeking fuller understanding.
- After Simeon's soaring prophecy of God's light and salvation revealed in Christ, he delivers a more ominous message to Mary that "this child" will cause many to "fall and rise" (echoing Mary's song in 1:52—"he has *brought down* the powerful . . . and *lifted up* the lowly," emphasis added), will provoke personal opposition, and will expose deep-seated "inner thoughts"; and through it all, blessed Mary will experience piercing psychic ("soul") agony. We see here the first "sign" of Jesus' difficult mission that will end in violent death. Salvation and suffering strangely swirl together in God's plan, leaving Mary—and Luke's readers—much to ponder.
- After learning that Jesus is not among the travel party returning home from Passover, both parents begin searching

for him and become "astonished" when they find him—three days later—in a seminar with the temple teachers. But Mary voices how she and Joseph truly feel about their missing son. Far from beaming about Jesus' precocity, they are beside themselves with worry and frustration. "Child, why have you treated us like this?" Mary demands. "Look, your father and I have been searching for you in great anxiety" (2:48). Jesus' somewhat insolent response—"Did you not know that I must be in my Father's house" (2:49)[8]—scarcely alleviates his parents' anxiety, least of all, we might imagine, that of "father" Joseph. But although Mary also does not fully grasp Jesus' meaning (2:50), she certainly knows about Jesus' *divine* paternity that increasingly guides his life. So as the young Jesus finally returns to Nazareth with his parents and remains "obedient to them," Mary has much to turn over "in her heart" about the mystery of Jesus' divine-human nature (2:51)—a pressing theological conundrum occupying thoughtful believers ever since.

As Mary models an ideal follower of God's will ("Here am I, the servant of the Lord; let it be with me according to your word," 1:38), so she represents an ideal interpreter of Luke's Gospel—internalizing and scrutinizing the story in all its wondrous dimensions.

John and Jesus

Although parental couples Zechariah/Elizabeth and Mary/Joseph and prophetic pair Simeon/Anna play important supporting roles in Luke's birth narratives, the main spotlight falls on the two infant sons, John and Jesus. The four aged figures represent a passing generation of God's faithful people in trying times still "looking for" (2:25, 38) divine restoration. With the advent of these two Spirit-filled children, the elders can now depart "in peace," as Simeon puts it (2:29), knowing that the youngsters will take up the mantle and further God's purposes for Israel and the world.

As dramatically as the birth stories set the stage for John and Jesus' starring roles in God's redemptive plot, they also make clear that one figure outshines the other: John may be a star, but Jesus Christ will be the "superstar" (to crib Lloyd Webber and Rice). One way or another, each canonical Gospel delicately negotiates the

John/Jesus relationship in order to establish Jesus' supremacy while still respecting John's significance. It is not an easy task. The historical details could admit different interpretations. John preceded Jesus in the public arena, his mission attracted large crowds and loyal disciples, and Jesus came to him to be baptized. These elements could easily suggest John's priority over Jesus and spark speculation among friends and foes alike that, after John's execution, Jesus took up the cause as a kind of John *redivivus* (cf. Luke 9:7-9, 18-19). Acts attests that, even after Jesus' death and resurrection, some followers of the "Way of the Lord" still looked primarily to John and his baptizing mission as the foundation of their faith (Acts 18:24–19:7). Therefore, early Christian evangelists could not simply assume their case for Jesus as Lord and Messiah vis-à-vis John: they had to *argue* it and still account for John's popularity in the process.

Luke builds his case for Jesus' primacy over John on several points that resonate with other Gospels. But Luke is unique in tracking the relationship back to the figures' conceptions and births, that is, back to the *roots* of the matter. With various materials (announcements, songs, prophecies) associated with John and Jesus' nativities, Luke constructs a comparative, projected profile of the two careers revealing that, although both John and Jesus "*will be great* in the sight of the Lord" (Luke 1:15, 32, emphasis added), Jesus will be a distinct notch *greater*. The following chart sketches how Luke reinforces this point through a pattern of stair-step or climactic parallelism.[9] John unquestionably holds a high rank in God's mission service, but Jesus ranks a marked step higher across the board.

John	Jesus
1. Filled with the Holy Spirit before his birth (1:15)	1. Conceived by the Holy Spirit (1:35)
2. Prophet of the Most High (1:76)	2. Son of the Most High (1:32)
3. Will turn many of the people of Israel to the Lord their God (1:16)	3. Will reign over the house of Jacob forever, and of his kingdom there will be no end (1:33)

John	Jesus
4. Joy and gladness; many will rejoice at his birth (1:14)	4. Good news of great joy for all people (2:10)
5. Neighbors and relatives celebrate birth (1:57-58)	5. Heavenly host and shepherds celebrate birth (2:8-14)
6. Will turn parents to children (1:17)	6. Obedient to parents, but holding highest allegiance to his Divine Father (2:49-51)
7. Will turn disobedient to wisdom of the righteous (1:17)	7. Filled with wisdom (2:40); increased in wisdom (2:52)
8. Grew and became strong in spirit (1:80)	8. Grew and became strong; increased in divine and human favor (2:40, 52)

THE PREPARER'S MISSION (3:1-20)

1. The Political Stage (3:1-2, 19-20)
2. The Biblical Script (3:3-6)
3. The Ethical Thrust (3:7-14)

Luke further clarifies the John/Jesus relationship through a *preparer/fulfiller* or *forerunner/culminator* arrangement.[10] Although John appears before Jesus, he is not, in this scheme, Jesus' predecessor or mentor. Rather, more like a publicist or advance man, John "prepares the way" for the arrival of "the Lord" and "Messiah" Jesus (Luke 3:4, 15). Fitting Luke's design of an "orderly" plot: as Abraham, Moses, David, and other venerable servants and prophets of God from Israel's past paved the way for Christ's coming, so John takes the baton, so to speak, for the penultimate leg, "straightening" and "smoothing" the course for Christ's final victory lap (3:4-5). More specifically, John's preparatory mission addresses key political, biblical, and ethical issues.

The Political Stage (3:1-2, 19-20)

As with Jesus' birth, his public ministry prepared by John takes place in the dominant environment of Roman imperialism (3:1-2). The players have changed in the thirty or so years (3:23) since Jesus' childhood, but the politics have largely remained the same. Tiberius now reigns as emperor, and the old provincial regime of Herod the Great (cf. 1:5)—the Roman-appointed client-"king" of the Jews—has been parceled into four districts: Judea, ruled by the Roman military official, Pontius Pilate; Galilee, ruled by the Herodian tetrarch Antipas (Herod the Great's son), and two surrounding regions under tetrarchs Philip (Antipas' brother) and Lysanias. The Jewish homeland remains under collaborative Roman and Herodian control. Jewish high priests, Annas and Caiaphas (3:2), retain oversight of temple affairs in Jerusalem, but they too "were subject to regulation and annual appointment by Rome."[11] The related missions of John and Jesus will unfold "not . . . in a corner" (Acts 26:26) but in the full light of scrutiny by powerful—and potentially punitive—political and religious authorities.

Herod's "shutting up John in prison" (Luke 3:20), which Luke reports earlier than Matthew and Mark, signals how threatening these rulers could be. John provokes his arrest by denouncing "all the evil things that Herod had done," especially his illicit adulterous union with brother Philip's wife (3:19). In the train of Israel's prophets, John's daring to speak truth to power sparks persecution. The following sections further explain John's commitment to biblical prophecy and ethics.

The Biblical Script (3:3-6)

Geographically, John's mission centers in the "wilderness" (or "desert," *erēmos*) of Judea around the Jordan River (Luke 3:2-3). Such a venue evokes potent biblical memories, such as the Israelites' wilderness trek to the promised land, their dramatic entry into the land across the Jordan, and the miraculous cure of Syrian commander Naaman's leprosy by dipping in the Jordan seven times. However, whereas these examples form part of the scriptural backdrop for John's mission, Luke pinpoints Isa 40:3-5 as the primary script that John follows.

The original prophecy arises from the sixth-century B.C.E. exile of God's people in Babylon. After a generation of displacement and despair, the prophet "cries out" a message of restoration and comfort, promising the people that God is coming to their rescue on a super-highway blazed through the hard wilderness terrain from Judah to Babylon. Now John takes up the prophetic mantle as "the voice of one crying out in the wilderness" and "prepar[ing] the way of the Lord" for his suffering and scattered people in the Roman Empire (Luke 3:4). The path is precarious—undulating across low valleys and high mountains, winding around crooked turns and rough patches—mirroring the jagged experience of beleaguered refugees. But the good news is that the Lord's advance prophet (John) and the Lord himself (God's Son, Jesus) are making the road "straight" (*eutheia*) and "smooth" (*leios*) as they reveal "the salvation of God" not only to Israel, but to "all flesh" (Luke 3:5-6). With God's highway thus paved, God's dispersed people will not simply be freed from exile. They can go home as well, bypassing and overriding the vast system of Roman roads symbolizing the long arm of imperial domination.

The Ethical Thrust (3:7-14)

It's not just Herod Antipas who feels the sting of John's ethical challenge. At the core of John's preparation for the Lord's arrival is his demand for the people's "repentance for the forgiveness of sins" (Luke 3:3), that is, a change of mind (*metanoia*), will, and character in accordance with God's holy purposes. Again, fully in line with Israel's prophets, John requires more than ethnic pedigree ("we have Abraham as our ancestor," 3:8) and ritual performance. Such matters are good and fine as far as they go—John preaches chiefly to Israelites ("children [of] Abraham") and practices baptism as his central rite—but they are no substitute for or guarantee of a faithful, "fruitful" life: " 'Bear fruits worthy of repentance' or face 'the fire' of judgment and alienation," he thunders (3:7-9). True children of Abraham coming through the Jordan's waters must live according to God's standards in God's land.

And this fruitful living must be demonstrated in concrete behaviors. Three groups seeking John's baptism ask him, "What then should we do?" (*Ti poiēsōmen*, 3:10, 12, 14); and John responds to each with crystal clarity (3:10-14):

Baptismal Seekers	John's Requirements
The "crowds"	Give extra clothing and food to the needy
Tax collectors	Collect no more than pre-scribed amount
Soldiers	Do not pad your income by extorting money from civil-ians through threats and false accusations

Jesus will also confront these groups, thus allowing us to monitor their character (moral) development over the course of Luke's narrative. The specific ethical requirements all have to do with material-financial behavior in a stratified have-and-have-not society. Here Luke's compassionate practical theology kicks in: at the heart of God's purpose for humanity is mutual care for each other's basic needs and rights. And still one more time (and not for the last time), Luke's teaching echoes biblical-prophetic theology. Resonance with Amos and Micah, though not cited, comes through loud and clear. The waters of baptism avail nothing unless "justice roll[s] down like waters, and righteousness [right dealings with others] like an ever-flowing stream" (Amos 5:24); and "what does the LORD require of you but to do justice, and to love kindness, and to walk humbly with your God?" (Mic 6:8).

PREPARING THE SON OF GOD (3:21–4:13)

1. Baptism in the Jordan River (3:21-22)
2. Genealogy (3:23-38)
3. Temptation in the Judean Wilderness (4:1-13)

As John the Baptist prepares the people for Jesus' advent as Lord and Messiah, the Father God and Holy Spirit prepare Jesus for his public mission. Although set apart from birth as God's Son con-ceived by the Holy Spirit, Jesus' filial identity and fitness for spiri-tual service must be confirmed as an adult before he begins his

115

work. Luke remains true to his aim to offer readers solid assurance (*asphaleia*) that Jesus fulfilled God's purpose throughout his career. The following three segments—the episodes of baptism and temptation split by a genealogy—are linked together by "Son of God" declarations (Luke 3:22, 38; 4:3, 9) and "Holy Spirit" manifestations (3:22; 4:1).

Baptism	"[T]he *Holy Spirit* descended upon him . . . and a voice came from heaven, 'You are *my Son*, the Beloved; with you I am well pleased'" (3:22, emphasis added)
Genealogy	"Jesus was about thirty years old when he began his work. He was the son (as was thought) of Joseph . . . son of Adam, *son of God*" (3:23, 38, emphasis added)
Temptation	"Jesus, full of the *Holy Spirit*, returned from the Jordan, was led by the *Spirit* in the wilderness. . . . The devil said to him, 'If you are the *Son of God* . . .'" (4:1, 3, emphasis added)

Baptism in the Jordan River (3:21-22)

As the appointed leader of God's people from wilderness wandering to settlement in God's kingdom, Jesus himself must lead the way through the transitional-baptismal waters of the Jordan. Even though John gathered the people and stirred the waters, Luke takes him out of the scene—into Herod's prison—just before Jesus' baptism (3:20). The baptismal mission is then described in passive terms without an instrumental subject: "Now when all the people *were baptized*, and when Jesus also *had been baptized*" (3:21, emphasis added). Baptized by whom? Whereas the tradition answers, "John the Baptist," Luke leaves the matter open. In biblical

116

language, ambiguous passive constructions often assume a *divine agent*, and in the present case, Luke may be acknowledging God's function as the true baptizer, the Creator who brings life and order out of watery chaos (cf. Gen 1:1-13; Exod 14:21-31; 15:1-19).

In any event, God's intimate involvement with Jesus' baptism is primary for Luke. Only Luke stresses that Jesus "was praying" at his baptism (3:21),[12] that is, in direct communion with God, who then answers by anointing Jesus with the Holy Spirit and affirming Jesus' favored status as God's Beloved Son (3:22). The direct heavenly annunciation (no angelic intermediary this time)—"You are my Son, the Beloved; with you I am well pleased"—echoes God's appointment of both a powerful ruler-messiah (Psalm 2) and a gentle, unassuming servant of justice (Isa 42:1-4).[13] God's chosen messiah is not John, but Jesus, as John himself frankly admits. Jesus' connection with God's dynamic Spirit stretches beyond John's vocation: John baptized with water, but the "more powerful" Jesus "will baptize . . . with the Holy Spirit and fire" (3:15-17). But this combustion of Spirit-power will heal more than hurt and establish justice more than vengeance. Paradoxically, God's mighty messiah is also a sensitive servant, restoring (not breaking) even "a bruised reed" and revitalizing (not snuffing) "a dimly burning wick" (cf. Isa 42:3).

Genealogy (3:23-38)

This genealogy is oddly placed, well into the plot of Luke's story and Jesus' adulthood (Matthew's opening genealogy is more logical) and seemingly disrupting the flow of Jesus' Spirit-directed course from baptism to temptation (3:22; 4:1). But Luke's expressed aim to write an "orderly" account deters us from hastily dismissing the genealogy as an awkward intrusion.

Apart from its location, Luke's genealogy differs from Matthew's in tracking Jesus' roots *backward* from *Joseph* (3:23) all the way to "*son of Adam, son of God*" (3:38, emphasis added) (rather than forward from Abraham to Mary). Coming on the heels of God's baptismal declaration of Jesus' divine Sonship, the genealogy immediately resists any tendencies to deny or downplay Jesus' humanity. Whereas the baptism scene draws Jesus' (and readers') attention heavenward (3:31), the genealogy brings him (and us) back to earth again—literally, to the first person created from earth: Adam from *adamah* (Heb. "earth, ground"), human from humus.

Like Adam, Jesus has no father but God (Joseph's paternity is only "supposed," 3:23), but is still human. As "son of Adam," the First Human, Jesus represents Every One; he is the Second or Last Adam (to use Paul's metaphors),[14] qualified to restore death-riddled humanity (the genealogy certifies each ancestor's death) to wholeness and salvation. But if Jesus is to redeem Adam's descendants, then *unlike* Adam, he must prove himself a faithful son of God, devoted wholly to God above all things in the face of self-serving temptations. Accordingly, the Spirit propels Jesus into the teeth of temptation in order to test his mettle. If he really is the anointed Son of God in human flesh, as the devil acknowledges, he must resist the devil's machinations, enticing Jesus to betray his true identity.

Temptation in the Judean Wilderness (4:1-13)

Introducing the devil into a story already featuring the activity of heavenly angels, divine voices, and the Holy Spirit in earthly affairs establishes an overarching context of cosmic conflict between good and evil powers. A spiritual fight rages for control of God's world and God's people. Salvation depends on the faithful and powerful mission of God's Messiah Jesus to defeat the devil and his minions.

Round one takes place just before Jesus begins his public ministry. No need to take the first step if Jesus is not ready for battle. He confronts the devil during a forty-day testing period in the wilderness, reprising in microcosm the ancient Israelites' forty years of wilderness trials (cf. Deut 8:2). To certify his fitness to lead God's people to salvation, Jesus must pass this final wilderness exam. In essence, this is a *test of power*, but in qualitative rather than quantitative terms. The issue is not how much power Jesus possesses. He comes to the wilderness "full of the Holy Spirit" (4:1) with all the firepower of heaven behind him. The devil makes no attempt to challenge Jesus' superior arsenal; he knows he's overmatched. Instead, the devil attempts to exploit Jesus' power against him. The crux of the examination is how Jesus will *use* the supernatural force he has: will he overcome or succumb to the notorious corruptive potential of absolute power? The devil shrewdly presents Jesus with three attractive opportunities, each designed to enhance Jesus' own interests over against those of God and other people. But each time, Jesus resolutely resists in accordance with a biblical mandate

118

from Deuteronomy, originally formulated to guide God's people out of the wilderness into "a land flowing with milk and honey, as the LORD, the God of your ancestors, has promised" (Deut 6:3).

Self-serving Temptations	Deuteronomic Rebuttals
Command stones to become bread	One should not live by bread alone **Deut 8:3**
Worship the devil in exchange for all the world's kingdoms	You should worship the Lord your God and serve only him **Deut 6:13**
Throw yourself off the temple pinnacle and trust God's angels to protect you	You should not tempt the Lord your God **Deut 6:16**

Jesus will defeat the evil powers that threaten humanity by overcoming evil with good; by sacrificing personal power for the good of others and glory of God.

- Rather than zapping stones into bread to satisfy his own hunger (which would have been ravenous after a forty-day fast), he reserves his feeding powers, as it were, for preparing a feast for five thousand out of a few loaves and fishes (see Luke 9:10-17).
- Rather than selling his soul to the devil in exchange for all the earthly empires (presuming an axis of evil between the devil and Rome), Jesus eschews worldly, tyrannical rule for exclusive, humble service of the Most High God, even if this requires the ultimate sacrifice (as it will, on a Roman cross).
- Rather than exploiting the temple as a circus arena for crowd-pleasing spectacle (think Evel Knievel), Jesus will not try God's patience with frivolous showmanship nor will

he allow the secularization of God's sacred house; when Jesus makes a dramatic scene in the temple precincts, it will be to challenge its gross misuse as a "den of robbers" (see 19:45-47).

Round one goes to Jesus, but it's not a knockout. The devil goes back to his corner and leaves Jesus alone "until an opportune time" (4:13). We can expect further tests of Jesus' wholehearted love for God and for others above self-interest as his mission unfolds.

CHAPTER 4

ESTABLISHING GOD'S MISSION IN GALILEE AND SURROUNDING AREAS

(Luke 4:14–9:50)

After successfully passing his examination in the Judean wilderness and Jerusalem temple (pinnacle), Jesus launches his mission in a different region. In Luke's account, Jesus will not return again to Jerusalem until the last days of his life, culminating in a series of temple conflicts (19:45–21:37) leading to his crucifixion on Skull Hill (23:33). After reappearing as risen Lord, Jesus ascends to heaven from nearby Bethany, after which his disciples "return to Jerusalem with great joy" and remain "continually in the temple blessing God" (24:50-53). Luke's Gospel begins (Zechariah's vision) and ends in the holy city, with special focus on the temple.

Within this Jerusalem frame, Jesus carries out an itinerant mission, first in the land of Galilee (and bordering areas) in 4:14–9:50, and then in a meandering course to Jerusalem in 9:51–19:44. The foundational Galilean phase begins, predictably enough, in Jesus' home village of Nazareth "where he had been brought up" (4:16). But not expected, except by those recalling the typical fate of Israel's prophets (4:24), is Jesus' violent rejection by his townsfolk, who drive him from their synagogue with foul intent to fling him off a nearby cliff! Somehow Jesus slips out of their hands and heads "on his way" (4:28-30). But a strong "caution" sign and "rejected prophet" tag hang over Jesus' mission from the outset. As Simeon had predicted, Jesus represents a provocative "sign that will be opposed" (2:34)—even on his home turf.

Understandably, Jesus never comes back to Nazareth and responds rather coolly to overtures from his family to patch things up (8:19-21; cf. 11:27-28; 12:51-53; 14:26). But he doesn't flee the area; he stays on the move but remains close to Nazareth, welcoming numerous seekers from many towns and villages throughout Galilee.

- "A report about him spread through all the surrounding country" (4:14).
- "And a report about him began to reach every place in the region" (4:37).
- "They had come from every village of Galilee" (5:17).
- "He went on through cities and villages, proclaiming and bringing the good news of the kingdom of God" (8:1).
- "When a great crowd gathered and people from town after town came to him . . ." (8:4).

Named towns on Jesus' Galilean itinerary include *Capernaum*, about twenty miles northeast of Nazareth on the northern shore of Lake Genessaret (Sea of Galilee), which Jesus visits multiple times (4:23, 31; 7:1), perhaps as his base of operations, and *Nain*, about ten miles southeast of Nazareth (7:11). We also learn that certain female disciples of Jesus hail from the western port cities of *Magdala*, a fish-processing center, and *Tiberias*, the provincial capital of Herod Antipas: Mary comes from Magdala (hence, the "Magdalene") and Joanna, "the wife of Herod's steward Chuza," comes from Tiberias (although the city is not named) (8:2-3). But Luke never places Jesus *in* these places and never mentions Tiberias or Sepphoris, another Herodian stronghold located just a few miles from the hamlet of Nazareth.[1] In Luke's narrative, Jesus catches the eye and ire of Herod Antipas in Galilee (9:7-9; cf. 13:31-32), but keeps his distance from major Herodian cities.

Although rooted in Galilee, Jesus' early mission begins to spill over into adjacent territories. The dynamic force of Jesus' mission is too strong to contain in one area. Twice he makes forays across the Galilean border: once, southeasterly across the lake to the largely Gentile district of the Decapolis, where he encounters a wild demoniac (8:26); and another time, northeasterly to Bethsaida in the more tolerant territory of Herod Philip[2] (Antipas' brother), where nearby, "in a deserted place," Jesus teaches, heals, and feeds a large crowd (9:10-17). On other occasions, seekers from regions around Galilee *come to* Jesus:

- "They had come from every village of Galilee and Judea and from Jerusalem" (5:17).
- "a great multitude of people from all Judea, Jerusalem, and the coast of Tyre and Sidon [in Phoenicia, northwest of Galilee]. They had come to hear him and to be healed of their diseases" (6:17-18).

Of particular interest is the pull from Judea and Jerusalem to Galilee. Word of Jesus' mission already reaches southward into the holy city and environs (see also 7:17). When Jesus later makes a "grand" entrance into Jerusalem a few days before his death, he comes with a reputation—good, bad, and mixed—already mounting and circulating among religious authorities and the general populace (19:28-40). One oddly placed and textually disputed verse even suggests that, though based in Galilee, Jesus' early preaching circuit also included excursions into "the synagogues of Judea" (4:44).[5] Whatever Jesus' precise itinerary and the social, religious, and political distinctions between Galilee and Judea, Luke does not press a hard and fast division between these areas' responses to Jesus. His messianic mission extends up and down first-century Palestine, throughout Galilee and Judea (and Samaria, too, as we shall see), provoking both enthusiastic and antagonistic reactions. Such a pattern keeps readers in suspense, never quite sure how any one group or individual might respond in any given locale, and it also cautions us against too readily locking characters into stereotypical boxes.

Interspersed among Jesus' mission ventures from town to town, where he expends great energy helping throngs of needy seekers, sometimes throughout the night (4:40-42), he makes several attempts at recuperative retreat either alone or with his closest disciples. Such getaways typically take place at an isolated "desert" (*erēmos*) or "mountain" (*oros*), traditional sites for spiritual reflection and divine (or demonic) encounters. Appropriately, during these periods Jesus devotes himself to *prayer* (*proseuchē*), sometimes (again) throughout the night (6:12). However much Spirit-power Jesus possesses, it is not inexhaustible; it needs replenishment through communion with God.

- "At daybreak he departed and went into a deserted place (*erēmon topon*)" (4:42).
- "But he would withdraw to deserted places (*erēmois*) and pray (*proseuchomenos*)" (5:16).
- "Now during those days he went out to the mountain to pray (*oros proseuxasthai*); and he spent the night in prayer (*proseuchē*)" (6:12).
- "He [Jesus] took them [the apostles] with him and withdrew privately to a city called Bethsaida. . . . 'Send the crowd away . . . for we are here in a deserted place (*erēmē topō*)' " (9:10, 12).
- "Once when Jesus was praying alone, with only the disciples near him . . ." (9:18).
- "Now about eight days after these sayings Jesus took with him Peter and John and James, and went up on the mountain to pray (*oros proseuxasthai*)" (9:28).

Despite his best-laid plans for privacy and prayer, however, the crowds soon discover Jesus' whereabouts and press in upon him in the desert (4:42; 9:11) or wait expectantly for him at the foot of the mountain (6:17; 9:37). In any case, Jesus happily welcomes the people and resumes his mission of bringing the good news of God's kingdom—"for I was sent for this purpose" (4:43).

Having surveyed the geographical and topographical lay of the land in Luke 4–9, we turn to uncover the main missiological and theological components. This section *establishes* the basic program of Jesus' mission, focused on three principal assignments: (1) *freeing and healing the afflicted* (restoration), (2) *feeding and feasting with "sinners"* (table fellowship), and (3) *calling and training followers* (discipleship). In carrying out these tasks, Jesus grapples with several key practical-theological issues discussed above (chapter 2): his ministry of *restoration* tackles problems related to *evil powers* and *displaced exiles*; his practice of *table fellowship* confronts a *stratified society*; and his *discipleship* agenda prepares his followers to deal with his fate as *crucified Messiah* (see 9:23) and *delayed Lord*, equipping them to carry on God's mission in his absence.

Although restoration, table fellowship, and discipleship provide useful categories for analyzing Luke 4–9, they should not be set off from one another into rigid interpretive compartments. The story of Jesus' mission flows from one type of work to another and often blends two or all three categories in the same incident. For example, at meal settings in 5:27-39 and 7:36-50 (table fellowship), Jesus welcomes wayward "sinners" into God's household (restoration), instructing them and other diners in the ways of the Lord (discipleship).

RESTORATION:
FREEING AND HEALING THE AFFLICTED

1. Removing a Loud Demon and Relieving a High Fever (4:31-44)
2. Cleansing a Leper and Curing a Paralytic (5:12-26)
3. Reaping a Grain Harvest and Restoring a Withered Hand—On the Sabbath (6:1-11)
4. Reviving a Centurion's Slave and Resuscitating a Widow's Son (7:1-17)
5. Liberating a Demon-Infested Man and Lifting Up a Pair of Afflicted Women (8:26-56)
6. Altering Jesus' Countenance and Alleviating a Boy's Convulsions (9:28-43)

In contrast to Matthew and Mark's brief accounts of Jesus' "astounding" teaching in the Nazareth synagogue, set later in his ministry (Matt 13:53-58; Mark 6:1-6), Luke expands the story considerably and pushes it back to represent Jesus' *first* public appearance. As the inauguration of Jesus' Galilean mission, this incident has a clear programmatic function in Luke's narrative, reinforced by Jesus' appeal to scriptural models.[4]

Attending his hometown synagogue on the Sabbath "as was his custom," Jesus takes his turn this particular week reading and commenting on the lectionary text. At the appropriate time in the service, Jesus stands, and a synagogue minister (or "attendant") hands him a scroll of Isaiah; Jesus unrolls it toward the end and reads a brief selection from Isa 58:6 and 61:1-2. He then rerolls the scroll, hands it back to the attendant, and sits down. The entire audience, comprised of Jesus' relatives and neighbors, "[fix their eyes] on him" and perk up their ears to hear his commentary (4:16-20). In the space of a few verses, Luke has dramatically slowed the pace and marked every movement of this solemn scene in the synagogue service. With the congregation in the story, we readers are poised on the edges of our seats for Jesus' "sermon."

The message is succinct and stunning: "Today this scripture has been fulfilled in your hearing" (4:21). Jesus intimates that he personally embodies the Isaiah prophecy: "today" Jesus dares to appropriate Isaiah's "me"—"The Spirit of the Lord is upon *me*/he has anointed *me*/he has sent *me*"—and to adopt Isaiah's redemptive vision as his own. The Spirit-anointed Jesus has been sent:

- To preach good news (*euangelisasthai*) to the poor
- To proclaim (*kēryxai*) freedom (*aphesis*) to the captives and sight to the blind
- To dispatch (*aposteilai*) the broken/oppressed (*tethrausmenous*) to freedom (*aphesis*)
- To proclaim (*kēryxai*) the year of the Lord's favor (Luke 4:18-19)

In the ensuing mission, we thus anticipate that Jesus will mediate "the Lord's favor" to poor, captive, blind, oppressed, and other unfortunate folk (cf. 7:21-22). Such favor will revolve around "good news" of release, remission, and restoration: the double emphasis on *aphesis* exploits a term connoting *release* from both slavery (emancipation) and sin (forgiveness); the appointed "year of favor" suggests the "Year of Jubilee," a biblically mandated amnesty period every fifty years for the *remission* of all incurred debts, foreclosed lands, and indentured slaves (see Lev 25:8-55);[5] and the identity of *tethrausmenous* ("the oppressed," NRSV) is rooted in the image of things "broken in pieces," like pottery shards, in need of *restoration*.[6] This overall liberating-restoring thrust of Jesus' Isaianic mission—directed toward those held captive by oppressive physical, psychological, sociopolitical, and spiritual forces—offers God's people poignant hope and vitality in a precarious environment beset by evil powers and displaced exiles.

Initially, Jesus' hometown audience seems encouraged by his wondrous and "gracious" announcement, but their amazement is also laced with skepticism and indignation. "Is not this Joseph's son?" they query (4:22), as if to say: "Who does he think he is, putting on such messianic airs? We've known him and his father for years; he grew up right here in our humble hamlet. How dare he assume Isaiah's prophetic authority!"[7] The matter of Jesus' questionable roots again rears its head, this time in his own native village! Sensing his townsfolk's doubts and resentments, Jesus does nothing but fan them into raging opposition. As if appropriating the vocation of Isaiah's prophetic servant weren't enough, Jesus proceeds to take up the mantles of Elijah and Elisha as well. And on top of that, he highlights their restorative missions to needy persons *outside Israel*: Elijah's miraculous feeding of a destitute Sidonian widow and Elisha's healing of a Syrian leper, Naaman (4:25-27; cf. 1 Kings 17; 2 Kings 5). We may now add the hungry, widows, and lepers to the list of broken people Jesus will aid in Luke's narrative. But they may not all be native Israelites, and they certainly will not be denizens of Nazareth. Sensing his relatives and neighbors' mounting resistance to his mission, Jesus makes no moves toward reconciliation; if they reject and persecute him—as many ancient Israelites violently spurned Elijah, Elisha, and other prophets—then Jesus will shake the dust off his feet and reach out to outsiders who will listen.

Prospects of a Gentile mission thus emerge early in Luke's story. As we shall see, however, the progress of this venture will be slow and difficult, and although conflict continues to simmer between Jesus and some of his fellow Jews, Jesus and his followers by no means turn their backs on their compatriots. Negotiating delicate relations among Jesus' restorative movement, other Jewish "parties" and people, and Gentile officials (like Naaman) and ordinary folk (like the Sidonian widow) becomes a major factor driving Luke's two-volume work (see discussion of religious pluralism in chapter 2).

Having previewed general types of people Jesus will free and heal, we proceed to specific cases. Luke has packed this section with twelve restoration incidents organized in six pairs, half of which "couple" male and female figures. All but two cases involve miracles in which Jesus brokers God's liberating power on behalf of demonized, diseased, or deceased persons.

Removing a Loud Demon and Relieving a High Fever (4:31-44)

Despite his sour experience in Nazareth, Jesus continues to proclaim God's message in Galilean synagogues on the Sabbath. In

127

one case, Jesus teaches in the Capernaum synagogue and then stays the rest of the Sabbath day and through the night at Simon Peter's house (4:31-44; cf. 5:8). In both ordinary settings (synagogue and house), however, Jesus performs extraordinary acts through the astounding "authority (*exousia*) and power (*dynamei*)" of his "utterance" (*logos*) (4:36). His teaching alone packs an unusual "authoritative" punch (4:32). But the effect is not simply revelatory and cognitive but also therapeutic (*therapeuō*, 4:40) and restorative. His word generates "power" as well as insight.

The first scene features Jesus' deliverance of a man tormented by "a spirit of an unclean demon" (4:33), and the second reports Jesus' relieving of Peter's mother-in-law's "mega-fever" (*pyretō megalō*, 4:38). In both cases, Jesus verbally "rebukes" (*epitimaō*, 4:35, 39; cf. v. 41) the virulent source of affliction: he directly commands the boisterous demon to "be silent" and orders both demon and fever to leave their victims—and they obey! In Luke's worldview, threats to human health thus take on a virtual persona of oppressive occupying forces; and with authority and power akin to a dominant royal or military Commander-in-Chief, Jesus controls the actions and movements of these evil powers by non-negotiable fiat (cf. 7:6-8).

Cleansing a Leper and Curing a Paralytic (5:12-26)

In these healing incidents, Jesus restores another pair of individuals beset by extreme ailments: a man "covered with" some kind of scales or skin eruptions known as leprosy (5:12) and another man so paralyzed that he has to be carried—on his bed—to Jesus (5:18). The cleansing of the leper recalls Elisha's ministry to Naaman (4:27), although notable differences also emerge: unlike Naaman, the leper Jesus encounters is neither a foreigner nor an official and takes no curative dip in the Jordan. The raising of the paralytic recalls Mary's announcement that God will "lift up" the powerless (1:52). Both miracles liberate men "captive" to their infirmities, allowing them to "go away" (*aperchomai*, 5:14, 24) from their confinement and rejoin the home-going journey of God's people: on Jesus' command, the formerly ostracized leper "goes away" to the priest for formal readmission into society; and the formerly immobilized paralytic "goes away" to his home, restored to family and friends. Both cases resonate with Isaiah 35's vision of Israel's glorious return from exile through the desert:

- Make firm the feeble knees . . .
- The lame shall leap like a deer . . .
- A highway shall be there, and it shall be called the Holy Way; the unclean shall not travel on it,[8] but it shall be for God's people . . .
- The redeemed shall walk there (Isa 35:3, 6, 8-9)

As Jesus cures "diseases" that rack the physical body, he also heals social "ills" that rend the body politic.[9]

In comparison with his previous "rebuke" of a debilitating demon and fever, Jesus expands his healing methods: while speaking a restorative word to the leper ("Be made clean"), Jesus also applies a therapeutic touch (5:13); and while commanding the paralytic to "stand up," Jesus also pronounces, "your sins are forgiven" (5:20-24). In the latter instance, Jesus makes no explicit causal connection between the man's sinfulness and lameness. By his own admission, he simply exploits the occasion to let the audience "know that the Son of Man [Jesus] has authority on earth to forgive sins" as well as power to heal (Jesus' mission encompasses both spiritual and physical restoration). This claim distresses the Jewish legal experts in the group—teachers of the law, scribes, and Pharisees—who worry that Jesus illicitly usurps divine prerogatives of forgiveness (5:17, 21). However, though Jesus indeed acts as God's judicial agent (Son of Man),[10] he intends no disrespect ("blasphemy," 5:21) toward God or disregard for the law. In fact, in the preceding scene, Jesus insists that the cleansed leper report for priestly inspection and make the appropriate offering—"as Moses commanded" (5:14; cf. Lev 13-14).

Reaping a Grain Harvest and Restoring a Withered Hand— On the Sabbath (6:1-11)

Legal issues again come to the fore in this pair of restoration scenes: what type of mission work is and is not "lawful" (6:2, 4, 9)—particularly *on the Sabbath* (five references, 6:2, 5-7, 9)? Jesus' previous Sabbath activity in the synagogue (healing the demoniac, 4:31-37) elicited queries of amazement, but not charges of impropriety. But in the present case, where Jesus "restores" (6:10) function to a man's paralyzed hand, "some" (not all, 6:2) legal experts ("scribes and . . . Pharisees")—who have been closely watching

(6:7) Jesus since his encounter with the bedridden man (see 5:17-39)—now become "filled with fury" at his alleged violation of Sabbath labor laws (6:11). Fiery opposition to Jesus' work extends beyond his disgruntled kinfolk in Nazareth.

The lawyers' objections to Jesus' Sabbath healing in the synagogue (why not wait another day to restore the withered hand?) are further fueled by his previous Sabbath allowance of his disciples' gleaning in the grain fields. A disturbing pattern of Sabbath violation seems to be emerging. As self-titled "lord of the Sabbath" (6:5), Jesus appears to do whatever he pleases on this sacred day, irrespective of legal restraint. However, the incidents in question do not admit to broad generalizations about Jesus' Sabbath observance (or lack thereof). These are special cases dealing with basic problems of hunger and health. Jesus' disciples are not harvesting their own fields with plow and sickle for storing in barns (cf. 12:17-19) or selling in markets; rather they hand-pluck leftover heads of grain at the edges of others' fields for their "daily bread," *as stipulated in Mosaic law "for the poor and the alien" in Israel* (Lev 19:9-10; 23:22; cf. Deut 24:19). The disciples had "left everything" (homes, businesses, fields) to follow Jesus (5:11, 28; cf. 18:18:28-29) and now live like wandering refugees. Perhaps they should have double-plucked the day before the Sabbath—as the ancient Israelites gathered a double-portion of manna (Exod 16:22-30)—but if circumstances were not conducive to such preplanning, Jesus was not about to deprive his "exiled" followers of basic sustenance. If David, while a refugee from Saul's kingdom, finagled a batch of sacred bread (reserved only for priests) for him and his (non-priestly) companions (Luke 6:3-4; 1 Sam 21:1-6), then surely the disciples of the messianic "son of David" are entitled to a little Sabbath gleaning. Moreover, wasn't the original intent of the Sabbath to "do good" and to "save life" (Luke 6:9), to preserve God's "good" creation in all its forms (cf. Gen 1:1–2:4)?

Bottom line: the Lukan Jesus aims to save and restore God's displaced and disabled people "today"[11]—even if, or maybe, especially if, that day is the holy Sabbath Day of Rest-oration. He keeps rehabilitating broken-down travelers for Isaiah's homebound highway through the desert: as he "[made] firm the feeble knees" and lame legs of the paralytic, he "strengthens the weak [right] hands" of the man in the synagogue (cf. Isa 35:3).

Reviving a Centurion's Slave
and Resuscitating a Widow's Son (7:1-17)

After Jesus interrupts a funeral procession in Nain and success-fully commands a deceased young man to "rise" (*egerthēti*, 7:14), the stunned crowd exclaims, "A great prophet *has risen* (*ēgerthē*) among us!" (7:16). Jesus also demonstrates this "rising" reputation by healing a centurion's slave in the preceding scene; and together these incidents cast Jesus in the prophetic mold of *Elijah and El-isha*, as Jesus intimated in his Nazareth sermon (cf. 4:25-27). The parallels are notable, but not perfect. Like Elijah, Jesus resusci-tates the son of a destitute widow and "[gives] him [back] to his mother" (1 Kgs 17:23; Luke 7:15), but the widow Jesus aids is from the Galilean village of Nain, not a Sidonian city like Zarephath or any other locale outside Israel; as Elisha cures a leprous Syrian general, Jesus helps a foreign military officer, but in this case he treats the dire illness of a Roman centurion's servant, not the offi-cial himself.

Although distinguished in gender and social status,[12] the Roman centurion and Galilean widow share a poignant concern for cher-ished household members either on or just over the brink of death. The centurion desperately seeks healing for a highly esteemed servant lying at death's door (7:2), and the widow bitterly weeps for her deceased "only son" (*monogenēs*) as the pallbearers carry him to his grave (7:12, 14). The widow's situation seems particu-larly grim, not only emotionally but also socially and economically, as she must now fend for herself, bereft of immediate (male) fam-ily support.[13] Along with the pallbearers, a "large crowd" from the village attends the widow's son's funeral, but we know nothing about their long-term commitment to her welfare. In any case, when Jesus comes on the scene, he becomes deeply concerned about *her*: "When the Lord saw *her* (*autēn*), he had compassion *for her* (*autē*) and said *to her* (*autē*), 'Do not weep'" (7:13, emphasis added). He then "comes forward," "touches" the coffin, halts the pallbearers, and proceeds to revive the dead son and return him to his mother (7:14-15). Jesus lets nothing come between him and this widow and son's restoration: he reaches out and makes con-tact, "touching" the corpse's bier as he earlier "touched" (5:13; 7:14) the leper's skin. Both contacts render Jesus "unclean," al-though only momentarily since he soon restores the afflicted men

131

to health and life. Although showing his compassion toward the infirm, these "defiling" gestures do not evince, as commonly claimed, Jesus' supercession of the Mosaic law. In performing good and necessary community functions, Jewish physicians, folk healers, morticians, and burial attendants (like the pallbearers in the present scene) often became ritually "unclean"—a "condition" easily remedied by legal-ritual process (washings and offerings). Like them, Jesus acts as a community servant, not as a rebel or radical.[14]

By stark contrast with his direct approach to the woman and her son, Jesus neither initiates nor makes any contact with the centurion or his servant. Whereas Jesus bypasses crowd and pallbearers to get to the dead young man, the centurion seeks Jesus' help for his ill servant through two sets of intermediaries: first, he dispatches some Jewish elders, who vouch that the centurion merits assistance because he "loves our people" and even "built our synagogue" (7:3-5); then, as Jesus nears the officer's home, he sends more personal "friends" (presumably Roman), who petition Jesus to "speak the word" dismissing the slave's infirmity with commanding authority akin to the centurion's. More than that, through these friends, the centurion acknowledges Jesus' *superior* authority: whereas the elders exclaim, "he is worthy" of attention (7:4), the centurion declaims, "I am not worthy" (or "fit," 7:6) to receive Jesus. Accustomed to being a powerful patron and commander of others, the centurion becomes a humble client and servant of Jesus in a remarkable act of self-abasement. So Jesus heals the slave without meeting the slave's master or entering his house. Whether speaking long distance to a Roman slave or up close to a Jewish son, Jesus' restorative reach extends far and near, to "everyone whom the Lord our God calls" (cf. Acts 2:39).

Liberating a Demon-Infested Man and Lifting Up
a Pair of Afflicted Women (8:26-56)

Though technically three miracle stories, the last two involving women—one with a bleeding disorder, the other with a fatal disease—are closely intertwined within a single extended episode (8:40-56); juxtaposing this incident with the preceding exorcism of a demonized man (8:26-39) effectively presents another pairing of male-female figures.

132

Delivering a demon-possessed man and reviving a dead child recall previous scenes, with a few new twists. As the unclean spirit in the synagogue loudly remonstrated with Jesus, "What have you to do with us?" before Jesus commanded the demon to leave (4:34-35), so the unclean spirit in the present case shouts in response to Jesus, "What have you to do with me?" (8:28). (Even the demons in Luke recognize Jesus' divine authority and total opposition to evil powers.) Both stories feature a curious use of pronouns: the *single* demon in 4:34 self-identifies as "us," while the *many* demons in 8:28 (cf. 8:30) refer to themselves as "me." Whatever else this terminology might signify, it suggests a tight solidarity among the evil powers that be (one for all, all for one). And, as the many demons adopt the name "Legion" (8:30)—after a large Roman military unit—this wicked alliance encompasses political as well as spiritual forces. Situating this legion-occupied victim "not . . . in a house [or synagogue] but in the tombs" across the Galilean border (into the Gentile territory of the Gerasenes), and depicting him as a denuded and uncontrollable wild man infested with enough violent impulses to drown a pack of pigs (8:27-29, 33) evoke an aggressive and destructive image of Roman imperial might in the Diaspora as well as Israel. Accordingly, the post-deliverance picture of the man "sitting at the feet of Jesus, clothed and in his right mind" (8:35) offers an encouraging image of restoration for oppressed exiles.

An official's (Jairus) desperate plea for Jesus to heal his dying child (8:40-42) echoes the centurion's concern for his beloved ill slave, except in this case the official is a Jewish synagogue leader, not a Roman synagogue builder, who directly invites Jesus "to come to his house" (8:41) instead of working through brokers. Jesus' resurrection of Jairus's "only" child (*monogenēs*, 8:42)—who dies before Jesus arrives—mirrors the event at Nain, except now the singular child is a daughter rather than a son and the distraught parent is a prominent official instead of a poor widow. These key distinctions among otherwise parallel scenes intimate Jesus' inclusive mission across lines of gender, ethnicity, and social status.

As for the woman plagued with a bleeding disorder for twelve long years, she not only shares certain matters with Jairus's twelve-year-old dying daughter (Jesus calls the woman "daughter" in 8:48), but also with the Gerasene demoniac who likewise suffered "a long time" (8:27) and lost everything he had (the woman "spent all she had on [ineffectual] physicians," 8:43). But the hemorrhaging woman also stands out from other afflicted persons in Luke's narrative in terms of her particular disease ("a flow of blood" [8:43-44]) and her initiatory healing contact with Jesus without his permission. Whereas Jesus deliberately touches the leper, the widow's son's bier, and Jairus's daughter (8:54), this woman breaks through the crowd, "comes up behind" Jesus, touches his clothing, and triggers a power surge that stops her bleeding (8:44-46; cf. 6:18-19). Jesus' flow of power (*dynamis*) stanches her flow of blood. Although the woman's surreptitious action takes Jesus by complete surprise ("Who touched me?"), he tenderly affirms this "daughter's" faith and bids her peace when she bows "before him" (8:47-48). Quite the opposite of invasive evil powers that shed blood and rupture lives and lands, Jesus surrenders his power to stop bloodshed and restore wholeness.

Altering Jesus' Countenance and Alleviating a Boy's Convulsions (9:28-43)

Luke presents yet another story of Jesus' rehabilitating an "only child" (*monogenēs*)—this time, a father's fitful (epileptic?), demon-possessed son (9:38). The three *monogenēs* references within a short narrative span (7:12; 8:42; 9:38)—all unique to Luke—accentuate the pathos of these healing/resuscitation scenes and the precariousness of family survival in an age of high mortality and displacement. The book of Tobit, set in a Diaspora context of suffering and exile, illustrates Israelite anxiety about only children and lost inheritances in the cases of Sarah and Tobias, each an only child with prospects of marriage to each other—but not altogether happy prospects since a rapacious demon (Asmodeus) killed all seven of Sarah's previous husbands on their wedding night!

- You know, O Master, that I [Sarah] am innocent of any defilement with a man, and that I have not disgraced my name or the name of my father [Raguel] in the land of my exile. I am *my father's only child (monogenēs)*; he has *no other child* to be his heir; and he has no close relative or other kindred for whom I should keep myself as wife. Already seven husbands of mine have died. Why should I still live? (Tob 3:14-15, emphasis added).
- He [Sarah's father, Raguel] has *no male heir and no daughter except Sarah only (monogenēs)*, and you [Tobias], as next

of kin to her, have before all other men a hereditary claim on her (Tob 6:12, emphasis added).

- So now, since I [Tobias] am *the only son* (*monos*) *my father [Tobit] has*, I am afraid that I may die and bring my father's and mother's life down to their grave, grieving for me—and they have *no other son* to bury them (Tob 6:15, emphasis added).

As it happens, Tobias marries Sarah, repels the jealous demon, and secures the future of their two families in exile, with hopes of ultimate restoration to the land of Israel (see Tob 14:5-15). Luke's triple stories of Jesus' reviving dead or demonized only children and restoring them to their parents (he "gave him back to his father" [9:42]) likewise assure God's threatened and scattered people of restored security through God's Messiah.

Although the afflicted only son in the present story does not die (like the widow's son and Jairus's daughter), he suffers terribly under the assault of a vicious evil spirit who "*seizes* him . . . *convulses* him until he foams at the mouth . . . *mauls* him . . . [and] *dashes* him to the ground" (9:39, 42, emphasis added). The last two verbs carry notions of "breaking, crushing in pieces" (*syntribō*) or "bursting, tearing in pieces" (*rhēgnymi*).[15] The first term appears frequently in the LXX in contexts of war and national destruction, and a close cognate (*diarrēgnymi*) denotes the Gerasene demoniac's (Legion) "breaking apart" of "chains and shackles" (8:29); the second term suits the savage, marauding habits of wild dogs or pigs (see Matt 7:6). By releasing such a badly battered boy from his tormentor and restoring him to his father, Jesus offers hope for liberating God's captive people oppressed by violent regimes.

This healing story follows close on the heels of an epiphanic mountaintop encounter between Jesus, Moses, and Elijah, witnessed by three of Jesus' closest disciples, Peter, James, and John. The remembrance and reemergence of the great prophets, Moses and Elijah, were often linked with Israel's eschatological hopes of restoration in biblical thought, as in the closing lines of the twelve "minor" prophets' corpus:

Remember the teaching of my servant Moses, the statutes and ordinances that I commanded him at Horeb for all Israel. Lo, I will send you the prophet Elijah before the great and terrible day of the LORD comes. He will turn the hearts of parents to their children and the hearts of children to their parents, so that I will not come and strike the land with a curse. (Mal 4:4-6; cf. Luke 1:16-17)

Moreover, by discussing Jesus' "departure [*exodos*], which he was about to accomplish at Jerusalem" (9:31), the three "glorious" figures envision Jesus' life and death (departure) as a liberating mission of God's people on a par with Israel's historic release (exodus) from harsh Egyptian slavery.

Given this backdrop, it's not surprising that Jesus' first action, "when they had come down from the mountain" (9:37), shows restorative signs associated with both Moses and Elijah: he liberates a convulsive boy enslaved by a brutal evil power and restores the heart—and body—of this only child to his desperate father. The conclusion aptly captures Luke's theological aim throughout this unit—to demonstrate "the greatness of God" on behalf of God's afflicted people (9:43).

TABLE FELLOWSHIP:
FEEDING AND FEASTING WITH "SINNERS"

1. Feasting with Tax Collectors and "Sinners" in Levi's House (5:27-39; cf. 7:18-35)
2. Reclining with a "Sinful" Woman in Simon's House (7:36-50)
3. Feeding Thousands in a Deserted Place (9:10-17)

Luke's Jesus likes food and fellowship. He spends considerable time and energy around the dinner table, functioning alternately as host, servant, and guest. As Robert Karris has stressed, "In Luke's Gospel Jesus is either going to a meal, at a meal, or coming from a meal. . . . Jesus loves to eat and gets himself in deep trouble with the religious leaders of his day because of his eating habits."[16] Although no doubt Jesus enjoyed himself, his culinary pursuits have more to do with spiritual instruction and social inclusion than personal pleasure. The symposium or "table talk" setting of many Lukan meals affords an optimal context for conversation and controversy, especially over Jesus' liberal practices of eating with "sinners" and feeding the masses, irrespective of social distinctions. Although reclining sideways, according to the custom of the day, Jesus uses the dinner table as a platform on which he takes a stand against certain forms of segregation and stratification in his society.[17]

Feasting with Tax Collectors and "Sinners" in Levi's House
(5:27-39; cf. 7:18-35)

Jesus goes beyond ivory-tower advocacy for "sinners." He recruits his closest mission partners among such folk. The first designated "sinner" (*hamartōlos*) in Luke, Simon Peter, becomes Jesus' first disciple, along with fellow fishermen, James and John (5:8-11; cf. discussion below); soon thereafter, Jesus enlists another man associated with "sinners," Levi the tax collector (5:29-30). With blunt audacity, Jesus challenges Levi at his tax office: "Follow me."[18] More accurately, Levi is stationed at a tollbooth or customs house around Lake Genessaret, collecting tolls, tariffs, and other duties on goods and produce crossing Herod Antipas' realm. John the Baptist has already exposed tax collectors' fraudulent tendencies to overcharge their customers for their own (and Herod's) advantage (3:12-13). Thus when Levi heeds Jesus' call, "leaves everything"— including his business—"and follows him" (5:27-28), Jesus disrupts Herod's exploitative economic system.[19]

The potential for further economic disruption increases as Levi promptly celebrates his new life by throwing a "great banquet" for Jesus in his home and inviting a "large crowd" of fellow tax collectors and other "sinners" (5:29). The prospect of empty tollbooths in Galilee would not have pleased Herod or his accountants. Another group becomes concerned for different reasons: certain Pharisees lament Jesus' cavalier mixing with sinful dinner guests (5:30). Deeply committed to honoring God and God's law in all aspects of life, the Pharisees sought to extend standards of holiness from the sacred temple to the everyday meal table. Thus *what* and *how* one ate and *whom* one ate with were not chiefly matters of personal taste, but spiritual duty. Accordingly, they did not eat and drink with "sinners," not because they despised such folk and had no interest in helping them but because the Pharisee's dinner table—like John's baptismal pool—represented God's ideal, righteous kingdom incorporating God's faithful and *already repentant* people. At this crucial point, Jesus disagrees in means but not ends. For him, the table is not so much a private place to showcase the holiness/wholeness of God's kingdom as a public venue to *share the opportunity* for becoming holy/whole. Hence he happily dines with "sinners" so that, during the course of the meal he might "call [them] *to repentance*" (*eis metanoian*, 5:32, emphasis added)—a significant

Lukan addition to Mark 2:17.[20] Sinners do not get a free lunch with Jesus: his table talk presses them with a call for change.

Jesus' dining habits further distinguish him from John the Baptist and the Pharisees. Members of both circles regularly practice the spiritual discipline of fasting, whereas Jesus encourages his disciples to "eat and drink" (5:33); moreover, whereas John is known for his abstemious diet, including teetotalism (1:15; 7:33), Jesus indulges enough to suggest, if not certify, his reputation as "a glutton and a drunkard," in tandem with being "a friend of tax collectors and sinners" (7:33-34). However, Luke makes clear that, although Jesus promotes feasting over fasting, he does not oppose John and the Pharisees' alternative asceticism. He himself fasted in preparation for his mission for *forty days* (a feat of Moses- and Elijah-like proportions [4:1-2]) and instructs his disciples to resume fasting after his death (in the meantime, they must celebrate the messianic cornucopia Jesus provides [5:33-35]). And Jesus wholeheartedly endorses John's prophetic mission and ascetic lifestyle (for John at least): "Among those born of women no one is greater than John" (7:28).

Reclining with a "Sinful" Woman in Simon's House (7:36-50)

The fellowship between Jesus and the Pharisees, despite their differences, continues with Simon the Pharisee's (distinguished from Simon Peter) inviting Jesus home for a meal (7:36). Tension soon fills the air, however, when a "sinner" woman from "the city" crashes the party and latches onto the reclining Jesus' feet (extended back from the table)—kissing them repeatedly, weeping over them profusely, anointing them with perfume, and wiping them with her hair (7:37-38). This makes for quite a "touching" scene in every sense of the word. With striking intimacy and passion, this woman poignantly (sensuously) conveys her deep love for Jesus. Simon the host, on the other hand, expresses a rather different sentiment, namely, suspicion about Jesus' permitting this woman's advances: "If this man were a prophet," Simon mutters to himself, "he would have known who and what kind of woman this is who is touching him—that she is a sinner" (7:39). He does not leap up and throw the sinful woman or Jesus out of his house, but he is bothered all the same.

Once again, the rub is Jesus' fraternizing with "sinners" at the meal table. "What kind" of sinner this woman is doesn't really matter (from Simon's viewpoint, any "sinner" would be out of place), although she seems to have a bad reputation about town. We cannot assume, however, as many interpreters do, that she must have been a prostitute and a rather notorious one at that! Luke never specifies her "sinful" occupation. The "sinners" we've met thus far have been fishermen or tax collectors: why then couldn't she be an unscrupulous businesswoman or merchant? (Acts features several working women—none of whom are prostitutes.)[21] The fact that she makes passionate, even erotic, contact with Jesus at a dinner party does not make her a spicy courtesan or symposium entertainer. Her copious weeping hardly fits the bill, not to mention her absorption in menial service: she gives Jesus a footbath, not a lap dance.[22]

Sensing Simon's misgivings, Jesus defends the woman's actions on two grounds. First, her kissing, washing, and anointing a dinner guest meet basic requirements of hospitality *that Simon failed to provide Jesus*; if anyone should be embarrassed here, it should be Simon (7:44-46). Second, her weeping and lavish expressions of love signify, in Jesus' book, gratitude for sins *already forgiven* (in a previous encounter with Jesus?): "I tell you, her sins, which were many, *have been forgiven* [*apheōntai*, Greek perfect tense]; hence she has shown great love" (7:47-48). "What kind of sinner" is this woman? A *forgiven* sinner is all that counts. As such, she has every right to a place at the table, even by Simon's standards.

Feeding Thousands in a Deserted Place (9:10-17)

What begins as a desert retreat between Jesus and his twelve disciples near Bethsaida becomes a day-long teaching and healing session with five thousand intruders on Jesus' privacy. By day's end, Jesus' annoyed disciples try to send the people away (finally!) to find their own food and lodging. But Jesus will have none of it; now playing the role of host, he commands his associates, "*You* (*hymeis*) give them something to eat" (emphasis on "you," 9:13). Suddenly stuck with a massive catering job, the disciples get even more frustrated when they manage to scrounge up only five loaves and two fishes. The math is not propitious: a thousandth of a loaf of bread per person, and the fish—forget it. So it seems the crowd will have to leave after all. But as it happens, Jesus divides the throng into units of fifty, takes the meager bread-and-fish fare, looks heavenward, blesses and breaks the food, and gives the pieces to his disciples to distribute to the people. Defying normal *principia mathematica*, Jesus provides enough such that "all . . . were *filled*," with *twelve baskets* of leftovers (9:13-17, emphasis added)!

The dramatic move from lamenting paltry resources in the desert to "gather[ing] up twelve baskets of broken pieces" (9:17) vividly reinforces Luke's messianic vision of re-"gathering" and restoring "broken" and displaced Israel (comprised of "twelve" tribes). Having heard "about the kingdom of God" and been healed of their infirmities (9:11), the people return home full and satisfied.

DISCIPLESHIP:
CALLING AND TRAINING TWELVE FOLLOWERS

1. Sailing on a Volatile Lake (5:1-11; 8:22-25)
2. Teaching on a "Level Place" (6:17-49)
3. Hearing on Various Levels (8:1-21)
4. Hanging on a Daily Cross (9:18-27, 43-50)

We focus more fully in this section on Jesus' commissioning and instructing a special cadre of *twelve associates*, sometimes just called "the Twelve" (8:1; 9:1). The number is not arbitrary, having been determined, along with the names, after a nightlong prayer vigil (6:12-15). We need no secret code to decipher that the twelve disciples (like the twelve baskets) represent the dozen tribes constituting "all Israel." Jesus appoints them as future "judges" of restored Israel under his messianic authority (cf. 22:29-30); but most important, Jesus *sends* (*apostellō*) them as apostles (*apostoloi*, "sent ones") to replicate his mission of "proclaim[ing] the kingdom of God . . . bringing the good news . . . curing diseases everywhere," and gathering the "broken pieces" of God's people (6:13; 9:1-2, 6, 17). At this stage, however, Jesus only entrusts the Twelve with limited assignments (9:1-6) and steps in where they fail (9:40-42); but every missionary has to start somewhere. Even as Jesus establishes his own mission, he starts preparing the twelve apostles to continue his work after his "departure" (9:31). They will play a major role in sustaining Jesus' movement during the interim between his death and *parousia*.

However, as significant as the Twelve are in Jesus' restoration program, they do not constitute the full body of disciples. Luke introduces Levi the tax collector as a dedicated follower of Jesus (5:27-29) but not in the list of the Twelve (6:14-15).[23] Likewise, Luke identifies Mary Magdalene, Joanna, Susanna, and "many others" *women disciples* who follow Jesus—*alongside* the Twelve (men)— and support the movement "out of their resources" (8:1-3). Honorable mention also goes to an anonymous "someone" who expels demons in Jesus' name; despite one of the Twelve's objection that "he does not follow with us," Jesus happily accepts this exorcist as a disciple: "Whoever is not against you is for you" (9:49-50).

Sailing on a Volatile Lake (5:1-11; 8:22-25)

Two episodes place Jesus in a boat with his disciples on Lake Gennesaret. First, he commandeers Simon Peter's fishing boat on the lakeshore while Simon and associates are washing their nets after an unsuccessful night of trolling. Initially, Jesus pushes out "a little way" and teaches the crowds gathered on the shoreline (5:1-3). After this public instruction, Jesus has Simon "put out into the deep water" for a more personal and "deeper" lesson. Suddenly the same lake that yielded no catch throughout the night delivers a huge haul into Simon's nets when he lets them down at Jesus' order (5:4-6). As the fish-filled vessel threatens to sink, it becomes an altar where Simon bows before Jesus in awe and humility: "Go away from me, Lord, for I am a sinful man" (5:8). But Jesus isn't going anywhere. In fact, it's Simon and his partners, James and John, who "leave everything" behind—including this bumper catch—to be *with* Jesus (5:11, emphasis added). And they leave with a specific mission strangely related to their profession: "From now on," Jesus asserts, "you will be catching *people*" (5:10, emphasis added). Catching fish, like collecting twelve baskets of leftovers, provides another vivid image of ingathering (restoring) God's people.

But puzzling elements of force also enter the picture. Commercial fishing violently drags fish out of their natural habitat for the purpose of killing and consuming them. The prophet Habakkuk used such imagery to lament Judah's pending destruction by the Babylonians:

> You have made people like the fish of the sea, like crawling things that have no ruler. The enemy brings all of them up with a hook; he drags them out with his net; he gathers them in his seine; so he rejoices and exults . . . for by them his portion is lavish, and his food

is rich. Is he then to keep on emptying his net, and destroying nations without mercy? (Hab 1:14-17)

If Luke figuratively exploits these negative facets of fishing, perhaps he does so with biting irony: *unlike* evil powers and oppressive regimes that capture and ravage God's people for their own violent ends, Jesus' disciples will catch and restore them to new life.[24] Or maybe Luke suggests something of a forceful, urgent process in bringing people into God's kingdom, along the lines of two later texts:

Go out into the roads and lanes, and *compel* (*anankazō*) people to come in, so that my house may be filled. (14:23, emphasis added)

The law and the prophets were in effect until John came; since then the good news of the kingdom of God is proclaimed, and everyone tries to enter it *by force* (*biazō*) [or *is forced* to enter it]. (16:16, emphasis added)

In the second lake scene, the boat carrying Jesus and his disciples fills not with fish, but with water from a sudden windstorm. The frantic disciples wake their sleeping Lord (Jesus is clearly not worried) and inform him of their crisis: "Master, Master, we are perishing!" (8:22-24). He then promptly calms the turbulent winds and waves with a commanding word. After rebuking the elements, Jesus chides the disciples—"Where is your faith?" (8:25)—though less sharply than in Mark ("Have you still no faith?" 4:40).

In any case, the disciples are slow to pick up on Jesus' lake lessons. But in their defense, these are big lessons to swallow—as big as all creation. For by taming chaotic waters and exercising dominion over fishes of the "sea" with but a word, Jesus proves his dynamic link with the Creator God of Genesis and his gracious purpose to remake a broken world in God's image (cf. Gen 1:1-10, 20-23, 26-28).

Teaching on a "Level Place" (6:17-49)

After choosing and calling the twelve apostles on a mountain, Jesus comes down to a "level place," where he "stands" and teaches them, as well as a huge audience gathered from Judea and Phoenicia (and presumably, Galilee) (6:12-17). Although the Twelve enjoy a special relationship with Jesus, they do not receive some body of secret, esoteric knowledge: Jesus' word is for everyone. This pedagogical scene, popularly called the "Sermon on the Plain," stands out from Jesus' "Sermon on *the Mount*" in Matthew, delivered from a *sitting* position (Matt 5:1-2), and from previous *seated* lectures and discussions in Luke (2:46-47 [temple]; 4:20-21 [synagogue]; 5:3 [boat]). These vertical inversions of place and position—mountain to plain/sitting to standing—spatially illustrate God's mission of social reversal, forecast by Mary (1:52) and John ("every mountain and hill shall be made low" [3:5]) and fulfilled by Jesus.

The content of Jesus' "plain" instruction aptly fits its location, "leveling" and even flipping prevailing strata and hierarchies.[25] Two pithy commands urge disciples to level the field between themselves and others (both enemies and friends) and, as much as possible, between themselves and their Heavenly Father:

> Do to others [including enemies], as you would have them do to you. (6:31)

> Be merciful [to "sinners" and "enemies"] just as your Father is merciful. (6:36; cf. 6:32-35)

Faithful discipleship manifests the core virtues of love (*agapē*), kindness (*chrēstotēs*), and mercy (*oiktirmos*) to all (6:27-36).

In a foundational series of "blessings" and "woes," Jesus goes beyond an ethic of mutual concern to a striking paradigm of social reversal (6:20-26).

Blessings	Woes
1. **Poor** possess the kingdom of God	1. **Rich** have all they're going to get
2. **Hungry** will be filled	2. **Full** will be hungry
3. **Weepers** will laugh	3. **Laughers** will mourn and weep
4. **Despised** (for Christ's sake) have heavenly honor like true prophets of old	4. **Pleasers** (of everybody) are like false prophets of old

The community of God's kingdom represents an alternative society, markedly different from the status quo. Whereas full realization of this kingdom lies in a future, ideal heavenly realm, Jesus also announces its *present* inauguration *on earth*: "Yours *is* (*estin*) the kingdom of God" (6:20, emphasis added); "Your kingdom come"— here and now (11:2); "Look, the kingdom of God is amongst (*entos*) you" (17:21). And Jesus demands that his followers not simply wait for some heavenly utopia but *actively work* with him now to establish God's loving, kind, and merciful rule (6:27-45). Calling Jesus "Lord, Lord" is not some wistful mantra but an urgent mandate to "do what I [Jesus] tell you" (6:46-47). And any so-called disciple who "hears [Jesus' words] and does *not* act" sets himself up for a disastrous "leveling" of his own life and "house" (6:48-49, emphasis added).

Hearing on Various Levels (8:1-21)

Jesus further develops this emphasis on hearing and doing what he says in the parable of the sower (8:4-15). Whereas he tells two other brief *parabolai* during his Galilean mission (5:36-39 [garments and wineskins]; 6:39 [blind leading blind]), the sower represents the most developed parable to this point, with the bonus of a detailed exposition of its meaning. The basic story is clear and simple: a sower sows seed on four types of ground with varying results—the first three disappointing and only the last producing a bumper crop (8:4-8). The allegorical lesson for the disciples is equally straightforward: "the seed is the word of God" (8:11) broadcast by Jesus and other prophets and teachers to four types of hearers who respond in various ways, three negative and one positive (8:11-15).

Jesus assumes a challenging environment, beset by diabolical forces that assault the faithful with difficult "testing" (*peirasmos*, 8:13) in desolate territory (trampled, rocky, thorny), as Jesus was tested (*peirazō/peirasmos*) by the devil in the wilderness (4:2, 13). And as Jesus overcame this testing by citing God's word (4:4, 8, 12), so his disciples must "hold fast" to God's word with "patient endurance" (8:15).

Proof of the disciples' steadfast commitment to God's message will be manifest in the "fruit" they bear in response to the word. Hearing must lead to heeding, acoustics to actions, if the word is to have any value. The word of God is a precious commodity that must be protected and practiced, lest it be "taken away." It's not simply *what* one

144

hears that matters; more critically, it's *how* one reacts. "Pay attention to *how* you listen" (or "look how you listen"), Jesus exhorts (8:18, emphasis added). And one should listen in such a way that highlights the gracious effects of God's word, like a "lamp . . . on a lampstand" (8:16-18), and exhibits faithful obedience to that word in the family of God: "My mother and my brothers," Jesus claims, "are those who hear the word of God and *do it*" (8:21, emphasis added).

PARABLE		MEANING	
Ground	**Seed**	**Hearer**	**Word**
Beaten Path	Trampled and eaten by birds	Hardened	Taken away by the devil
Rocky	Sprouts but withers for lack of moisture	Fickle	Sparks initial faith but fails in time of testing *(peirasmos)*
Thorny	Sprouts but choked by thorns	Cluttered	Choked by worries, riches, and pleasures of life
Good Soil	Produces hundred-fold harvest	Steadfast	Produces "fruit-ful" character with "patient endurance"

Hanging on a Daily Cross (9:18-27, 43-50)

At a solemn moment of assessment, Jesus—"praying alone with only his disciples near him"—asks his confidants, "Who do the crowds say that I am?" (9:18). After the disciples report popular belief in Jesus' prophetic identity (someone like John or Elijah), Jesus turns the searchlight on the disciples themselves: "But *you all*, whom do *you* say I am?" Then Peter promptly—and correctly—answers: "The Messiah//Christ (*Christos*) of God" (9:20).

But how will Jesus carry out his role as God's messianic agent? On this critical issue, Peter and associates have the right title, but not the right job description. Knowing this deficiency, Jesus "sternly orders and commands" his disciples "*not* to tell anyone" about his Messiah-ship until they fully understand what that means (9:21, emphasis added). In particular, they must come to grips with his vocation as a *suffering* Messiah. Three times Jesus drives home the point: first, he plainly informs his followers that he "must undergo great suffering," culminating in public execution (9:22); then, on a mountain, he discusses his "departure" (*exodos*) with Moses and Elijah in the groggy presence of three disciples (including Peter) (9:30-32); and finally, after healing a man's convulsive son, Jesus announces his ominous fate of being "betrayed into human hands" (9:44). Hints of Jesus' ultimate resurrection and glorification also emerge (9:22, 29-32), but the dominant accent falls on his impending passion (*paschō*, "suffering") *and the pattern it provides for discipleship.*

Here the matter becomes very personal—and painful—for Jesus' followers. As he faces suffering and death as part of his messianic mission, Jesus also charges his deputies with the same assignment: "If any want to become my followers, let them deny themselves and take up their cross daily and follow me" (9:23). Shockingly, Jesus calls the disciples to a self-sacrificing, cruciform way of life, both in the sense of a "daily" *style of life* and a paradoxical *means to life* ("those who lose their life for my sake will save it," 9:24). Appreciating the difficulty of all this death-and- cross-speak, Jesus urges his associates, "Let these words sink into your ears" (9:44). Once again, Jesus raises the importance of proper hearing (cf. 9:35). But this is hard to take in: the image here is not taking up a miniature cross for ornamentation but a real one for crucifixion. And, in fact, the disciples "did not understand" (9:45) Jesus' strange talk about his own *and their* dying-and-rising or losing-life-to-save-it. Beyond that, although they shy away from asking Jesus for clarification, the disciples have no qualms arguing among themselves about "which one of them was the greatest" (9:46-48). Their preoccupation with social status couldn't be further from Jesus' emphasis on sacrificial service.

But such misunderstanding will not persist. The striking narrative aside that "meaning was concealed from them" (9:45) leaves room for future flashes of insight. As we have seen, the concept of crucifixion did not jibe with popular messianic expectations; and if the image of a crucified Messiah was horrifying, how much more that of crucified *disciples*! But after Jesus' resurrection, his followers will begin to apprehend their Lord's way of the cross more fully, especially through their experiences of suffering for Christ's name reported in Acts. As they face persecution and, in some cases, death (Stephen [Acts 7:54-59]; James [12:1-5]) for their faith, they discover renewed "boldness" (4:13, 29-31) to persevere in God's life-giving mission and remarkable growth in the messianic community (2:41; 4:4; 6:1, 7). As they share Christ's suffering *together* in "one heart and soul" (4:32)—bearing each other's burdens "day by day" (2:46; 5:42) and mutually sacrificing for the common good (taking up the cross is a community project)[26]—"great grace" breaks out "upon them all" (4:33). Sacrifice indeed leads to salvation; those who lose their lives for Jesus' sake find them anew (see 2:37-47; 4:23-37; 5:12-42).

EXPANDING AND INTERPRETING GOD'S MISSION ON THE WAY TO JERUSALEM

(Luke 9:51–19:44)

In this largest segment of Luke's Gospel—the so-called Central Section or Travel Narrative—Jesus expands and interprets his God-anointed mission en route to Jerusalem. In terms of *expanding* the mission, as Jesus branches out from Galilee southward into Samaria and Judea, he confronts, recruits, and presents a number of new personnel (mostly in parables). Appropriating Jesus' "lost-and-found" motif central to this unit (15:1-32; cf. 19:10), we may broadly characterize his extended journey to Jerusalem as a search-and-rescue mission restoring God's "lost" people.

Many of these people fit character types already featured in Luke: (1) *disciples*, now a band of seventy instead of twelve (10:1, 17); (2) *women*, including two new named female followers, Martha and Mary (10:38-42); (3) *Pharisees and lawyers*, again at meal settings but now, at times, more sharply criticized by Jesus (11:42-44); (4) *rich and poor*, with continued "woe" to the wealthy (6:24; cf. 1:53) but also a positive example of a "lost" rich man (Zacchaeus) whom Jesus "seeks and saves" and who, in turn, seeks and hosts Jesus (19:1-10); (5) *fathers, sons, and slaves*, now featured in a series of parables rather than healing incidents. Beyond these human figures, Jesus continues to battle and overcome (6) *Satan and demons*, even as some critics start accusing him of collaborating with such evil powers (11:14-23). Two new dramatis personae also emerge in Luke's central section: (7) *Samaritans*, representing something of a middle group between Jews and Gentiles, but tipping more toward the "foreigner" side (*allogenēs*, 17:18); and (8) *the blind and seeing (again)*, mentioned in 4:18 and 7:22, but not developed until this segment (Luke's only sight-restoring miracle story occurs toward the journey's end in 18:35-43). Much of Luke 9:51–19:44 coheres around these eight character groups.

A. Disciples
    1. Prospective Disciples (9:57-62)
    2. Seventy Disciples (10:1-17)
    3. Fearless Disciples (12:4-12)
    4. Divided Disciples (12:49-53)
    5. Self-Sacrificing Disciples (14:25-33)
    6. Forgiving and Faithful Disciples (17:2-6)
    7. Childlike Disciples (18:15-17)
    8. Praising Disciples (19:29-40)

B. Women
    1. Hospitality of Martha and Mary (10:38-42)
    2. Healing of a Bent Woman (13:10-17)
    3. Parable of the Widow and Unjust Judge (18:1-8)

C. Pharisees and Lawyers
    1. Woes of Hypocrisy (11:37-54; 12:1-3)
    2. Parables of Hospitality (10:25-37; 14:7-24)
    3. Coming of God's Kingdom (17:20-21)
    4. Parable of Haughty Pharisee and Humble Tax Collector (18:9-14; cf. 16:14-16)

D. Rich and Poor
    1. Parable of the Rich Fool (12:13-21)
    2. Parable of the Rich Man and Poor Lazarus (16:19-31)
    3. Jesus' Encounter with the Rich Ruler (18:18-30)
    4. Jesus' Encounter with the Rich Tax Collector, Zacchaeus (19:1-10)

E. Fathers, Sons, and Slaves
    1. Parable of a Friend and Father at Midnight (11:5-8)
    2. Parables of Watchful and Faithful Slaves (12:35-48)

3. Parable of a Father and Two Sons (15:11-32)
4. Parable of Dishonest Steward (16:1-13)
5. Parable of Unprofitable Servants (17:7-10)
6. Parable of Slaves and Pounds (19:11-27)

F. Satan and Demons
   1. Vision of Satan's Fall like Lightning (10:17-20)
   2. False Accusation of Alliance with Beelzebub, Ruler of Demons (11:14-26)
   3. Healing of Bent Woman "Bound by Satan" (13:10-17)

G. Samaritans
   1. Incident of the Inhospitable Samaritan Village (9:51-56)
   2. Parable of the Good Samaritan Traveler (10:25-37)
   3. Healing of the Grateful Samaritan Leper (17:11-19)

H. Blind and Seeing (Again)
   1. Seeing Signs of the Times (11:29-36; 12:54-56)
   2. Seeing the Kingdom of God (17:20-37)
   3. Seeing Again and Following Jesus (18:35-43)

As for *interpreting* God's mission, the great bulk of Luke's Central Section is taken up with Jesus' teachings and sayings, with less emphasis on Jesus' miracles—five (11:14; 13:10-17; 14:1-4; 17:11-19; 18:35-43) versus eleven in the previous section. Jesus offers more interpretive commentary about God's purposes along this extended trek to Jerusalem than in any other segment. Much of this discourse comes in the form of *parables—nineteen* or so (the category is debatable in a few cases) compared to three during the Galilean mission, and many of these parables appear only in Luke.

In chapter 1, I discussed a number of aspects pertaining to Luke's overall literary form. But we must also appreciate Luke's use of more particular speech-forms, especially one as pervasive as parables in this section. In basic terms, parables represent snippets of typical, everyday family or business life in which Jesus drives home a particular point or lesson. The characters in these stories are usually unnamed, stock figures (Lazarus excepted in 16:19-31), and the lessons have wide application to a general audience or target subgroup; although often sparked by an individual's query or comment, Jesus' parables speak to broad religious

THE GOSPEL OF LUKE AND ACTS OF THE APOSTLES

and social issues. And they do so, not with the simple and gentle moralizing of a fable, but more with the complex and edgy satirizing of a parody. Jesus offers little explanation for most parables (the decoded parable of the sower excepted [8:11-15]); he usually leaves hearers (and readers) hanging and puzzled, often with a troubled scowl (is he mocking us?) or bemused smirk (that's absurd!). Whatever point Jesus makes feels more like a punch, but we're never quite sure who or what gets knocked down in the process. Concluding his fine survey of *What Are They Saying About the Parables?* David Gowler remarks

> There are no spectators in the dialogic world of parable; all partici-
> pate. . . . Parables not only challenge and loosen the grip of estab-
> lished norms and relations in the dominant culture, but they contain
> and engender a criticism (and sometimes a mockery) of the official
> social order and ideology, and . . . parables can also vigorously cri-
> tique "peasant culture" as well. Parables offer up instead another
> alternative: Jesus' view of reality.[1]

Whatever the specific issues addressed in the parables (see below), they demonstrate Jesus' liberating, "alternative" mission that challenges the status quo, the powers that be, and, indeed, all types of people across society's spectrum.

Although we might organize our analysis of Luke's Travel Narrative around the character groups and parable clusters outlined above, such topical approaches can lose sight of the journey's "orderly" progression. But precisely what "order" Luke follows here is not at all clear. In chapter 1, I examined two schemes scholars have proposed: one fitting a Deuteronomic framework, the other a chiastic pattern. Even though both models account for some material, neither represents a perfect fit without undue fiddling. In line with Luke's occasional citation of Deuteronomy, his frequent casting of Jesus as a prophet-like-Moses, and his appropriation of the wilderness-journey motif, the Deuteronomic scheme has much to commend it, though not as a structural straitjacket; likewise, although several noncontiguous scenes match up in chiastic-like pairs, several passages stand on their own with loose relationship to the rest of the account. In fact, on the face of it, the whole of Luke's Central Section appears highly episodic and thinly connected. Perhaps most surprising for a travelogue, we discover *no* specific place names until Jesus' final stops in Jericho and at the

Mount of Olives (near Bethpage and Bethany) before entering Jerusalem (18:35; 19:1, 29).[2] In lieu of a detailed itinerary, Luke gives only the barest hints of Jesus' movements from "a village of the Samaritans" (9:52) to "a certain village" (10:38), then a "certain place" (11:1), "one of the synagogues" (13:10), "one town and village after another" (13:22), "the region between Samaria and Galilee" (17:11), and so on. Beyond providing the interpreter with a general lay of the land, a map is pretty much useless. If we attempt to retrace Jesus' steps, *we* risk becoming "lost"!

A smattering of sparse travel notes, clustering around four main stages of the journey, keep the story "going" steadily toward Jerusalem, but with little concern for the precise route. Observe the repetition of *poreuomai* and cognates, a common term for "go, proceed; travel, journey."[3]

- **Stage 1:** "When the days drew near for him to be taken up, he set his face to go (*poreuesthai*) to Jerusalem" (9:51).
- **Stage 2:** "Jesus went through (*dieporeueto*) one town and village after another, teaching as he made his way (*poreian*) to Jerusalem" (13:22). "Yet today, tomorrow, and the next day I must be on my way (*poreuesthai*), because it is impossible for a prophet to be killed outside of Jerusalem" (13:33).
- **Stage 3:** "On the way to Jerusalem Jesus was going through (*poreuesthai*) the region between Samaria and Galilee" (17:11).
- **Stage 4:** "Then he took the twelve aside and said to them, 'See, we are going up to Jerusalem' " (18:31). "As they were listening to this, he went on to tell a parable, because he was near Jerusalem" (19:11). "After he had said this, he went on (*eporeueto*) ahead, going up to Jerusalem" (19:28). "As he came near and saw the city [of Jerusalem], he wept over it" (19:41).

In order to maintain some sense of narrative "order" and to follow Jesus' path as best we can, the analysis below coordinates with the four stages intimated by the travel notes. But before embarking on our interpretive trek, we briefly consider possible reasons for recounting such a long journey with so few signposts. In contrast to Jesus' determined focus at the outset of the march—"he *set his face* to go to Jerusalem" (9:51, emphasis added)[4]—his *feet* seem in no particular hurry to reach his destination; rather he appears content to drift from nameless village to village, place to place, engaging a variety of people and spinning numerous parables as he goes—something like a traveling bard. Is there some purpose to this perambulating, some method to the meandering? In Luke's narrative world—resonating with Deuteronomy and Israel's "moving" experiences of exodus, wilderness wandering, and exile—Jesus' *wandering* journey, recovering the "lost" and delivering Moses-like instructional speeches en route to Jerusalem, emerges as a new restoration venture (rescue mission) on behalf of God's scattered people.

Furthermore, unlike other segments in Luke and Acts, where characters and plot follow a carefully charted course, the Gospel's more loosely mapped Central Section allows for delays and detours in God's mission (including delaying Christ's *parousia*) and assures readers of God's continuing guidance (through Christ's teaching) along the slow and snaky path of discipleship. More often than not, the biblical God's purposes have been realized not in a simple straight line but in a complex circuitous maze, demanding maximum trust and patience from God's people. As Second Isaiah asserts, from an exilic context, "God's ways are not our ways"—they are infinitely "higher" (Isa 55:8-9). And, we might add, they're often a good bit longer and windier than we might prefer.

STAGE 1: SETTING HIS FACE TOWARD JERUSALEM (9:51–13:21)

1. "Nowhere to Lay His Head" (9:51-62)
2. "I Watched Satan Fall from Heaven" (10:1-20; 11:14-26)
3. "Go and Do Likewise" (10:25–11:13)
4. "Beware of the Yeast of . . . Hypocrisy" (11:33–12:3, 54-56; 13:10-17)
5. "Do Not Worry about Your Life" (12:4-34)
6. "I Came to Bring Fire to the Earth" (12:35–13:9)

In this initial stage, our survey coheres around six key sayings of Jesus. A quick glance at terminology signals an environment of displacement ("nowhere," "fall from heaven"), distress ("woe," "worry," "fire"), and opposition ("Satan," "hypocrites"). From the start, this journey promises some rough going. How rough it gets will become clearer as we examine the wider content and contexts of Jesus' pronouncements.

"Nowhere to Lay His Head" (9:51-62)

Jesus speaks here as the "Son of Man," his favorite self-designation, representing paradoxical roles: on the one hand, he commands extraordinary authority to forgive sins (5:24), govern the Sabbath (6:5), and execute final judgment (9:26); on the other hand, he suffers a slanderous reputation as a glutton and drunkard (7:34) and murderous rejection by earthly authorities (9:22, 26). As with his Messianic identity, so as Son of Man, Jesus is *both* a sovereign *and* a suffering figure. The present case falls more on the suffering side: Son of Man Jesus can't even muster enough authority to secure a decent place to sleep ("nowhere to lay his head" [9:58]) during his many travels. He has no illusions about this final trip to Jerusalem; it will not be a cushy excursion with sojourns in fancy villas or five-star hotels. But that's nothing new in Luke. Jesus' earthly life began in a stable and animal trough attached to a "no vacancy" inn (2:7); now, during his itinerant mission, even the animals have it better: "foxes have holes and birds of the air have nests" (9:58), but Jesus has no place to rest (unless you count the bottom of a boat in the middle of a storm [8:22-23]).

The Travel Narrative's opening incident confirms Jesus' displaced, vagabond status, as he and his companions find no welcome in a Samaritan village. The situation betrays historic rivalry between Samaritans and Jews concerning the true people of God and heirs of ancient Israelite religion (discussed in chapter 2). The Samaritans based their claim on their own version of the Torah (Samaritan Pentateuch), accentuating Mt. Gerizim near Shechem as the sacred center of worship. On the other side, apart from maligning Samaritans' supposed mixed blood (half-Assyrian), most Jews adhered to the Prophets as well as the Law and looked to Mount Zion (temple mount) in Jerusalem as the most holy place. Such ethnic-religious conflict was deep-seated and hotheaded, sometimes resulting in bloodshed.[5] So it's not surprising to find some Samaritans rejecting Jesus precisely "because his face was set toward Jerusalem" (9:53). The fine points of Jesus' Jewish faith are not the issue, as they were in the Nazareth synagogue (4:16-30) and in debates with Pharisees and lawyers; now his basic identity as a Jerusalem-oriented Jew is enough to set the Samaritans against him. By the same token, the fact that Samaritans spurn the Jewish Jesus and his Jewish followers is enough to spark a violent counterplot from two of Jesus' party: James and John want to torch the place, Elijah-style (9:54). Clearly, little love was lost between Samaritans and Jews.

But Jesus is on a different kind of mission. As he suffers rejection and homelessness, Jesus responds not by lashing out at the inhospitable Samaritans but by challenging his *disciples*, both present and prospective. He addresses four cases, the first dealing with James and John, the last three with would-be followers.

- First, he "turns," locking in on the volatile sons of Zebedee, "rebukes" their fire-breathing proposal, and moves on (*poreuomai*) to another place (9:54-55). In his recovery mission to the lost, Jesus has no intention of fanning the flame of ethnic-religious conflict.
- Second, he dampens the enthusiasm of a prospective disciple who claims he "will follow Jesus wherever he goes." This is where Jesus announces he has "nowhere to lay his head" (9:57-58). Far from affirming the man's pledge, Jesus lets him know that "wherever" is in fact "nowhere" permanent or predictable.
- Third, when another interested follower asks for prior leave to "go and bury my father," Jesus shows no sympathy and not a little absurdity in his response: "Let the dead bury their own dead" (which effectively means the dead will go *un*buried), "but as for you, go and proclaim the kingdom of God" (9:59-60). Jesus brooks no excuses or exigencies (including honorable ones like family burial) in carrying out God's urgent mission. The household of God, the faithful family of those who heed Jesus' word (cf. 8:19-21), takes precedence over natural family ties.
- Finally, Jesus rebuffs another prospect simply wants to bid his family farewell, a la Elisha, who eventually left father and mother to take up Elijah's mission (1 Kgs 19:19-21). But Jesus cuts no slack. His way is a tough row to hoe: "plowing" his path to Jerusalem allows no looking or going back (9:61-62).

Simply put, Jesus does not negotiate with disciples. Although something of an anti-Caesar and anti-Herod figure (only first-class travel and accommodations for them [cf. 7:25]), Jesus commands full general-like authority over his followers. Nothing and no one will deter his pressing messianic march to Jerusalem for the sake of God's kingdom.

"I Watched Satan Fall from Heaven" (10:1-20; 11:14-26)

As Jesus resists the drag of earthly encumbrances, so he persists in defanging cosmic evil powers ("snakes and scorpions" [10:19]) that threaten his mission. In fact he ratchets up the attack as he now dispatches seventy advance agents of God's kingdom, in two-member teams, to cure diseases and cast out demons in "every town and place where he himself intended to go" (10:1). The six-fold increase from twelve (9:1-6) to seventy or seventy-two[6] deputies suggests (1) escalating hostility from malignant forces; (2) Jesus' need for greater assistance as the mission expands, much like Moses' appointment of *seventy* elders to help manage the Israelites' wilderness journey (Num 11:14-30); and (3) perhaps a harbinger of the kingdom's outreach to the ends of the earth, encompassing the full "Table of Nations" numbered as *seventy* (Hebrew text) or *seventy-two* (LXX) in Genesis 10. Although Jesus sends forth his ambassadors as vulnerable "lambs into the midst of wolves" with no material supplies ("carry no purse, no bag, no sandals"), he arms them with the authority of his name to subdue "all the power of the enemy" (10:3-4, 19). And the result is cataclysmic—for Satan!—whom Jesus "watch[es] . . . fall from heaven like a flash of lightning" in the wake of his agents' campaign (10:17-18). Such imagery is metaphysical, not physical (no literal "fall" from the sky) or meteorological (no actual lightning bolt), but registers all the same a major cosmic defeat for Satan and his demons.

But final victory cannot be claimed yet in Jesus'—or Luke's—day. "The kingdom of God has *come near*" (10:9, 11, emphasis added) but not all the way. Signs of continuing conflict still demand keen vigilance and, sometimes, retributive justice. Although Jesus' messengers find some receptive houses offering temporary room and board, they also enter inhospitable towns that turn them away. Such rejection is scarcely surprising, given their previous experience in Samaria and Jesus' expectation of homelessness. But *not* expected is Jesus' sudden shift in policy toward resistant people: instead of eschewing vengeance against hostile audiences and simply moving on to another venue, as in the Samaritan incident, Jesus now advises his followers to "wipe off" their feet and stomp out "in protest against" hardhearted towns, anticipating scorching divine reprisals that make Sodom's fate seem like a harmless brushfire (10:10-12). A certain volatility in Jesus' mission cannot be denied. In the heat of battle against evil powers, stern judgment must temper cheap mercy; but enforcing such judgment is best left in God's hands. The fire will either fall or it won't; that's God's business. Jesus' disciples need not, should not, "command fire to come down from heaven and consume" their opponents (9:54-55).

As recalcitrant people continue opposing God's kingdom, so Satan and his demons keep fighting, keep getting up after they fall, even keep coming back after they're cast out! Wielding the "finger of God" against Satan's "castle" (11:20-21), as Moses did against Pharaoh's palace (see Exod 8:19), Jesus delivers afflicted persons from demonic oppression. But Jesus does not always consign expelled demons to final destruction in a watery abyss, as he did with Legion (cf. Luke 8:31-33). Some wander through "waterless regions" seeking a new habitat, but finding none they marshal seven "more evil" spirits and repossess the former victim with greater malice (11:24-26). The inauguration of God's kingdom through Jesus Messiah opens the way to liberation from evil powers but does not guarantee permanent peace for God's people without their due diligence. They must fill the void left by evil spirits with the Holy Spirit, whom "the heavenly Father give[s] . . . to those who ask him!" (11:13).

"Go and Do Likewise" (10:25–11:13)

As well as sketching a long, meandering course, Luke's Travel Narrative also offers some surprising twists and turns along the way. Up to this point, Jesus has been rebuffed by Samaritans in particular and received scant hospitality from anyone. The present segment, however, casts a different light on these matters. First, in interpreting the Torah's two foundational "love" commandments—love God wholeheartedly (Deut 6:5) and love your neighbor as yourself (Lev 19:18)—Jesus tells a parable that features a *Samaritan*, of all people, as the loving model worthy of emulation ("Go and do likewise," Luke 10:37) by *Jewish* religious leaders, represented by a lawyer, whose questions and comments trigger Jesus' story (10:25-29), and a priest and Levite featured in the tale. Whereas this clerical tandem "passed by" a stripped, beaten, "half dead" fellow-Jew ("from Jerusalem") on the roadside without lifting a finger, a Samaritan "was moved with pity" for the poor victim, tended his wounds, "brought him to an inn, and took care of him" (10:30-35). Far from dumping the man in a stable or manger (cf. 2:7), the Samaritan secured him a room and bed inside the inn—on the Samaritan's tab—as long as needed. Such portrayal of a "good," caring, hospitable Samaritan would have been hard for first-century Jews to swallow, as Luke 9:51-56 confirmed (inhospitable Samaritans/vengeful Jewish disciples). By standard Jewish definition, Samaritans were "no good"—if they had any role to play in Jesus' story, it would be the *robbers*! And frankly, any Samaritans in Jesus' audience would not have been any happier with the parable: a typical Samaritan response to finding a dying Jew in a ditch would be "good riddance," not going the extra mile to nurse the victim back to health.

Thus, the punch Jesus delivers in the parable of the good Samaritan drives home the universal thrust of the "love" commands: genuine love for God and for God's people bursts through all boundaries of ethnic and religious hatred. Such an emphasis both challenges and affirms the Torah. Deuteronomy's foundational mandate to love God with one's whole being (Deut 6:5) is linked antithetically with the martial order to "utterly destroy" all non-Israelite peoples inhabiting the promised land, to "make no covenant with them and show them no mercy" (Deut 7:2). Behind this ethnic cleansing policy runs a certain moral logic that idolatrous nations, if allowed to survive, would inevitably turn Israel away from exclusive devotion to God. Whether Hittites, Girgashites, or Canaanites in Moses' day, or Samaritans in Jesus' time, "other" peoples are branded as irremediable enemies of the Israelites/Jews (Deut 7:1-6). Jesus' parable of a loving, merciful, "neighborly" Samaritan obviously resists Jewish (or any other kind) of xenophobia and ethnocentrism. But this is *not* a radical new idea in Jewish social ethics, for the same Torah that advances ethnic cleansing in Israel's land also advocates inclusive love to "outsiders." As Leviticus 19 initially stresses neighborly love toward fellow Israelites, the same chapter ultimately expands the love ethic to all resident "aliens":

You shall not take vengeance or bear a grudge against any of your people, but *you shall love your neighbor as yourself*: I am the LORD. (Lev 19:18, emphasis added)

When an alien resides with you in your land, you shall not oppress the alien. The alien who resides with you shall be to you as the citizen among you; *you shall love the alien as yourself*, for you were aliens in the land of Egypt: I am the LORD your God. (Lev 19:33-34, emphasis added)

Israel's history is too fraught with her own tragic experiences of oppression and alienation to tolerate such heinous practices within her borders.

As Jesus shares the hospitality story of the good Samaritan to illustrate exemplary love for God and others, he tells another hospitality tale—the parable of the friend at midnight—to demonstrate the fullness of God's love for God's children. One neighbor-"friend" rudely awakens another at midnight, seeking three loaves of bread so he can feed a visitor (yet another friend) who has caught him by surprise, with empty cupboards. The sleeping friend, snugly tucked in for the night with his children, is not disposed to get up and help his bread-seeking neighbor, but because the seeker keeps knocking and making a pest of himself, the sleeper finally rises and meets the need (11:5-8). A simple story of friendship and persistence—one friend nagging another on behalf of a third friend—but with a deeper meaning concerning God's friendly, fatherly care of God's people. The argument follows a classic "how much more" line of reasoning: if an irritable, earthly father will eventually meet a pesky neighbor's request for bread, "how much more" will the gracious "heavenly Father give the Holy Spirit to those who ask him" (11:13)—and also give "our daily bread" that Jesus earlier taught his followers to pray for (11:3).

Sandwiched between the two parables where Jesus teaches about hospitality is a brief, but significant, episode where he *receives* hospitality from sisters Martha and Mary. Whether or not he "lays his head" down for the night, he clearly rests for a spell in these women's home. Both sisters attend to Jesus but in different ways: Martha "welcomes him into *her home*" (she seems to be the household head) and "serves/ministers to (*diakoneō*)" him with "much service/ministry (*diakonia*)," Mary—much to Martha's annoyance—simply sits at Jesus' feet and listens to his teaching

(10:38-42). Because Jesus affirms Mary's attentiveness over against Martha's complaint about her sister's idleness, many interpreters have assumed Jesus' subordination of Martha's action to Mary's contemplation, or in other words: hearing the word trumps doing the work. But despite Jesus' strong defense of Mary's "good" (*agathē*) choice in the present situation ("there is need of only one thing" [10:42]), the larger narrative context has stressed that *both hearing and doing are needful*, indeed, that hearing must lead to doing and doing must reflect obedience to God's word (see especially 8:4-21). Moreover, although Jesus rebukes Martha's "worry" over her many tasks (which likely include meal preparations, although no "kitchen" duty is specified) and her irritation with Mary's lack of help, he in no way denigrates Martha's acts of hospitality and service. How could he? Martha's ministerial activity and hospitality follow in the footsteps of the good Samaritan (sans the frustration) and prepare the way for the feisty midnight bread-seeker (another anxious host) in Jesus' parables. Of course, in order to get the points of these parables, one must first give heed to Jesus' word, which is precisely what *Mary* exemplifies. Luke's story presents Martha and Mary as complementary partners in discipleship, not competing rivals. Followers of Jesus should go and do/hear, hear/do likewise.

"Beware of the Yeast of . . . Hypocrisy" (11:33–12:3, 54-56; 13:10-17)

Jesus' concern for faithful practice, not merely profession, of God's word heightens in his sharp denunciations of hypocritical religious leaders. Along with lawyers (11:46) and synagogue leaders (13:15), the Pharisees bear the brunt of Jesus' critique: "Beware of the yeast of the Pharisees, that is, their hypocrisy" (12:1). Here the image of "yeast" suggests rotten and hidden attitudes and motives that corrupt the whole of one's being and behavior. A key dimension of Jesus' light-bearing mission involves exposing these dark recesses of religious pretense (see light-darkness imagery in 11:33-36; 12:2-3).

This anti-hypocrisy campaign comes to a head at another meal encounter with Pharisees and lawyers (11:37-54). These devotees of the Torah remain interested in Jesus' teaching and mission. As in 7:36, another Pharisee invites Jesus to his "sacred" table (11:37), offering hospitality and fellowship with no expressed intention to trap or shame Jesus. But again Jesus proves to be a more disgruntled than gracious guest. Where he previously faulted Simon the Pharisee for not providing him water to wash his feet (7:44), now—when given water to wash his hands—he *doesn't use it*! (11:38). Instead he launches into a tirade about the Pharisees' tendency to overemphasize external washings (hands, cups, dishes) as a whitewashing of internal grime (wickedness, greed) (11:39-41). From this introit, he then crescendos into a set of six blistering "woes to you" (11:42-52). Needless to say, this invective spoils the party. They never get to dinner, and the tide turns against Jesus. When he leaves the house (one suspects he's "invited" to leave), the legal experts now become "very hostile toward him" and more inquisitorial, "lying in wait for him, to catch him in something he might say" (11:53-54). Notice the "woes" that set them off, the first three targeted at the Pharisees, the second three at lawyers.

Woes to Pharisees	Woes to Lawyers
Neglecting justice and the love of God, even though faithful in tithing (11:42)	Loading people with legal burdens while providing no assistance (11:46)
Loving best seats in the synagogue and greetings in the marketplace (11:43)	Approving ancestors' virulent repudiation of the prophets (11:47)
Being like unmarked graves, concealing their lifeless identities from passersby (11:44)	Taking away the key of knowledge (11:52)

Luke's narrative often lumps together, in various combinations, Pharisees, lawyers, teachers of the law, and scribes with little distinction (5:17, 21, 30; 6:6; 7:30; 14:3). These groups share a deep devotion to the Mosaic law. In the present context, however, Jesus' "woes" against Pharisees and lawyers address the two parties' hypocrisy somewhat differently: whereas the Pharisees often fall short, in Jesus' estimation, of *practicing* the law they so vigorously profess, especially in seminal matters of justice and mercy, the lawyers chiefly fail in *teaching* the law in a "prophetic"[7] manner that opens hearts and minds to God's will (they misappropriate the "key of knowledge"). The focus on *practice* fits the lay Pharisaic movement's emphasis on living out the law in every aspect of life; the concern with *teaching* suits the lawyers' more professional status as legal scholars and judges. Jesus has no major problem with sincere, dedicated Pharisees and lawyers, and he's certainly not opposed to the law; indeed, he advocates strict adherence: "it is these [commandments] you ought to have practiced [justice, love], without neglecting the others [tithing]" (11:42).

Though not explicitly identified with Pharisees, lawyers, and scribes in Luke's writing, "leaders of the synagogue" (*archisyn-gagōgoi*) closely sympathize with such Torah-honoring groups and also merit Jesus' "hypocrite" label, albeit not universally (Luke allows for variable responses within character groups). As we have seen, Jesus responded graciously to the pleas of Capernaum's synagogue ruler (Jairus) for his ailing daughter, stopping at nothing (including the daughter's death!) to save the child (8:40-56). But when Jesus heals a "daughter of Abraham" (13:16) from a chronic, crippling condition "in one of the synagogues" and draws fire from the leader for healing on the Sabbath, he retorts by calling this critic a "hypocrite" (13:10-15). Again, the conflict does not reflect Jesus' opposition to Sabbath law but rather his commitment to the law's fullest implications. Reminding the synagogue ruler that he and fellow congregants have no qualms about watering their livestock on the Sabbath, Jesus wonders how they can possibly question his Sabbath liberation of a woman who had suffered "eighteen long years . . . [of] bondage" to Satan's back-breaking oppression (13:15-16).[8] Though Jesus does not cite it, the Deuteronomic version of the fourth commandment reinforces his point. The main motive for resting (and *rest*oring) one's entire household on the Sabbath—including son, daughter, and male and female slave, as well as "your ox or your donkey, or any of your livestock" (Deut 5:14)—recalls the Israelites' bitter suffering under Egyptian bondage, when they were worked to death every day of the week (Deut 5:12-15). Observing the Sabbath rest affirms God's purpose of freedom and restoration for God's people. What better way, then, to celebrate and perpetuate this purpose than by freeing and

163

restoring a "bent" (13:11) and "bound" (13:16) daughter of Abraham—*on the Sabbath*!

"Do Not Worry about Your Life" (12:4-34)

The travel discussion now turns more pointedly to Jesus' "friends" (12:4) or "disciples" (12:22; cf. 12:1—"when the crowd gathered by the thousands . . . he began to speak *first* to the disciples," emphasis added). And it also turns to the future, specifically, to hardships Jesus' followers can expect down the road (after Jesus' departure), be they extraordinary judicial trials, "when they bring you before the synagogues, the rulers, and the authorities" (12:11) or everyday burdens of "life, what you will eat, or . . . what you will wear" (12:22). The instruction has particular relevance for subsequent generations of Jesus' disciples: Acts reports several trials of Jesus' emissaries before hostile authorities (as well as clashes with Satan's agents) and various crises surrounding food shortages (6:1-6; 11:27-30) and other physical needs. Hearers of Luke's story in the throes of displacement and deprivation perk up their ears for Jesus' coping strategies.

On the surface, his advice is alarmingly simple, if not naïve: "Don't worry [12:11, 22, 29], don't be afraid [12:4, 32], it's going to be all right." Easy for Jesus to say. But underlying these hollow platitudes are solid principles grounded in the faithful character and action of the Holy Spirit and God the Creator/Father. Once again, practical and pastoral questions call forth theological and analogical ("how much more") answers (cf. 11:9-13).

- "Do not worry about how you are to defend yourselves or what you are to say; *for the **Holy Spirit** will teach you at that very hour what you ought to say*" (Luke 12:11-12, emphasis added; cf. 21:12-15; Acts 6:8-10; 7:55-60).
- "Do not worry about your life, what you will eat. . . . Consider the ravens . . . ***God** feeds them. Of **how much more** value are you than the birds!*" (Luke 12:22-24, emphasis added; cf. 12:6-7).
- "Do not worry about your life . . . what you will wear. . . . But *if **God** so clothes the grass of the field . . . **how much more** will [**God**] clothe you—you of little faith!*" (Luke 12:22, 28, emphasis added).

- "Do not keep worrying. For it is the nations of the world that strive after all these things, and *your Father knows that you need them. Instead, strive for [God's] kingdom, and these things will be given to you as well*" (Luke 12:29-31, emphasis added).
- "Do not be afraid little flock, for it is *your Father's good pleasure to give you the kingdom*" (Luke 12:32, emphasis added).

The focus falls on divine protection and provision of life's basic necessities (as during Israel's wilderness journey), not on acquisition and prosperity (as during Israel's territorial "conquest"). In fact, Jesus ultimately matches simple assurance of God's care with a jolting challenge to God's people to "sell your possessions, and give alms" (12:33). "Striving for God's kingdom" demands primary investment in God's business, in God's reign of love and justice.

The parable of the rich fool (12:13-21), sandwiched between two anti-worry discourses (12:4-12, 22-34), features a dramatic counterexample of one whose investment portfolio is wholly wrapped up in selfish, not godly, interests. From Jesus' perspective, such a materialistic attitude toward life is something worth worrying about: "Take care! Be on your guard against all kinds of greed; for one's life does not consist in the abundance of possessions" (12:15). In all his stockpiling of abundant goods and scheming of luxurious retirement, the "rich fool" factors God completely out of his life. But here's where he proves most foolish, since the eternal God cannot be factored out of human existence, especially in comparison with ephemeral goods. God determines life and death, and "this very night"—long before the "many years" the rich man planned for—God determines the terminus of this man's days, beyond which his possessions will be worthless (12:19-20). The parable provides compelling rationale for living a life that is "rich toward God" (12:21) until death or the final restoration of God's kingdom, the time of which God alone sets (cf. Luke 12:39-40, 46; 21:34-36; Acts 1:6-7; 17:31).

"I Came to Bring Fire to the Earth" (12:35–13:9)

For a journey that begins with Jesus' rebuking two disciples' desire to call down celestial fire upon an unwelcoming Samaritan village (9:54-55), his sudden declaration—"I came to bring fire to the earth, and how I wish it were already kindled" (12:49)—strikes a startlingly different note (or match, should we say). Here Jesus appears as a fire-breathing prophet-like-Elijah or an agent of God's fiery judgment—and, in fact, this is not an entirely new role in Luke's Gospel. We may recall Jesus' prior threat in this section of Sodom-like fire-and-brimstone retribution against any town that rejects his messengers (10:12); and even earlier, Jesus' fiery fore-runner (cf. 3:9) predicted a similarly incendiary mission for his "more powerful" successor: "He will baptize you with the Holy Spirit *and fire.* His winnowing fork is in his hand, to clear his threshing floor and to gather the wheat into his granary; but the chaff he will *burn with unquenchable fire*" (3:16-17, emphasis added). In his aggressive march against evil forces, attending his redemptive mission for the "lost," Jesus presses toward Jerusalem with holy firepower (not conventional weaponry).

So who gets burned, and why? The fire Jesus brings functions to rouse the complacent from a false sense of peace and to divide honorable members of God's true family from fraudulent pre-tenders ("Do you think that I have come to bring peace to the earth? No, I tell you, but rather division!" [12:51]). The blaze will rip through households, illuminating faithful kin "who hear the word of God and obey it" (11:28; cf. 8:21), along with slaves "whom [their] master will find at work when he arrives" (12:43), and smoking out unfaithful fathers and their families who "did not prepare [them-selves] or do what was wanted" (12:47-53). Apart from Luke's major religious distinction between those who fear Israel's one God and those who serve multiple deities, he also marks a "divided peo-ple" *within Israel* across all strata, based on differing responses to God's message and Messiah.[9] And he is not shy about predicting judgment for those who respond wrongly.

But appreciating that fire can easily spread too far and too fast and spark enormous anxiety, Pastor Luke also carefully qualifies the experience of divine judgment. Three points stand out in this unit:

- Although judgment inevitably involves a degree of suffering and deprivation, all such experiences are not products of just retribution. Put another way, those who suffer are not necessarily more evil than those who prosper. Recalling horrible incidents (otherwise unknown) in which Pilate bru-tally "mingled the blood" of Galilean Jews with their sacrifices to God and the Tower of Siloam fell on eighteen Jerusalemites, Jesus resists branding these victims as "worse sinners" than those untouched by these or any other tragedies (13:1-4). For one thing, the cruel governor Pilate and the crumbling Siloam tower are scarcely models of God's righteous judgment, and for another, the burden of repentance from sin falls equally upon all human beings, regardless of their present fortune (13:5).

- God's justice, far from being a knee-jerk response to unfaithfulness, is tempered with patience. As a vineyard owner and his gardener cultivate an unfruitful fig tree for three, even four, years before cutting it down (13:6-9), so God and God's Messiah will nurture God's wayward, unproductive people (vineyards and fig trees are stock metaphors for Israel; cf. Isa 5:1-7; Jer 8:13; Ezek 15:1-8; Hos 9:10; Mic 7:1) for an extended period before exercising stern discipline.

- Although not developing a concept of Christ's substitutionary sacrifice for sin, Luke drops hints of Christ's personal identification with human pain and punishment. Jesus not only administers a "baptism with fire"—he experiences it as well. Notice the parallel statements: "I came to bring fire to the earth, and how I wish it were already kindled! I have a baptism with which to be baptized, and what stress I am under until it is completed!" (12:49-50). God sent Jesus to go *through* the fiery swell of judgment *with* God's fragile people in order to rescue the lost and perishing.

STAGE 2:
MAKING HIS WAY TO JERUSALEM (13:22–17:10)

1. Humility and Hospitality (13:22–14:24)
2. Repentance and Service (15:1-32; 17:1-10)
3. Cost and Conflict (14:25-33; 16:1-30)

At this juncture, Luke reiterates Jesus' primary mission of "teaching" as he travels "through one town . . . after another" and the solemn necessity of making "his way to Jerusalem" ("I *must be* [*dei*] on my way" [13:22, 33, emphasis added]).[10] Jesus' strong identification with biblical prophets, like Isaiah and Jeremiah, who confronted God's people and their rulers in Jerusalem and provoked virulent opposition to their messages, especially spurs him forward. Jesus knows the terrible fate that awaits him (13:33). That predatory "fox," Herod Antipas, is already seeking to kill him (13:31-32), as he executed John (9:7-9) and will eventually collude with Pilate at Jesus' trial in Jerusalem (23:6-25).

As he approaches the holy city as a maverick prophet, Jesus also comes, in a poignant shift of self-image, as a mother "hen," vulnerable to rapacious "foxes," but more importantly, beckoning her scattered "brood" under her protective wings. But with this scenario a larger tragedy looms—not only the death of God's Messiah (hen), but also the refusal of God's children (brood) to huddle together in God's household under God's rule (wings): "How often have I desired to gather your children together as a hen gathers her brood under her wings, *and you were not willing*" (13:34)! Unsheltered because of their own recalcitrance, the people of Jerusalem face the terrible prospect of mass destruction, which indeed occurs in 70 C.E. at the hands of the Roman army. From the other side of this devastating loss, Luke aims to assure his readers that there was—and is—no failure with God's care and compassion. In God's Son and Prophet Jesus, God persistently extended saving arms (wings) until they were stretched on a Roman cross; and despite being rejected then, these sheltering arms remain open to receive and restore God's beleaguered children.

Even with the end of Jesus' long, hard road weighing on his mind, he still has much to say about the scope and values of God's kingdom he advances on earth. Among other materials, this section features three of Jesus' longest parables in Luke: the great banquet (14:7-24; actually two related table stories), the lost son (15:11-32), and the rich man and poor Lazarus (16:19-31).

Humility and Hospitality (13:22–14:24)

As he makes his way to Jerusalem, Jesus proclaims the way of God's bountiful kingdom, symbolized as a great feast in God's house, in paradoxical terms: both narrow and wide, calling for both humility and hospitality. One must "strive to enter [the banquet hall] through the *narrow door*," before God ("the owner of the house") *shuts it* permanently (13:24-26, emphasis added). One must not presume any place at God's table, least of all the place of highest honor: "some are last who will be first, and some are first who will be last" (13:30). But just as God's kingdom reverses social and religious hierarchies, so it traverses ethnic and geographical boundaries. Although the banquet entrance is narrow, the invited guests will stream widely "from east and west, from north and south, and will eat in the kingdom of God" (13:29).

Aptly, Jesus reinforces these dimensions of God's royal feast at another dinner party hosted by a Pharisee. This is Jesus' third invited meal in a Pharisee's home (cf. 7:36-50; 11:37-52). Despite escalating tensions (the Pharisees keep entertaining Jesus so they can "watch him closely," 14:1), each party continues eating and debating with the other, and the Pharisees even warn Jesus about Herod's murderous plots (13:31). Jesus, however, persists in tweaking certain Pharisaic scruples by performing another Sabbath healing—this time curing a man suffering from dropsy (excessive fluid retention) in the home of a "leader of the Pharisees" (14:1-3).[11] Host and guests offer no direct objection, but their "silent" response suggests more disquiet than acquiescence (14:4-6).

Jesus then expounds his perspectives on humility and hospitality in two new table tales. First, as he observes the guests' crass jockeying for the most prestigious seats, closest to the host, Jesus muses about a *wedding* banquet—a vivid image of the climactic fulfillment of God's covenant "marriage" with God's people—where places of honor take on heightened significance.[12] In this scenario, Jesus advises taking the "lowest," least conspicuous spots, lest the host (God) shuffles the seating arrangement at the last minute, leaving those who shamelessly claimed the best places at "high table" thoroughly humiliated when forced to relinquish their choice seats. Better, in Jesus' scheme, to start "low," humbly grateful for any space at the feast, and let God advance rather than demote one's station: "For all who exalt themselves will be humbled, and those who humble themselves will be exalted" (14:11; cf. 13:30). Seeking God's favor is one thing; presuming upon it is quite another.

Having put the guests in their places, so to speak, Jesus turns to challenge the host's guest list. Rather than follow the customary protocol of inviting "friends or . . . relatives or rich neighbors"—in other words, those who can enhance one's reputation and recip-rocate the invitation—the truly honorable host will invite "the poor, the crippled, the blind, and the lame" (14:13, 21). And more than simply invite these unfortunates, the host in Jesus' parable of the great dinner dispatches messengers to the city's "streets and lanes" in order to "bring" them in (14:21). Of course, those unable to walk or see or afford transportation could scarcely bring themselves. Ironically, those on the A-list, with every means of attending the dinner, snub the host with flimsy excuses regarding prior family and business obligations. It's their loss. The host will not be mocked or thwarted: their refusals just leave that much more room for even more distant, outcast guests. Hence, the host sends servants further, to the outlying "roads and lanes" on the city's edge, "compelling" the most marginal squatters to the munificent feast (in the ancient *polis*, elites typically resided in the inner city, while the "suburbs" housed the most squalid ghettos) (14:17-24).[15] This image of God's gracious messianic banquet presents another facet of Luke's kaleidoscopic portrait of inclusion across social and demographic lines and restoration of disabled and displaced victims.

Repentance and Service (15:1-32; 17:1-10)

As we have seen, Luke's emphasis on repentance offers little comfort or cheap grace to complacent sinners. Jesus' longest parable (unique to Luke) furthers this theme by featuring a wayward and wasteful son who "[comes to] himself," repents of his sin, and returns to his father seeking forgiveness (15:11-32). Although Luke does not measure impiety on a sliding scale, this "lost son" appears as an extreme "sinner," spiraling out of control until he hits rock bottom:

- As the younger son, he asks for his share of the inheritance now, effectively wishing his father were already dead and spurning the elder brother's oversight of the estate (15:11-12).[14]
- He then turns his back not only on his immediate family but also on his national heritage, by bolting to "a distant (*makran*) country" (15:13)—a self-inflicted exile.
- In his new environment, he promptly "[squanders] his property in dissolute living" (15:13), including consort with prostitutes (15:30).
- Now utterly destitute—and in the midst of a "severe famine"—he finds what little work he can, and even less food, slopping a pack of pigs (no one's, but especially no Jew's, dream job) (15:14-16).

170

It's hard to imagine a worse condition, unless it's that of the Gerasene demoniac who also wallowed pathetically, in his own way, among a swine herd before Jesus delivered him (8:26-39). But whereas this man was beset by a Legion of malevolent spirits, the prodigal son has only himself to blame—as he finally realizes.

In the muck and mire of moral and material poverty, the younger son finally resolves to confess his sin to both heavenly and earthly fathers (15:18) and to return home, no longer with filial status (he assumed that had been forfeited), but perhaps as a "hired hand" (15:19). Hope of restoration thus emerges, but with serious caveats and no guarantees. This precarious situation recalls the exile of ancient Israel in the eighth through sixth century B.C.E., the focus of intense debate among Old Testament prophets, priests, poets, and sages. The classic Deuteronomic stance, represented in Jeremiah, Lamentations, and Proverbs, as well as Deuteronomy, regarded national defeat and dislocation as a sign of God's displeasure with disobedient Israel, an act of divine discipline. The restoration of God's people thus depended heavily on their repentance and rededication to God's way. However, other viewpoints, expressed in Habakkuk, Job, and lament Psalms, placed the onus more on God's apparent forgetfulness and fickleness: "Why do you forget our affliction and oppression?" (Ps 44:24); "Lord, where is your steadfast love of old, which by your faithfulness you swore to David?" (Ps 89:49).

Jesus' parable deftly negotiates these tensions. The prodigal son takes the Deuteronomic road back home, laden with humility and remorse. As rehearsed (15:18-19), the young man delivers his abject confession to his father (15:21). But it falls on deaf ears. The father virtually ignores his son's confession—but *not out of anger or rejection*; instead the father is so consumed with love and joy over his son's return that he couldn't care less about apologies or probations. Notice how compassion and celebration in vv. 20 and 22-24 swallow the confession in v. 21.

- **Compassion**: "But while he was still far off (*makran*), his father saw him and was filled with *compassion*; he ran and put his arms around him and kissed him" (15:20, emphasis added).
- **Confession**: "Then the son said to him, 'Father, I have sinned . . .'" (15:21).

171

• **Celebration**: "But the father said to his slaves, 'Quickly, bring out a robe. . . . And get the fatted calf and kill it, and let us eat and *celebrate*; for this son of mine was dead and is alive again; he was lost and is found'! And they began to *celebrate*" (15:22-24, emphasis added).

While affirming Deuteronomic mandates of repentance from sin and obedience to God, Luke also assures his readers—in whatever "exiles" they may experience and however far they have wandered—of God's overwhelming, steadfast love for God's people. An honored place at God's banquet table remains open for the "last" and the "lost."

Not all, however—especially those who remain faithful—rejoice in such gracious openness toward undeserving "sinners." The parable's elder brother—like certain "Pharisees and . . . scribes . . . [who] grumble[ed]" against Jesus' table fellowship with "tax collectors and sinners" (15:1-2)—decries the homecoming party thrown for his lowlife little brother while he, the good and noble son, was out "slaving" in his father's fields (15:25-30). The father takes this complaint seriously but does not concede its validity. He responds to his firstborn with a key statement about this family's economy: "Son, you are always with me, and all that is mine is yours" (15:31). Unlike the typical arrangement, where the household head divvies up a finite set of resources (limited goods), such that one family member's gain is another's loss, in this father's domain (representing God's kingdom) all hold the father's riches in mutual trust (shared goods).[15] There's enough fatted calf for everyone and plenty of room in the banquet hall for all to dance and feast (15:25). Far from diminishing anyone, restoring the lost son only enhances the entire family's—including the loyal son's—potential for joy; more than that, "there is joy in the presence of the angels of God over one sinner who repents" (15:10; cf. 15:6-7, 32). The whole cosmos yearns for God's prime directive of restoration (cf. Rom 8:22-23).

This emphasis on the open, reciprocal community of God's kingdom not only motivates lost sinners to faith and repentance but also liberates the faithful for forgiveness and service. In the secure environment of God's boundless love, there is no ladder of special privilege to climb or pot of limited favor to claim. So, as Jesus tells his disciples, if a sibling in the faith keeps stumbling and repenting, even "seven times a day," God's household offers forgiveness every time (Luke 17:3-4); and after working in "the field" (17:7; like the elder brother), the faithful laborer-disciple further serves the master at supper, assured there will be plenty "later [the laborer] may eat and drink" (17:8).

Cost and Conflict (14:25-33; 16:1-30)

In these texts, Jesus refers to an array of figures across the social spectrum: father, mother, wife, children, brothers, sisters (14:26; 16:28), builders (14:28-30), warrior-kings (14:31-32), wealthy landowner, household manager, debtors, slaves (16:1-13), opulent homeowner, and homeless indigent (16:19-31). Such characters inhabit an agonistic world, exacting a high cost of economic resources and high level of social tension. Candidly acknowledging these hardships of life, Jesus does not facilely claim to remove them. In fact, he sees them as inevitable stepping-stones to God's kingdom. The greatest blessings often come at the heaviest price and through the stiffest opposition. Yet again, Luke's Jesus tempers God's grace with gravitas.

For example, framing brief illustrations about the necessity of cost counting—whether a builder calculating materials before tackling a project or a king sizing up personnel before waging war (14:28-32)—Jesus lays out, in no uncertain terms, what it costs, materially and personally, to be his disciple. In short, it costs *everything*:

- It costs *family*: "Whoever comes to me and does not hate father and mother, wife and children . . . *cannot be my disciple*" (14:26, emphasis added).
- It costs *life*: "Whoever comes to me and does not *hate . . . even life itself*, cannot be my disciple. Whoever does not *carry the cross* and follow me cannot be my disciple" (14:26-27, emphasis added).
- It costs *possessions*: "None of you can become my disciple if you do not *give up all your possessions*" (14:33, emphasis added).

Such strong, totalizing language smacks of hyperbole to modern ears, but Jesus seems to say this with a stern, straight face (no reassuring eye wink). He pulls no punches in making his rigorous demands of discipleship.

173

From this pointed discourse, Jesus moves to more figurative reflections on cost and conflict in two parables in Luke 16. In the puzzling parable of the dishonest manager, the title character weasels out of a predicament by *dis*counting certain costs. Comparisons and contrasts with the lost son are striking. Like the prodigal son, the dishonest manager "squander[ed] his [master's] property" and stood to lose his position in the household (16:1-2). Unlike the son, however, who wasted his father's wealth in a faraway country, the steward depletes the estate from within (here, evidently, the master goes away and leaves the steward in charge [cf. 19:12-13]). But even more unlike the son, rather than owning up to his mismanagement and throwing himself on his master's mercy, the steward connives to protect himself by arbitrarily reducing debts owed by his master's clients. The goal is not so much to cook the books and cover up his master's losses but rather to make "friends" with his master's debtors such that they now *owe him* favors—like taking him in when he loses his job! (16:3-7). Here Jesus showcases a "shrewd" manipulation of the patronage system,[16] which even the master in the story can't help but admire (16:8) and no doubt brings a smile to hearers and readers (like we might enjoy, even root for, the clever thief in a classic heist movie).

More surprising, however, is Jesus' apparent approbation of the shifty steward: "And I tell you, make friends for yourselves by means of dishonest wealth so that when it is gone, they may welcome you into the eternal homes" (16:9). Does the dishonest manager suddenly become a model of wise discipleship? For his basic shrewdness?—perhaps (simpleminded faith is no virtue in a complex world [cf. 16:8]). But for his wastefulness and fraudulence?—hardly. I take Jesus' point in 16:9 as sharply ironic, tipped off by references to "when it is gone" and "eternal homes." Jesus stresses once again the *vulnerability* and *temporality* of wealth: it is quickly depleted ("gone") and bankrupt beyond this evil world (it is *not* "eternal"). So, to paraphrase, Jesus seems to quip: "Go ahead, follow the lead of the crooked manager in the parable, if you dare, and bet your eternal soul on the friends you buy off and the security they provide. And see what it gets you." Of course, it's an absurd, losing proposition; no more than the rich fool in an earlier parable can this dishonest steward depend upon his manipulation of money to guarantee an "eternal home" in God's kingdom (cf. 12:13-21). Actually, the more precise image is of an "eternal *tent* (*skēnē*)"—

Through his comments on these actions, in parables and dialogue, Jesus betrays his own urgency. Like the persistent widow in the parable, Jesus pushes hard toward Jerusalem, pressing his case for God's just and merciful rule (18:3-5); and as he tolerates no obstacles stopping little children from coming to him, he lets nothing and no one stop him from fulfilling his mission (18:16). The road continues to be treacherous, however. As "Son of Man," a prominent title in this section (17:22, 24, 26, 30; 18:8), Jesus envisions his role as chief agent of God's final judgment on behalf of God's persecuted people (cf. Luke 21:25-36; Acts 7:56-60; Dan 7:9-27; Rev 1:12-20). But this glorious destiny, when the Son of Man has "his day" (Luke 17:24), will emerge out of the bitter crucible he shares with the poor and oppressed: "But first he must endure much suffering and be rejected by this generation" (17:25). Paradoxically, humiliation marks the path to exaltation (18:14; cf. 14:11).

Recognizing the Kingdom of God (17:11-37)

The language of "kingdom" inevitably raises questions of time and place: for example, *when* was David's kingdom established (c. 1000 B.C.E.), and *where* was it located (land: Israel; capital: Jerusalem)? "Kingdoms" are the stuff of historical timelines and maps. Not surprisingly, then, from Jesus' day until ours, religious folk have passionately (sometimes bitterly) debated: *when* is God's kingdom coming, and *where* will we find it? Vital questions, to be sure, but easily misdirected. When certain Pharisees asked Jesus "when the kingdom of God was coming" (a good, legitimate concern), he promptly raised the discussion to a metaphysical level. This is not just another empire having its day in the sun. This is *God's eternal* kingdom, and it "is not coming with things that can be observed," nor is it something one can point to and say, " 'Look, here it is!' or 'There it is!' " (17:20-21). God's kingdom defies chronology and cartography: it is neither now nor later, here nor there. In some cosmic sense, it is *always* and *everywhere*.

But Jesus does not leave the matter floating in some mystical or philosophical sphere of ideas. For all its transcendence, the kingdom of God remains a concrete, not merely conceptual, reality that engages God's world and God's people. Jesus emphatically announces to his Pharisaic interlocutors: "For in fact, the kingdom of God is *en hymin*"—that is, either "within you" or "among you"

177

(perhaps Luke has both meanings in view). Whether we read "within" or "among," in this unique Gospel statement[17] God's kingdom has a present, palpable dimension that deeply affects earthly, human experience, that brings God's justice and mercy to bear on this world now (cf. below on 18:1-14). The kingdom of God (*basilea tou theou*) thus represents the experience of God's rule or realization of God's will (whenever and wherever) more than God's "country" or territory or seat of God's authority. Alternative translations, such as "rule of God" or "dominion of God," perhaps capture the dynamic quality of God's *basileia* better than "kingdom."[18]

However, although Jesus' followers, in his own and in Luke's time, had profound experiences of God's rule through Christ "within/among" them, they knew God's mission was not complete. If nothing else, the inescapable presence of Herodian-Roman tollbooths around the Sea of Galilee and of imperial soldiers in Caesarea, Jerusalem, and across the Roman Empire made clear that God's kingdom had not fully arrived. Add the crushing memory in Luke's era of Rome's brutal suppression of Jewish rebels and razing of Jerusalem in 66-70 C.E., and questions about the efficacy of God's rule on earth became very hard to squelch. In the face of these doubts and fears, Jesus assures his followers that better days are coming, climaxed by the pyrotechnic *parousia* of the Son of Man (17:24). The present flickers of God's just and merciful kingdom within/among God's people portend its ultimate (eschato- logical), permanent (eternal) blaze ignited by the returning Son of Man.

So when can we expect this glorious event? What banner day can we mark on the calendar? Only God knows (cf. Acts 1:6). For Jesus' part, he simply announces that the Son of Man will return during an age of hardship for the faithful and of preoccupation with basic matters of life like eating/drinking and marrying/parenting—which could pretty much describe *any* age. To be sure, Jesus specifically compares the notorious ages of Noah and Lot, which were unexpectedly overtaken by divine cataclysmic judgment (Luke 17:25-28). But he does *not* highlight any immoderate or immoral aspects of their consuming and commingling; rather he focuses on their banal going-through-the-motions of mundane life, without a moment's care about God's restorative vision for the world. The challenge for God's people is not to get stuck in the rut of business as usual, but to press forward in faith and hope day after day, age after age—never looking back ("Remember Lot's wife" [17:32]), never banking on one's resources ("Those who try to make their life secure will lose it" [17:33])—but ever longing for the full realization of God's rule on earth.

Seeking the Justice and Mercy of God (18:1-14)

Beyond looking for the Son of Man's final establishment of God's rule, what can God's people do to hasten its coming, to "[seek/]strive (*zēteō*) for [God's] kingdom" (12:31)? Once again, Jesus urges his followers to *pray* for God's rule (cf. "Your kingdom come," 11:2), not as a wistful last resort, but as a fruitful first response of faith, specifically imploring God to act with *justice* and *mercy*—the hallmarks of God's rule—in an unjust and unforgiving world. This section features two parables about the efficacy of prayer with a female and male exemplar, respectively, each the target of insensitive antagonists.

	Luke 18:1-8	**Luke 18:9-14**
Protagonist	Persistent Widow	Tax Collector
Antagonist	Unjust Opponent and Judge	Self-Righteous Pharisee
Prayer Focus	Boldly Pleading for Justice	Humbly Pleading for Mercy

The widow in the first parable finds herself in a double bind, pleading for *justice* against (1) a personal oppressor ("*my* [unjust] opponent") before (2) an unscrupulous judge who "had no fear of God and no respect for anyone" (18:2-3). We don't know the particulars of this woman's case, but widows, whether poor or wealthy, were vulnerable to economic exploitation by predators who "devour widows' houses," as Jesus later decries (20:47).[19] In any event, this widow does not accept her fate without a fight. Although the magistrate is not inclined to help her (or anyone else), she pesters him enough that he eventually gives in to her demands—"so that she may not wear me out by continually coming" (18:5). The image of "wearing me out" (*hypōpiazō*) is pugilistic, along the lines of "giving me a black eye" (cf. 1 Cor 9:27),[20] creating a slapstick scene sure to entertain the parable's hearers (think "little ole lady" deck-ing Mike Tyson), while still making a serious point about justice. Persistence pays off; evil powers can be overcome (worn out) by determined action. The widow's "might" makes right.

But the parable's primary point, remember, is about the action of *prayer*. Jesus relates this story "about their need to pray always and not to lose heart" (18:1). The widow thus models the disciple's call to "wear out" God, as it were, with urgent petitions for justice on earth. The judge, with responsibility for executing justice, plays the God and Son of Man parts—or rather, *counter*-parts! As a thor-oughly *unjust* judge, he is the very antithesis of the righteous God and Son of Man. But if such a shameless and shameful human judge can eventually be coaxed (coerced) into acting justly, *how much more* (cf. 11:13) will "God grant justice to his chosen ones who cry to him day and night"—and do so promptly (18:7)! And how much more will the Son of Man come, establish God's just rule, and vindicate God's oppressed people! "And *yet* (*plēn*)," there's also a flip side (parables may spark multiple meanings), concerned with the people's preparedness to receive the Son of Man: "When the Son of Man comes, will he find faith on earth?" (18:8). Divine *dikaios* (justice) calls forth human *pistis* (faith) in the sense of both *trustful dependence* upon God, who alone establishes perfect justice, and *faithful persistence*, like the oppressed widow, in pursuing as much justice as possible in an evil world while wait-ing (actively!) for the climactic realization of God's kingdom.

In the second parable, Jesus imagines a scene in the temple with two figures deeply engaged in prayer, but with different postures and purposes. A Pharisee "[stands] by himself" (or "for the sake of himself" [18:11]) and prays *about* himself (not *for* himself or others), trumpeting his self-righteousness before God in derisive contrast to a laundry list of dirty "sinners," including "this tax collector"—the other figure in the parable. This Pharisee (who does *not* represent *all* Pharisees in Luke's narratives, much less in first-century history) particularly sets himself apart from this and other tax collectors —notorious for lining their pockets at taxpayers' expense—by extolling his own financial sacrifice at the end of his preening litany: "I fast twice a week; I give a tenth of all my income" (18:12). For his part, the tax collector offers no self-defense to the Pharisee or to God. With head bowed low, he "[stands] far off (*makrothen*)" (18:13), ironically as alienated from God and overcome with remorse in the Jerusalem temple as was the dissolute lost son in a "distant (*makran*) country" (15:13, 18-19, 21). Moreover, his chest thumping ("beating his breast" [18:13]), far from a self-adulating gesture (think gorillas or gladiators) conveys penitent self-mortification consonant with his one succinct plea: "God, be merciful to me, a sinner" (18:13; contrast the Pharisee's long-winded prayer-speech). Whereas the widow in the previous parable boldly pleaded for justice, this tax collector humbly begs for *mercy*; but his petition is granted as surely as the woman's ("this man went down to his home justified" [18:14]). The twin virtues of justice and mercy, in dialectic balance and tension, constitute the primary goals of God's rule and the most valuable gifts God grants to those who seek God and God's kingdom.

Entering the Kingdom of God (18:15-30)

The multifaceted image of God's kingdom negotiates other dialogic elements. Regarding human engagement with God's rule, Jesus recently disclosed God's sovereign, active presence "within/among" God's people (17:20-21; see above); put another way, whether people know it or not, they are already *in* God's pervasive kingdom, subject to God's rule as well as indebted to God's grace. Now Jesus stresses the need to "enter" this kingdom (18:17, 24-25). *But how can one enter a realm one already occupies?* Such a question falls back into the literalist trap of treating God's kingdom as a place or territory rather than a way of being and living. "Entry" language focuses figuratively on people's responses to God's rule, that is, how they buy in to God's kingdom, how they live and act

	Luke 18:15-17	Luke 18:18-30
Example	*Positive:* Little Children	*Negative:* Rich Ruler *Positive:* Itinerant Disciples
Objection	Adults Only	Mission Impossible
Entrance Key	Receiving God's kingdom as a little child	Believing in God's power to save

within the realm of God's justice and mercy. Again Luke expounds an issue in a pair of stories featuring both positive and negative examples and judgments. In these two episodes, however, Jesus appears as a participant instead of a storyteller.

In the first incident, Jesus happily receives small children brought to him for blessing, just as he helped Jairus' ailing daughter (8:40-42, 49-56) and another father's convulsive son (9:37-43). Not all, however, are so sanguine about these tots' clustering around Jesus. In particular, his disciples "sternly order" parents and guardians to stop bothering Jesus with their children (18:15). We are not told why the disciples are so overwrought about the children's gathering. Perhaps they want to buffer Jesus from undue burdens as he approaches Jerusalem, or maybe they dismiss these little ones altogether as nobodies and nuisances, with nothing to contribute to Jesus' movement.[21] In any case, Jesus will have none of it. He welcomes these youngsters with open arms and prohibits his disciples from blocking their way (18:16). For as Jesus sees it, the kingdom of God, far from being an "adults only" club, "belongs" just as much to children; indeed, it belongs *only* to those who *both* embrace *and* emulate little ones: "Truly I tell you, whoever does not receive the kingdom of God as a little child (*paidion*) *will never enter it*" (18:17, emphasis added). God's kingdom is fundamentally a *pediatric community*, a nurturing and training household for the *children of God*. Jesus does not spell out how one should receive God's rule "as a little child," but we may assume wholehearted responses of humility (lowliness), faith (trust), and even joy (gratitude) emphasized thus far in Luke and more commonly—and genuinely—expressed by the young and innocent.

In the second scene, the focus shifts from little children to a wealthy ruler—at the opposite end of the social spectrum. Given what Jesus has just suggested about entering God's kingdom, the prospects are not good for this "very rich" (18:23) official. His success would more likely breed pride and self-sufficiency than childlike lowliness and dependency. But in fact this man respectfully approaches Jesus as "Good Teacher" (although Jesus takes affront, since, as a devout Jew, he insists, "No one is *good* but God alone" [18:19, emphasis added; cf. Deut 6:5]) and has a serious discussion about eternal life and divine law. When he confesses his adherence to God's commandments "since my youth," we have no reason to doubt his sincerity (Jesus doesn't). Here we meet a "good" rich man humbly seeking the wisdom of a "good" teacher concerning the One Good God of Israel. But for all this ruler has going for him, he's not "good" enough. In addition to keeping God's laws (which Jesus affirms), Jesus requires that the rich man sell everything he has and give the proceeds to the poor (Luke 18:22). But such an extraordinary demand is not easily met, provoking a first response of deep "sadness" or "distress" (18:23).[22] Note well that the wealthy ruler does not brush off or scoff at Jesus' mandate; he takes it quite seriously, agonizing over its incredible cost. Note also that Luke does not report, as the other Synoptic Gospels, that this man *left* Jesus at this point (*contrast* Matt 19:22 with Mark 10:22—"he *went away* grieving"). The prospect remains that the ruler might overcome his fears and follow Jesus yet.

How might this happen? Not easily, to be sure, but not impossibly either. "Looking at" the distressed man (with love and concern),[23] Jesus acknowledges, "How hard it is for those who have wealth to enter the kingdom of God," that is, to comply with this kingdom's radical distributive (not acquisitive) economy. It's so hard in fact that a camel has a better chance of jumping through the eye of a needle (the knobby humps, sort of like bulging money bags, don't easily fit any opening) (18:24-25). But first and foremost, this is *God's* kingdom, where *God's* purposes and policies are carried out and where *God* has total control and final say. And if God wills a rich person's change of heart toward possessions and includes such a person in God's kingdom, then so it shall be. Making the impossible possible is foundational to God's messianic rule on earth through God's Son Jesus (18:26-27; cf. 1:37). In truth, all who give themselves over completely to God's care (like a child) are drawn by God's power and love. Except for actual children, it's not a natural thing to do: the poor cling to their scant property as much, if not more, than the wealthy. Only God makes people fit for God's kingdom. Peter may pipe up to Jesus, "Look, we have left our homes and followed you" (18:28), but he and fellow disciples would have never taken a first step without God's magnetic pull through Christ. And having lost everything "for the sake of the kingdom of God," the preposterous promise that they will thereby gain "very much more" now and for eternity can only be fulfilled by God's grace and power (18:29-30).

STAGE 4: GOING UP TO JERUSALEM (18:31–19:44)

1. Missing and Seeing the Son of Man/Son of David (18:31–19:10)
2. Rejecting and Receiving the Lord and King (19:11-44)

As the destination at last comes into view, this final and shortest stage of Luke's Travel Narrative contains as many references to Jerusalem (four) as the previous stages combined, in mounting anticipation of Jesus' dramatic *drawing near* (19:11, 41; cf. v. 37) and *going up* (18:31; 19:28) to the holy city. Moreover, Luke sharpens the scenes leading up to Jesus' Jerusalem entrance with increased vividness and detail, commanding the reader's close attention. We suddenly know precisely where Jesus is and how he approaches Jerusalem: he enters Jericho (northeastern Judea, a few miles west of the Jordan River), heads southwest toward Bethany and Bethphage (approximately ten miles), and then a short distance to the Mount of Olives on the eastern edge of Jerusalem (18:35; 19:1, 29, 37). Moreover, for the first time in the journey we see Jesus using a special mode of travel (besides walking), namely, "a colt that has never been ridden" (not just any mount) procured in an unusual way (see below); and we also receive the fullest profile of any person Jesus meets on the trek (19:1-10).

- **Name**: Zacchaeus, the *only* name in the Travel Narrative outside of Jesus, Peter, James, John (rarely), poor Lazarus (in one parable), and a few Old Testament figures
- **Profession**: "*chief* tax collector," not just another tax man
- **Physical description**: "short in stature"
- **Double location**: up a sycamore tree/in his house

This lively last leg of the journey features six tightly connected scenes that we may organize in two ways. First, although I have downplayed chiasm as a structuring device for the entire Central Section, I think it has merit in this segment. The following outline sketches a chiastic pattern, highlighting both *parallel elements* of violence and hiddenness (A/A'); approaching, shouting, obstructing, and praising (B/B'); and *counterpoint elements* of distributing/ multiplying money and saving/slaughtering wrongdoers (C/C').

184

A. Jesus Predicts His Death in Jerusalem (18:31-34)
- Violent death
- Truth "hidden (*kryptō*) from them" (18:34)

B. Jesus Heals a Blind Beggar (18:35-43)
- "As he approached (*engizō*) Jericho" (18:35)
- Shouting (*krazō*) and shushing (*epitimaō*) (18:38-39)
- "All the people, when they saw it, praised (*ainos*) God" (18:43)

C. Jesus Saves a Tax Collector (19:1-10)
- Giving away and paying back percentages of money (19:8)
- Ending: *saving* the lost (19:9-10)

C'. Jesus Tells a Royal Story (19:11-27)
- Entrusting and multiplying percentages of money (19:13-15)
- Ending: *slaughtering* the enemies (19:26-27)

B'. Jesus Makes a Royal Entrance (19:28-40)
- "When he had come near (*engizō*) Bethphage and Bethany" (19:29)
- Shouting (*krazō*) and shushing (*epitimaō*) (19:39-40)
- "The whole multitude . . . began to praise (*aineō*) God joyfully with a loud voice for all the deeds of power that they had seen" (19:37)

A'. Jesus Bemoans the Destruction of Jerusalem (19:41-44)
- Violent destruction
- Truth "hidden (*kryptō*) from your eyes" (19:42)

A simpler scheme, followed in the exposition below, divides the six scenes into two units of three, both focused upon *divided audience responses* to God's rule in Jesus Christ: the first unit develops a *visual* theme around the polarity of missing/seeing Jesus as Son of Man/Son of David (18:31–19:10); the second develops a *relational* antithesis of rejecting/receiving Jesus as Lord and King. Both units have particular relevance to Luke's readers struggling with their own mixed responses to Jesus' physical absence and delayed reappearance as final judge (Son of Man), Messiah (Son of David), and agent of God's dominion (Lord/King) in a world still subject to powers of evil and corruption.

Missing and Seeing the Son of Man/Son of David (18:31–19:10)

In this unit's three scenes, Jesus deals with different individual or group characters: (1) the twelve disciples (18:31-34), (2) an anonymous blind beggar (18:31-34), and (3) a tax collector named Zacchaeus (19:1-10). All face obstacles to "seeing" either physically or intellectually, but ironically, only the latter two figures—who meet Jesus for the first time—press through in faith to receive "sight" (the apostles remain in the dark). The following outline isolates the main points of "visual" comparison and contrast.

Jesus Predicts His Death in Jerusalem (18:31-34)
- Twelve disciples were blind ("understood nothing") to Jesus' teaching
- What Jesus said about his impending death "was hidden from them"

Jesus Heals a Blind Beggar (18:35-43)
- Blind man cries out to Jesus, pleading for mercy
- Crowd attempts to silence him
- He cries out "even more loudly"
- Jesus welcomes him and restores his sight
- He demonstrates "faith" and "follows" Jesus

Jesus Saves a Tax Collector (19:1-10)
- Diminutive tax collector Zacchaeus wants to see Jesus
- Crowd blocks his view
- He runs ahead and climbs tree "to see [Jesus]"
- Jesus invites himself to Zacchaeus' house and blesses it
- Zacchaeus confesses his commitment to honesty and generosity

The disciples' main "blind spot" continues to surround Jesus' forecasts of his execution. On two occasions just before embarking on the Jerusalem journey, Jesus began preparing his followers for his tragic death (9:21-22, 43-44) but to no avail: they didn't grasp what he was saying and were too "afraid to ask him" for further instruction (9:45). Now toward the end of the journey, with his demise imminent, Jesus tries a third time with the most vivid details yet, predicting that he will be "handed over [betrayed] to the Gentiles [Romans] . . . mocked . . . insulted . . . spat upon . . . flogged . . . kill[ed]" (18:32-33). Jesus also appends to this horrible list the hope of resurrection ("on the third day he will rise again"). But the disciples don't pick up this positive note any more than they understand the litany of suffering. The third time is not a charm but rather a sad sign of how confused they remain about Jesus' crucifixion and resurrection. Their picture of Jesus as mighty Son of Man, Lord, and Messiah had no room for a Roman *cross*. Such an odious image was simply not in their Christological frame of reference, and as we have seen, the "scandal" of the crucified Christ persisted in the post-resurrection generations of Paul and Luke.

How can disciples, then or now, wrap their minds around a cruciform faith? Although offering no great exposition in the present text, Luke does provide a couple of hints. First, Jesus stresses that the terrible fate awaiting him in Jerusalem fulfills "everything that is written about the Son of Man by the prophets" (18:31). A sample text or two would have been helpful. We don't know what particular prophetic-biblical images Jesus has in view—something surrounding the concepts of "suffering servant" or "righteous sufferer" perhaps—but fine points remain hazy. Still, the claim that scripture prepares the way for Jesus' bitter end provides a basis for believing that his violent death (somehow) serves a divine purpose. Second, the comment in *passive voice* that the truth about Jesus' fate "*was hidden* from them" (18:34, emphasis added) shifts the final burden for understanding *away* from the disciples. The full significance of Jesus' death is *beyond* them. Although the quest for *hidden* knowledge can be frustrating (ignorance is not bliss), it can also inspire hope. The limits of human comprehension open up prospects of *divine revelation*. What God conceals, God can reveal; and from Luke's perspective, what God conceals, God *will* reveal: "For nothing is hidden that will not be disclosed, nor is anything secret that will not become known and come to light" (8:17; cf. 10:21-24).

Jesus' ensuing encounters with a blind beggar and chief tax collector follow similar plots: a visually challenged man approaches Jesus, is obstructed in some way by crowds surrounding Jesus, presses through the blockade, and captures Jesus' gracious attention. However, though closely linked in Luke's narrative, these two figures also form something of an odd couple. In terms of status, they occupy opposite rungs on the social ladder: one, a lowly, disabled beggar, with little chance of advancement; the other, a high-level, well-off C.E.O. (or C.T.O., "chief tax officer"). This unusual pairing serves Luke's emphasis on bringing together the people of God from all walks of life.

Matthew and Mark give particular attention to the blindness incident, placing it immediately before Jesus' grand entry into Jerusalem. Moreover, Mark *names* the blind man (Bartimaeus), and Matthew doubles the effect with *two* blind men (Matt 20:29-34; Mark 11:46-52). By contrast, Luke downplays the blind man somewhat (anonymous, single figure) in favor of the unique and fuller portrait of Zacchaeus. This man has a "rich" and varied profile. Beyond being materially rich and at the top of his profession, he also has some strikes against him. His tax collecting business for Herodian-Roman interests scarcely endeared him to the general population that labeled him a "sinner" (19:7), and however long on cash he might have been, his abnormal shortness of height counted as a marked disability and liability. Being a "short sinner" (or maybe, a "wee little weasel") was not a status (or stature) one aspired to in the first-century world.[24] But it makes no difference to Jesus. In response to Zacchaeus' desire to see him, he makes time at this urgent stage of the journey (though "hurriedly," 19:5-6) to have dinner in this tax collector's home, despite the crowd's "grumbling" perception of impropriety.

As it happens, Zacchaeus defies expectations (another slap at stereotypes). Far from being greedy and exploitative, he announces his commitment to giving "*half* of my possessions . . . to the poor" and restoring any overcharges he might have made *fourfold*! Although commonly regarded as evidence of his "conversion" in Jesus' presence, Zacchaeus in fact uses *present* tense verbs—"I give (*didōmi*) to the poor . . . I pay back (*apodidōmi*)" (compare NRSV's "I *will* give . . . *will* pay back")—suggesting an ongoing pattern of behavior (19:8). This is more of a *confirmation* than conversion story, which Jesus himself confirms. Zacchaeus may not be distributing *all* his goods to the poor, as Jesus recently required of the rich ruler, but *half* is not half bad. It will do just fine as evidence that "salvation has come to this house, because he [Zacchaeus] too is a son of Abraham" (19:10).

Rejecting and Receiving the Lord and King (19:11-44)

"Near Jerusalem" (19:11, 41), Jesus tells his last parable on the journey and makes his way along "the path down from the Mount

188

of Olives" (19:37) toward the city's eastern gates. The parable sets the stage for the final procession with several common elements revolving around royal authority and kingdom business.

	Parable of Pounds (19:11-27)	**Final Approach to Jerusalem (19:28-44)**
Royal Figure	Nobleman "receiv[ing] royal power" (19:12, 15)	Jesus the Lord (19:31, 34) and King (19:38)
Itinerary	Returning from "distant (*makran*) country" (19:12)	Heading into holy city (19:28, 37, 41)
Attendants	Ten slaves, focus on three (19:13, 16-24)	Twelve disciples, focus on two (19:29)
Assignment	"Do business" with ten pounds (*minas*) for nobleman's estate	Bring one never-ridden colt for Jesus' transport
Audience Response	Citizens of the country "hated" and rejected royal nobleman's "rule over us" (19:14)	Multitude praises God loudly for Jesus "the king who comes in the name of the Lord" (Pharisees object to crowd's outburst) (19:37-39)
Final Judgment	"Harsh" ruler orders enemies slaughtered "in my presence" (19:22-27)	Heavy-hearted Jesus "weeps" over obstinate Jerusalem as he forecasts enemies' razing of city (19:41-44)

Through the parable, Jesus compares his future coming (*parousia*) to that of a returning nobleman. Luke thus juxtaposes two royal "visitations" of Jesus in inverted temporal order: first (via the parable), his promised, but delayed, return—after an indeterminate absence in a "distant" realm[25]—as an exalted agent of the Sovereign's (God's) kingdom ("having received royal power [from God]," 19:15); and second, his present, imminent entry into Jerusalem on a commandeered ("the Lord needs it," 19:31, 34), never-ridden colt[26] along a red-carpet route festooned with cloaks and shouts of adoration—all fit for a king. Simply put: although Jesus' reign as Israel's divinely appointed king officially commences with his entry into Jerusalem, it must await final establishment at a later appearance (*parousia*).

Not so simple, however, are the mixed reactions and consequences each "coming" generates. Starting with the parable, in the indefinite interim between the nobleman's departure and return with royal power, two groups remain active: his *servants* carry on their master's business with varying degrees of faithfulness, and his *opponents* scheme to block his rule. When the nobleman eventually returns as king, he metes swift and strict judgment to these subjects—(1) rewarding his productive servants according to the measure of their successes, (2) stripping one timid servant's responsibility and resources for lack of initiative, and (3) rounding up his enemies and brutally eliminating them (19:15-27)! This is not a man to mess with; he comes back with iron royal might and is not afraid to use it. Coming directly after the statement, "For the Son of Man came to seek out and to save the lost" (19:10), the parable of the pounds is a bit of a shock to the system. This Son of Man (nobleman) ferrets out and punishes both non-doers and evildoers.

The first coming mitigates this "harsh" (19:22) portrait somewhat, but not completely. Whereas Matthew, drawing on Zech 9:9, places Jesus on the colt of a *donkey* (*onos*; *hypzygion*) as a sign of the king's *humility* (Matt 21:2-7), Luke neither identifies the colt's (*pōlos*) species nor cites Zechariah's prophecy. Though clearly not galloping in on a warhorse, Luke's Jesus approaches Jerusalem not so much with humility as with divine regal authority amid paeans of praise "for all the deeds of power that they [the crowds] had seen, saying, 'Blessed is the king who comes in the name of the Lord! Peace in heaven, and glory in the highest heaven'"

190

(19:37-38). At this time, however, Jesus does not exercise his authority with a heavy hand, like that wielded by the nobleman in the parable. When "some . . . Pharisees" decry the mob's hailing a new king (likely to provoke severe Roman reprisals), Jesus censures them but does not have them slaughtered! (Luke 19:39-40). Moreover, on the crest overlooking Jerusalem, Jesus, anticipating violent opposition from the city's officials, *weeps* over their blindness and obstinacy (reminiscent of the "weeping prophet," Jeremiah). This poignant scene is unique to Luke. Pathos tempers retribution—*but does not cancel it*. Through his tears, Jesus announces with horrid detail the devastation that Jerusalem invites for its rejection of God's Messiah—a "crushing" defeat under the hammer fist of a vicious army (19:41-44). The allusion to Jerusalem's demolition by Roman forces in 70 C.E. is painfully clear.

So how exactly does this pair of narratives (parable of pounds/ "triumphal" entry) help Luke's readers struggling with both the delay in Jesus' return and the horror of Jerusalem's destruction? What pastoral-theological message do they convey? In brief, they issue both a *challenge* and *comfort*. The challenges include

- Remain faithful and fruitful during the interim, however long it lasts. The task of advancing God's reign on earth falls in part on God's servants. Remarkably, Christ enlists his followers as junior partners in the business of God's kingdom (19:13).
- Find what "the Lord needs" to further God's rule and get it (19:31-33). All earthly possessions given by God should be pressed into serving God's interests.
- "Praise God joyfully" (19:37) for signs of God's rule and senses of Christ's powerful presence that break into this present environment of evil and suffering. Don't let fear or cynicism squelch occasions for ebullient celebration.

And for comfort:

- Know that Christ acknowledges and will reward faithful service (19:26). Persevering labor in God's kingdom will not be in vain.
- Rest assured that in God's time, God will send Christ to earth again with total "royal power" (19:15) to vanquish evil forces

and vindicate God's suffering people. Justice will ultimately reign.
- Hear and feel the compassionate Lord crying with God's people over lost opportunities and the tragic fall of God's holy city. By "weeping" (19:41) with those who "weep," Christ deeply sympathizes with those broken and shattered by sin and death—and is moved to restore them to wholeness (see 7:13-15, 44-50).[27]

CHAPTER 6

DEFENDING GOD'S MISSION IN JERUSALEM AND JUDEA

(Luke 19:45–24:53)

Ever since Jesus lamented—"I must be on my way, because it is impossible for a prophet to be killed outside of . . . Jerusalem, Jerusalem, the city that kills the prophets" (13:33-34)—we have anticipated his joining the ranks of God's spurned and slain prophets soon after entering the holy city. That tragic time has come. Jesus now enters his final days (commonly known as his "passion"), culminating in execution on a Roman cross.

Of course, simply knowing—from both narrative forecast and historical hindsight—that such a terrible fate awaits Jesus does not lessen its shock or explain its significance. The "scandal" of Christ crucified begs for explanation in every generation, not least the initial ones closest to Jesus' death (c. 30 C.E.), compounded by the recent trauma of Jerusalem's destruction (the "death" of the city that "killed" Jesus in 70 C.E.). Who's responsible for all this madness? Why did these horrible events happen? Where is God in all this? Luke's Passion Narrative aims to provide some answers.

Apart from Jesus (dominant role), Satan (cameo last gasps to steal the show in 22:3, 31), and angels (two brief appearances in 22:43; 24:4-7, 23), the characters in this "passion play" fall into six main groups: the first three featured in several scenes; the latter three more limited.

1. **Jerusalem Authorities**: Jewish leaders/temple rulers variously clustered as chief priests, scribes, elders, Sadducees,

and members of the Council (or Sanhedrin, 22:66; 23:50); and the Roman governor Pilate (partly in consultation with Herod Antipas, 23:6-12)

2. **Jerusalem Population**: variously designated as "the people" (*laos*) (most frequently), "persons" (*anthrōpoi*), and "crowds" (*ochloi*)

3. **Jesus' Twelve Apostles**: with special focus on Judas and Peter

4. **Cross Bearers**: Simon of Cyrene (carries Jesus' cross) and two "criminals" crucified beside Jesus (23:26, 32-43)

5. **Women Disciples and Examples**: poor, but generous, widow (21:1-4); weeping "Daughters of Jerusalem" (23:27-28); and Mary Magdalene, Joanna, and other Galilean women (23:55–24:11, 22)

6. **Emmaus Disciples**: Cleopas and companion (24:13-35)

The first group, comprised of Jewish and Roman officials, uniformly opposes Jesus and bears primary responsibility for Jesus' death (a Roman centurion [23:47] and Jewish Councilman [23:50-54] are notable exceptions).[1] The next three groups have mixed reactions to Jesus: the Jerusalem people and Jesus' apostles are mostly supportive of Jesus, but sadly turn their backs on him at the end in betrayal (Judas), denial (Peter), and affirming rulers' cries for crucifixion (people); the pair crucified on either side of Jesus diametrically split in their opinion of him. The final two groups—women and Cleopas and companion (possibly Cleopas's wife)—evince wholehearted sympathy with Jesus, while still struggling with grief and confusion. Such wide and varied character reactions to Jesus' passion, if not mirroring readers' responses to the story, at least reflect something of readers' complex struggles with the trauma of a crucified Messiah.

TEMPLE TESTS AND TIMES (19:45–21:38)

1. Questions and Answers (20:1-8, 20-44)
2. Signs and Stones (19:45-48; 20:9-18, 45-47; 21:1-38)

Although Jesus senses the Jerusalem authorities' mounting resistance to his mission, he does not hide out, wise avoid confrontation. In fact, his first act in the city—bouncing the merchants out of the temple compound (19:45)—effectively challenges the temple's leadership and arouses suspicion. Thereafter he continues pushing the envelope by setting up his own shop "every day" in the temple area, teaching "all the people" mesmerized by his message. Framing texts demarcating this unit set the mood of tension between religious leaders and laity (*laos*) surrounding Jesus' popular daily lectures.

> *Every day he was teaching in the temple. The chief priests, the scribes, and the leaders of the people* kept looking for a way to kill him; but they did not find anything they could do, for *all the people* were spellbound by what they heard. (19:47-48, emphasis added)

> *Every day he was teaching in the temple*, and at night he would go out and spend the night on the Mount of Olives, as it was called. And *all the people* would get up early in the morning to listen to him in the temple. (21:37-38, emphasis added)

Questions and Answers (20:1-8, 20-44)

The open forum of the temple's outer courts encourages debate between teachers and audiences. In particular, Judean temple hierarchs (chief priests, scribes, elders, Sadducees)—on their home turf—would predictably confront maverick religious teachers, like the Galilean Jesus. Luke presents four terse, but tense, exchanges between Jesus and the temple leaders around issues of *politics* (Jesus' authority; paying taxes) and *theology* (resurrection relations; Davidic Messiah). In the opening three cases, the temple rulers interrogate Jesus, and he fires back a response; in the last case, however, Jesus turns the tables and poses a question—which elicits *no answer*.

Topic	Questions	Answers
Jesus' Authority	*Chief priests, scribes, and elders:* "By what authority are you doing these things? Who is it who gave you this authority?" (20:2)	*Jesus:* "Did the baptism of John come from heaven, or was it of human origin?" (20:4)

Topic	Questions	Answers
Paying Taxes	*Chief priests and scribes:* "Is it lawful for us to pay taxes to the emperor, or not?" (20:22)	*Jesus:* "Give to the emperor the things that are the emperor's, and to God the things that are God's" (20:24)
Resurrection Relations	*Sadducees:* Concerning a widow who had seven husbands—"In the resurrection, . . . whose wife will the woman be?" (20:33)	*Jesus:* "In the resurrection from the dead [they] neither marry nor are given in marriage . . . because they are like angels and are children of God" (20:35-36)
Davidic Messiah	*Jesus:* "David thus calls him [the Messiah] Lord [cf. Ps 110:1]; so how can he [also] be his [David's] son?" (20:44)	*None*

For his part, Jesus shows considerable rhetorical skill in setting his interlocutors back on their heels. He responds indirectly, answering questions with questions and having the last word with memorable punch lines. As the authorities question his authority, Jesus does not shy away from the challenge. He staunchly defends himself and his mission, but in a way that glorifies *God* as the supreme authority. One way or another, both implicitly and explicitly, Jesus brings the discussion back to his supporting role in advancing *God's rule*: (1) Jesus' authority, like John's, derives not from "human origin," but from God (20:4); (2) Jesus insists that humans pay due homage to God and give "to God the things that are God's"

(20:24); (3) since God "is God not of the dead, but of the living" (20:38), the "children of God" have the hope of resurrection and eternal life with God (compare the Sadducees "who say there is no resurrection," 20:27); and (4) the Lord God appoints Israel's Messiah to "sit at *my right hand*, until *I make* your enemies your footstool" (20:42-43, emphasis added; cf. Ps 110:1).

Although extolling God's sovereign authority over all, Jesus not only submits himself to God, but also subverts all competing authorities not aligned with God's will—whether based in the Jerusalem temple or the imperial halls of Rome. Whatever the emperor's own notion of divine privilege, his "things" are manifestly *not* "the things that are God's." Even though the people of God may pay taxes, they must not pay homage, reserved for God alone, to Caesar. Ultimately, God will render to Caesar and other evil powers all the "things" they have coming for oppressing God's people.[2]

Signs and Stones (19:45-48; 20:9-18, 45-47; 21:1-38)

When Jesus is not fielding questions in the temple about his mission, he exposes signs of the temple establishment's corruption and of the temple edifice's demolition. Jesus leads with his most dramatic audio-visual sign, driving out sellers of sacrificial animals (among other things) essential to temple business and punctuating his action with critical prophetic commentary from Isaiah and Jeremiah (19:45-46).

	Text Cited by Jesus	**Prophetic Context**
Isaiah 56	"My house shall be called a house of prayer" (Isa 56:7)	Restored temple (house) as site of covenant faithfulness and refuge for "the outcasts of Israel" and "others . . . besides those already gathered"—including foreigners, eunuchs, and indeed, "all peoples" (Isa 56:1-8)

	Text Cited by Jesus	Prophetic Context
Jeremiah 7	"But you have made it a den of robbers" (Jer 7:11)	Jeremiah's temple sermon denouncing worshipers' false sense of security amid practices of idolatry and injustice toward "the alien, the orphan, and the widow" and pronouncing judgment upon God's polluted "house" (Jer 7:1-15)

As a faithful Jew devoted to serving God in the temple since childhood (cf. 2:22-52), Jesus is beside himself, a la Jeremiah, with the leaders' despicable misappropriation of God's sanctuary as a haven for robbers rather than refugees and as a hotbed of injustice against outcasts (like foreigners and eunuchs) and the homeless (aliens, orphans, widows) rather than a house of prayerful worship and merciful ministry. If this is the way the rulers conduct temple business, then it might as well cease (symbolized by the merchants' expulsion). Later Jesus especially castigates the scribal authorities for "devour[ing] widows' houses and for the sake of appearance say[ing] long prayers" (20:47), thus falling dismally short of Isaiah's call for sincere prayer and Jeremiah's for social justice. In stark, ironic contrast, the next scene features a "poor widow" commended by Jesus for contributing "all she had to live on"—her last two coins—to the temple treasury (21:1-4). Though vulnerable to losing her meager "house" to rapacious temple officials, she nonetheless gives everything she has to God's "house," trusting in God's faithful care even when the custodians of God's sanctuary fail to carry out God's will.

From driving out temple merchants and citing Isaiah and Jeremiah, it's not surprising that Jesus proceeds to predict (again) his own death and rejection, like a dislodged "stone," at the hands of corrupt "tenants" and "builders" of God's estate (20:9-19)[5] as well as the fall and destruction of God's city and temple—"not one [beautiful] stone will be left upon another" (21:5-6; cf. 21:7-36). Jeremiah became the target of false accusations and death plots for his protests against injustice in the temple and his predictions of Jerusalem's destruction by Babylonian forces; and (Second) Isaiah sympathized with God's "suffering servant" and struggled with weary exiles after Jerusalem's demise in 587 B.C.E. The tragic constellation of unfaithful leaders, rejected prophets, imperial sieges, and ultimately—Jerusalem's destruction—in Jesus and Luke's first-century C.E. world eerily echoes late seventh- and early sixth-century B.C.E. Judean religion and politics. History repeats itself in the worst sort of way.

But a long historical view also provides grounds for hope. Out of the ashes of defeat and exile—even as just deserts for Israel's covenantal disloyalty to God and neighbor, as the Deuteronomic prophets would have it—Jeremiah and Isaiah both envisioned Israel's redemption from sin, restoration to the promised land, and reconstruction of Jerusalem and its temple. The God of steadfast love cannot abandon God's people, and indeed, the latter decades of the sixth century B.C.E. witnessed a return from exile, a reconstitution of Judean society, and the rebuilding of the temple—not on the grand scale of "former days," to be sure, but still a solid footing to start fresh. Modulating to a higher key, Luke's Jesus sounds forth a stirring hope for God's "captive" and "trampled" people (21:24): from the depths of their despair, at their tensest moment of "fear and foreboding," (21:26) "they will see 'the Son of Man coming in a cloud' with power and great glory. Now when these things begin to take place, stand up and raise your heads, because your redemption is drawing near" (21:27-28). "Near" may not be "now" for Luke's readers, but it's a good place to begin anew and to become "alert" (21:36) to the Son of Man's full restoration of God's kingdom.

TRIALS AND ERRORS (22:1–23:25)

1. Passover Plots (22:1-62)
2. Trying Times (22:63–23:25)

The enigma of Christ's crucifixion, to the extent that it poses a "problem" for Christians today, often finds a salvation solution with heavy Pauline accents. Why did Jesus die an excruciating, unjust death? Answer: to provide the perfect sacrifice for the sins of the world, thereby opening the way to forgiveness and reconciliation with God. The cross represents God's chief instrument of salvation.

Although this concept constitutes a core theological conviction for many believers, it does not remove all the knots and splinters, so to speak, from the cross for every follower of Christ. A "scandal" is not so easily explained.

For all his love of Paul, the author of Luke and Acts does not develop a theology of Christ's sacrificial atonement beyond a few hints (see "forgiveness of sins" in Luke 24:47; Acts 2:38; 5:31; 10:43; 13:38-39; broadly, but not directly, tied to Jesus' death).[4] Luke has no doubt that Christ's crucifixion (vindicated by resurrection) was an integral part of God's saving purpose, not a sad accident of history; but Luke does not work out a systematic exposition of the cross within God's redemptive plan. Other questions come to the fore, more practical than theological—or better, more practical-theological. As with any murder mystery or unjust execution, Jesus' violent death triggered a basic investigative agenda: (1) *Agents*: Who did it? Who's responsible? (2) *Motives*: Why did they do it? What did they hope to gain? (3) *Means*: How did they do it? What did they use? (4) *Time*: When did they do it? What was the time of death?

We have some indisputable evidence. We know the killing "weapon" and who ultimately wielded it: even non-Christian historians acknowledged Jesus' death on a *Roman cross* at the hands of *Roman soldiers*.[5] But murders of popular figures are seldom that simple. What accomplices and collaborators, what plots and conspiracies, led to the fatal event? Trusting God's sovereign control of what happens in this world is more difficult in some situations than others, and it is never more difficult than in experiences of *excruciating suffering by innocent people of God*—especially the unfathomable *crucifixion of God's Holy Son and Messiah*. It's too much to ask Luke's readers simply to accept the cross, without discussion, as God's will. Even Jesus had his doubts just before his arrest (22:42). We need to know more about the *story* of Jesus' death to understand God's purpose more fully. Who was involved *besides God*, or whom did God "use" to bring about Jesus' crucifixion (if this indeed was God's desired end)? How did it unfold? By reenacting the crime and events leading up to it, Luke's narrative seeks to bring some clarity and closure to Christ's followers.

Passover Plots (22:1-62)

Luke sets Jesus' last night and last meal during "the festival of Unleavened Bread, which is called the Passover (*pascha*)" (22:1;

cf. 22:8, 11, 15). This is not just any arbitrary "time of death" but a significant season on the Jewish calendar commemorating the glorious "exodus" of ancient Israelites from Egyptian exile and slavery (see Exodus 11–13). Celebrating this festival during subsequent periods of foreign domination, like that of Roman rule in Jesus' day, would naturally inspire fresh dreams—and not a few revolutionary schemes—of Jewish independence and liberation. Accordingly, in first-century Jerusalem, Roman security forces remained on high alert throughout Passover week. A popular "liberator" of the poor and oppressed such as Jesus (cf. Luke 4:18-21) disrupting temple business (19:45-48) would merit special surveillance.

However, while suggesting this tense political backdrop to Jesus' final Passover, Luke focuses first upon both *cosmic* and *internal* plots against Jesus' life. This thing is both bigger and closer to home than Rome. These plots curiously intertwine as:

- *Satan* reemerges and "enter[s] into *Judas* . . . one of the twelve," impelling him to *betray* his Master to the priestly authorities who "were looking for a way to put Jesus to death" (22:3-6, emphasis added; cf. 22:47-53).
- *Satan*, desiring "to sift all of you [the twelve] like wheat," manages provoking *Simon Peter* (despite his false bravado) to *deny* Jesus three times before priestly servants (22:31-32, 54-62, emphasis added).
- An "*angel from heaven*" nurtures Jesus during his prayerful struggle over his fate, while *the disciples sleep* (22:39-46, emphasis added).

None of this takes Jesus by surprise. He knows the battle he faces. In terrible "anguish, he prayed more earnestly, and his sweat became like great drops of blood," like a soldier or athlete pushed to the limits of endurance (22:43-44).[6] He entertains no illusions about his disciples' loyalty: at this last supper, he predicts Judas' betrayal and Peter's denial—denouncing the former ("Woe to that one by whom he [the Son of Man] is betrayed," even though such a fate has been pre-"*determined*" by God! [22:21-22]) but interceding for the latter ("I have prayed for you that your own faith may not fail; and you [Simon], when once you have turned back, strengthen your brothers" [22:31-32]). As for the disciples as a group, Jesus acknowledges their support ("You are those who have stood by me in my trials" [22:28]), even as he laments their shortcomings:

"Why are you sleeping?" (22:46); "No more of this!" (swordplay against Jesus' arrest party [22:49-51]).[7] Jesus further knows that, even at this critical hour, his apostles remain more concerned about their status ("which one is greatest") in God's kingdom than any service they might offer him or each other (22:24-27).

What does this extended Passover story have to say about and to Jesus' followers, including Luke's readers? From the first generations following Jesus' death, early Christians gathered regularly to observe the Lord's Supper (Eucharist/Communion) "in remembrance" of Jesus, as he commanded (22:19), memorializing his last meal on that fateful "night when he was betrayed" (1 Cor 11:23-26). The intense experiences of that passion night—including the reactions of the first disciples—thus remained very much alive in the Christian community. Later believers could scarcely help identifying with the Twelve in some way. As Judas suddenly turned against Jesus (we have no inkling of his treachery until this late stage of Luke's narrative), may we, too, not suffer bouts of disloyalty to Christ for financial gain (Luke 22:4-5) or some other reason? Do we not still look about the room and wonder, "Which one of them [or us!] it could be who would do this" (22:23). If the stalwart Simon Peter ("Rock") buckled under pressure and denied Jesus, are we not also susceptible to momentary lapses of faith? And who among us has not locked horns with and lorded ourselves over other Christian brothers and sisters to serve our delusions of "greatness"?

The Passover incidents in Luke 22:1-62 do not so much address *why* Jesus had to be crucified (beyond the bare statement that God "determined" it [22:22; cf. v. 42]) as *how* his followers should (and did) respond in the face of his crucifixion. This is theology in *action* more than explanation. Whatever its purpose, the stark reality of Christ's bitter, unjust suffering cannot be sidestepped or sugarcoated. To follow Christ is to follow the Crucified One and to carry the cross: that is nonnegotiable, and "woe" to any disciple who resists. But we may also rest assured that this same Crucified Christ, present in the Lord's Supper, prays that "[our] own faith may not fail" in times of severe trial—even when we are too weary to pray for ourselves.

Trying Times (22:63–23:25)

From cosmic and internal plots against Jesus' life, Luke's Passion Narrative turns to a rapid run of *judicial proceedings*. Arrested by temple police (22:47-53) and detained in the high priest's residence throughout the night (22:54-62), Jesus is rudely hauled at break of day before (1) the *Jewish Council,* or "Sanhedrin," a kind of Supreme Court for local Jewish affairs comprised of chief priests and elders (22:63-71), who then hand him over to (2) *(Pontius) Pilate*, the Roman governor and chief military officer in Judea (23:1-5, 13-25), who, before authorizing Jesus' crucifixion, sends him to (3) *Herod (Antipas)*, the ruler of Galilee, who happens to be in Jerusalem at this time (23:6-12). We may track the main elements of these three "trials" as follows:

	Jewish Supreme Court	**Herodian Jurisdiction**	**Roman Military Tribunal**
Judge	The "Council" (Sanhedrin)	Herod Antipas, tetrarch of Galilee (at Pilate's request)	Judean governor Pontius Pilate
Prosecutors	Elders, chief priests, scribes	Chief priests and scribes	Chief priests, leaders of the people, and the people/crowds
Issues/ Charges	*Religious Blasphemy:* "If you are the Messiah, tell us . . . Are you then the *Son of God?*" (22:67, 70, emphasis added).	Jesus' reputation as a miracle/sign-worker	*Political Treason:* "We found this man perverting our nation, forbidding us to pay taxes to the emperor, and saying that he himself is the *Messiah, the king*" (23:2, emphasis added).

	Jewish Supreme Court	Herodian Jurisdiction	Roman Military Tribunal
Jesus' Defense	"If I tell you, you will not believe. . . . But from now on the Son of Man will be seated at the right hand of the power of God. . . . You say that I am [the Son of God]" (22:67-70).	"No answer" (23:9) and no sign	"You say so"—terse response to Pilate's direct question, "Are you the king of the Jews?" (23:3).
Jesus' Treatment	Mocking, beating, blind-folding, taunting ("Prophesy! Who is it that struck you?" [22:64])	Contempt and mock investiture (with "elegant [royal] robe" [23:11])	Flogging and release (23:16, 22)
Final Verdict	"Guilty" of blasphemous misrepresentation on the basis of Jesus' self-incriminating testimony (without supporting witnesses)	Jesus sent back to Pilate as "not guilty" and undeserving of death penalty	Under mob pressure, Pilate overturns his own "not guilty" verdict and "hand[s] Jesus over [to be crucified] as they wished" (23:25).

Luke scarcely presents these "trials" as models of jurisprudence or "due process." We might better designate them "mock trials," in the dual sense that they involve verbal and physical mocking of Jesus while making a mockery of justice. We see no careful sifting of evidence or weighing of testimony. Various parties hastily insult, interrogate, and indict Jesus alone, with little concern for deliberation, corroboration, or hearing witnesses for the defendant. The "shotgun" proceedings end with mob-like rule, as the leaders and people "all [shout] out together, 'Away with his fellow!' . . . 'Crucify, crucify him!'" (23:18, 20)—and Pilate acquiesces. Whether by aggression or concession, Jews, Romans, and Roman-sympathizers (like Herod) collude in Jesus' execution.

Luke greatly overdraws the bloodthirsty disposition of the Jerusalem population in the trial stories. He provides no rationale for the crowd's sudden about-face from hailing Jesus' royal entry into the city and hanging on his every word in the temple to joining the priestly authorities' pleas for crucifixion (in fact, earlier the leaders delayed seizing Jesus because *"they were afraid of the people"* [22:2; cf. 19:47-48]). But even with these inconsistencies, the impression of *some* Jewish complicity in Jesus' death is hard to shake in Luke. As for Pilate and Herod, though appearing less rabid than Jesus' Jewish opponents, they are no less culpable. Their self-interested, power-broking cronyism ("that same day Herod and Pilate became friends" [23:12]), spineless capitulation to the mob (supposedly, neither Herod nor Pilate find Jesus guilty of capital crimes), and reputation for ruthlessness (cf. Herod's beheading of John the Baptist [9:7-9] and Pilate's well-known record of brutality) condemn them as accomplices. Ultimately, the buck stops with Pilate: the decision to execute Jesus goes on his record. All in all, Luke casts the net of blame for Jesus' crucifixion widely. Throw in the betraying, denying, and self-absorbed disciples, and we are hard pressed to find anyone on Jesus' side at this stage. Again, rather than pointing the finger at someone else, readers are spurred to examine their own faithfulness to Christ and commitment to justice (cf. 22:23).

Shifting from portraits of Jesus' adversaries to that of Jesus himself in these "trying" moments, two characteristics stand out: his *innocence* and his *reticence*. Ironically, *three times* Pilate pronounces Jesus *innocent* of anything meriting death (23:4, 14, 22). Although this judgment does not stop Pilate from having Jesus flogged and crucified (Pilate suffers his own "denials" of Jesus' identity), it certifies for Luke's readers the terrible injustice Jesus endured. In no way does he deserve this fate; there's nothing good about his crucifixion in and of itself. Whatever good God might bring out of this heinous act is all to God's credit, a testament to God's amazing grace in an evil world.

Whereas judges, accusers, and agitated crowds have much to say during Jesus' "trials," Jesus himself is remarkably *reticent*, content for the most part with simple affirmative responses ("You say that I am" [22:70]; "You say so" [23:3]) or "no answer" at all (23:9). He mounts no elaborate rhetorical defense (as do Peter, Stephen, and Paul in Acts)[8] and issues no scathing rebuke (though 22:67-69 has some bite to it). He exudes a quiet acceptance—purchased, however, at the price of agonizing prayer (22:42-44)—of the suffering he must experience *as part of his vocation* as Son of God and Messiah-King (he confesses both roles under interrogation). Thoughtful readers will find it hard to match Jesus' reticence and confidence; in fact, his remarkable demeanor opens a flood of questions about Jesus' self-understanding of his death. But, nonetheless, in readers' struggles for fuller knowledge about Jesus' scandalous crucifixion, the assurance that Jesus himself *knew what it was about and accepted it* provides a basis for faith and hope.

DEATH AND LIFE (23:26–24:53)

1. Crucifixion and Burial (23:26-56)
2. Resurrection and Appearances (24:1-53)

The closing scenes in Luke's Gospel focus on the climactic events surrounding Jesus' crucifixion and resurrection. Although Jesus is obviously the central figure, a number of other characters—some familiar, some new in Luke's story—also appear; in fact, all the character groups listed above in the Passion Narrative are represented in these concluding episodes. Luke thus places a strong final accent not only on what happens to Jesus but also on *how a variety of people respond* to Jesus' experiences. Whereas some responses are predictable, others prove more surprising; and together they provide a rich fund for readers' reflections.

Crucifixion and Burial (23:26-56)

This unit supplies basic data for Jesus' obituary:

- **Place of Death**: a site near Jerusalem called "The Skull" (or "Cranium" [*Kranion*] [23:33]), probably descriptive of a hill with a natural cranial shape, but also suggestive of its unnatural, morbid use as a public execution venue littered with skeletal remains—by any reckoning a horrible place to die.
- **Time of Death**: three o'clock in the afternoon, at the end of a three-hour ordeal on the cross during which "*the sun's light failed (eclipsed)*" (23:44-45); this anomalous phenomenon of midday darkness betokens a sort of cosmic anguish over this terrible travesty of justice—even the sun can't bear to look upon it.
- **Place of Burial**: "a rock-hewn tomb where no one had ever been laid" (23:53), which provides a decent burial (rather than leaving the mutilated corpse for the birds and dogs to pick)[9] but also an isolated one, apart from kin; ancient tombs typically housed the remains of several family members, and in any case, this tomb belonged to one Joseph of Arimathea, not Joseph (or anybody else) of Nazareth.[10]

More importantly, at these times and places of Jesus' death and burial, we find various people attending to him in various ways, including a trio of voices taunting Jesus to "save himself" if he's truly the Messiah-King (23:35-39) but also some notable "minor" figures that buck stereotypes and complicate readers' reactions.[11]

- **Jewish Authorities**. The religious leaders launch the first salvo daring Jesus to "save himself" as he (supposedly) "saved others" (23:35). God counters their mockery, however, by ripping the temple curtain in two (23:45)[12]—another symbol, like driving out the merchants, of the present temple establishment's moral bankruptcy. But suddenly, just after Jesus' death, a member of the Jewish Council named Joseph requests Jesus' body and arranges for its burial (23:52-53). This is not some ruse to hinder Jesus' followers from mourning his death. Joseph is a "good and righteous man . . . waiting expectantly for the kingdom of God" (23:50-51; cf. Simeon in 2:25-28). If not a disciple, Joseph had at least publicly opposed the Council's "plan (*boulē*) and action" against Jesus (23:51). Not all Jewish authorities resisted God's purpose (*boulē*) in Christ (cf. also Gamaliel in Acts 5:33-39 [*boulē*, v. 38]).[15]

- **Roman Authorities**. The Roman soldiers supervising Jesus' crucifixion chime in with their own "Save yourself!" gibe, punctuated by crass gambling for Jesus' clothing and cruel offers of "sour wine" (Luke 23:34, 36-37). But again, a remarkable counterexample emerges. A centurion at the scene (likely the officer-in-charge), overwhelmed at the sun's darkening, the curtain's tearing, and Jesus' bellowing his last words, "praised God and said, 'Certainly this man was innocent'" (23:47). This is not the first or last Roman centurion in Luke's work to honor Israel's God and Jesus Messiah (see Luke 7:1-10 and Acts 10:1–11:18).

- **Cross Bearers**. Even though Jesus had called upon his disciples to carry the cross with him (Luke 9:23), they want nothing to do with it when the critical moment arrives; they're nowhere to be found. Ironically, even Jesus does not carry his cross—but not because he's escaping crucifixion. Presumably because he's too debilitated from flogging to bear the heavy load, his executioners commandeer one Simon of Cyrene to carry the cross "behind Jesus" (23:26). With stinging irony now, this random bystander and visitor to Jerusalem assumes the proper posture of self-denying discipleship in the absence of Jesus' longtime followers. He will not be the last North African Cyrenean to follow Jesus (see Acts 2:10; 11:20; 13:2). As for the pair of cross-bearing criminals who die alongside Jesus, one joins the derisive "Save yourself" chorus (adding "and us!" [23:39]), the other again defies expectations—affirming Jesus' innocence, in contrast to his own guilt, and pleading for Jesus' mercy "when you come into your kingdom" (23:40-42).

- **Jerusalem Population**. From their tragic lapse into a thunderous mob clamoring for Jesus' crucifixion, the "people" (*laos*) gradually resume sympathizing with Jesus. "A great number of the people *followed* him" (the basic response of discipleship) to Skull Hill (23:27); they then "stood by, watching" the grisly spectacle, but *not* participating in the religious leaders' mockery (23:35); and finally, after witnessing all the phenomena surrounding Jesus' death, "all the crowds . . . returned home, beating their breasts" in overwhelming sorrow (23:48). Jesus' own people by no means close their hearts to God's Messiah; the stage is set for an explosive renewal of repentance and faith among myriads of Jews in Jerusalem (see Acts 2:37-42; 4:4; 21:20).

- **Women Disciples and Examples**. On the way to Jesus' execution, before the general populace grasps its infamy, a group of devoted women, "Daughters of Jerusalem," commence "beating their breasts" and loudly lamenting Jesus' impending death (23:27-28). Luke later introduces another group of women: those "who had followed him [Jesus] from Galilee" and witnessed his death from "a distance" (23:49), but then observed "the tomb and how his body was laid" so they might return (after the Sabbath) to anoint Jesus' corpse with "spices and ointments" (23:55-56). Women from Judea and Galilee "spice" the story of Jesus' death and burial as models of persisting love and faithfulness within an otherwise putrid environment of violence and injustice.

Although the drama of Jesus' death involves many players, none is more active than Jesus himself—up to his very last breath. In contrast to his reticence in the trial scenes, he makes several significant pronouncements en route to and during his crucifixion. First, in response to the wailing women, Jesus demonstrates remarkable sympathy *for them* to the neglect of his own suffering. "Do not weep for me," he pleads, "but weep for yourselves and for your children" (23:28). As he wept over complacent Jerusalem's pending destruction by enemy forces (19:41-44), so he commiserates with the terrible fate awaiting these innocent "Daughters of Jerusalem" and their children when Jerusalem falls (23:27-31). About to endure his own violent and unjust death, Jesus bewails the slaughter of other innocents as casualties of war and oppression.

While hanging on the cross, Jesus goes beyond sympathy in voicing confident hope in God's salvation for others and himself. Three "famous last words" of Jesus, all unique to Luke, counter the three "save yourself/us" taunts from Jewish leaders, Roman soldiers, and one of the criminals crucified with him.

- **"Father, forgive them; for they do not know what they are doing" (23:34)**.[14] It's one thing to forgive a paralyzed man with no particular history of wickedness (5:18-24) or even a well-known "sinner"-woman who showers Jesus with lavish love (7:44-50). But it's quite another for the innocent Jesus to forgive his executioners who, though maybe not knowing the full story of "what they are doing" (or how God might redeem "what they are doing"), can scarcely ignore the blood on their hands. Here Jesus wondrously practices what he has preached: "Love your enemies . . . pray for those who abuse you" (6:27-28). Such action is of a piece with his recent healing of one of his captors, a henchman of the priestly authorities whose right ear had been severed by one of Jesus' impetuous disciples (22:49-51; found only in Luke).

- **"Truly I tell you, today, you will be with me in Paradise" (23:43)**. In response to one criminal's affirmation of "fearing God" and deserving judgment and his request to be remembered in God's kingdom (23:40-42), Jesus does more than pledge some future consideration. He announces that "*today*" (*sēmeron*) this man will join Jesus in the realm of "Paradise." Jesus continues to "save the lost" through the final moments of his and others' earthly lives, charting the way to restored Edenic life transcending death. Death does not have the last word. The kingdom of God advanced by Jesus is an eternal realm of hope and renewal.

- **"Father, into your hands I commend my spirit" (23:46)**. Jesus remains hopeful up to his final breath. Although not "saving himself" and not quite anticipating *bodily* resurrection, Jesus prays with confidence that God will save and sustain his "spirit" after death. This is a far cry from his "cry of dereliction" in Matthew 27:46 and Mark 15:34 ("My God, my God, why have you forsaken me?"), drawn from Ps 22:1. Luke's Jesus takes his cue from another psalm forged in a period of intense affliction; the full statement reads: "Into your hand I commit my spirit; you have redeemed me, O LORD, faithful God" (Ps 31:5).

This final utterance, rooted in the psalter, encapsulates a fundamental theological hope in *the faithful God who redeems Israel's suffering Messiah and people for restored life in God's kingdom*. Luke works out no theory of sacrificial atonement, but he holds up the cross of Christ as a master portrait of God's commitment to work out good for God's people, even in the most desperate situations.

Resurrection and Appearances (24:1-53)

Although the first and last of Jesus' three predictions of his death also included brief forecasts of his resurrection "on the third day" (9:22; 18:33), none of his followers recalls this datum or expects any vitality in Jesus' corpse when the day arrives. We soon learn from "two men in dazzling clothes," who appear to Mary Magdalene and other Galilean women at Jesus' *empty* tomb, that Jesus indeed "has risen" from the dead. Only then does the light dawn in the women's memory (24:8). Their report of Jesus' resurrection, however, fails to convince two groups of auditors: Peter and the apostles, who dismiss the women's testimony as an "idle tale" (24:10-11); and Cleopas and companion, "astounded," but not assured, by the women's announcement (24:21-22). Both of these groups eventually believe when the risen Jesus appears to them in bodily form—but even then, it takes some time to realize his true identity. At first they remain clueless, confused, and frightened. Recognition comes not so much through visual epiphany as through the *hearing of Jesus' word* and *sharing of food with Jesus*. The main elements of these "recognition scenes" may be charted as follows.

	Mary Magdalene and the Women (24:1-10)	Cleopas and Companion (24:13-35)	Simon (Peter) and the Apostles (24:10-12, 34-53)
Location of Jesus' Body	Missing from tomb when the women come to anoint his body	Walking with the pair on the Emmaus road until he "vanished from their sight" (24:31)	Suddenly appears in their midst in Jerusalem until, after leading them out to Bethany, "he withdrew from them and was carried up into heaven" (24:51)

	Mary Magdalene and the Women (24:1-10)	Cleopas and Companion (24:13-35)	Simon (Peter) and the Apostles (24:10-12, 34-53)
Reaction of Jesus' Followers	"Perplexed" and "terrified" (24:4-5)	"Astounded" at women's testimony, but not believing; dashed hopes of Israel's salvation; at first did not recognize Jesus' presence (24:13-24)	Dismissed women's testimony as "idle tale" (24:10-12); "terrified" when Jesus appears, despite his "Peace" greeting, believing he was "a ghost" (24:36-38); "disbelieving and still wondering," despite his invitation to touch his hands and feet (24:39-41)
Recognition of Jesus through *Food*	None	"When he was at the table with them, he took bread, blessed and broke it, and gave it to them. *Then their eyes were opened, and they recognized him*"—just before he "vanished from their sight" (24:30-31, emphasis added)	When Jesus asked for something to eat, "they gave him a piece of broiled fish, and he took it and ate it in their presence" (24:41-42)

	Mary Magdalene and the Women (24:1-10)	Cleopas and Companion (24:13-35)	Simon (Peter) and the Apostles (24:10-12, 34-53)
Recognition of Jesus through *Word*	After being reminded of Jesus' prediction by two "dazzling" messengers, the women "remembered his *words*" (24:4-8, emphasis added)	"Then beginning with Moses and all the prophets, he interpreted to them the things about himself in all the *scriptures*"—especially about the Messiah's path to "glory" through suffering (24:26-27, emphasis added). "Were not our hearts burning within us while he was . . . opening the *scriptures* to us? (24:32, emphasis added)	"He opened their minds to understand the *scriptures*"—from the Law, Prophets, and Psalms—concerning the Messiah's suffering and subsequent resurrection from the dead (24:44-46, emphasis added)

Christians of Luke's and later generations might think that Jesus' first followers had distinct advantages over them in understanding Jesus' crucifixion, believing in his resurrection, and coping with his physical absence and delayed return. But Luke's story of the first days following Jesus' death describes experiences remarkably similar to those of subsequent disciples. No one witnesses Jesus' actual resurrection and exit from grave clothes and tomb. Mary Magdalene (and other women) and Simon Peter (later)

213

observe the *effects* of resurrection—empty tomb and limp linens—but these clues may admit other explanations, such as reburial at another site or grave robbing. Thereafter the risen Jesus appears to various disciples, but *not* in a readily recognizable form and *not* for expected or extended visits. His popping in and out of Emmaus and Jerusalem and then ultimately "withdrawing" into heaven do not make for deep assurances about Jesus' living, abiding presence. Such assurances of fellowship with Christ, as well as insights into the purpose of his crucifixion, more consistently come through sacraments of food and word, Eucharist and Scripture, breaking bread in remembrance of Christ's body and blood and opening the Bible in search of God's purposes for God's suffering servant-Messiah and his people Israel. And such sacraments are as available to Luke's community (and ours) as they were to Christ's earliest followers just before and after his ascension (see Acts 2:41-47; 17:11; 20:7).

CHAPTER 7

HIGHLIGHTING GOD'S MISSION FROM JERUSALEM TO THE "ENDS OF THE EARTH"
(Acts 1–28)

Interpreters commonly view Acts 1:8 as a structural blueprint for the entire book: "But you will receive power when the Holy Spirit has come upon you; and you will be my witnesses in Jerusalem, in all Judea and Samaria, and to the ends of the earth." This text is strategically significant because (1) it represents Jesus' final commission to his followers before "a cloud" whisks him away to heaven (1:9), (2) it recognizes the critical role of the Holy Spirit in equipping Jesus' followers for continuing his mission in his absence, and (3) it broadly charts the centripetal movement of the early church's mission from Jerusalem (Acts 1–7), through the surrounding land of Israel (Judea and Samaria; Acts 8–12), and toward the "ends of the earth" (Acts 13–21). It's not a perfect map of Acts' plot: the story runs selectively, not comprehensively, throughout "*all* Judea and Samaria"; the final destination in Rome moves the plot more to the "center of the empire" than the "ends of the earth"; and the narrative loops back to Jerusalem and Judea (Caesarea) at key junctures. But as a *general outline* of the book, Acts 1:8 is not a bad place to start.

We may further track Acts' development in line with the four stages of mission progress observed in Luke's Gospel.

215

- **Preparing God's Mission in Jerusalem (Acts 1–7)**. God prepares Jesus' followers for mission by pouring out the Holy Spirit on "all of them" (2:4), adding thousands of new believers to their number (2:41; 4:4), and forging them into a worshiping and caring community "of one heart and soul" (4:32) that gathers regularly in the temple and in private homes (2:42-47; 4:32-37; 5:42). Preparation also involves dealing with conflict both within the community (5:1-11; 6:1-7) and from temple authorities (3:1–4:31; 5:12-42; 6:8–7:60), like those who challenged Jesus.
- **Establishing God's Mission in Judea, Samaria, and Syria (Acts 8–12)**. The early church's first mission ventures outside Jerusalem result from the religious establishment's increasingly violent opposition, spearheaded by "grand inquisitor" and persecutor, Saul (7:58–8:3; 9:1-2). The mission's border-crossing outreach thus commences in ironic fashion: as the young Jewish messianic community *scatters* under pressure from hostile, evil powers, it *spreads* Christ's gospel to other peoples—specifically, Samaritans (8:1-40) and Gentiles in Caesarea (10:1–11:18) and Syrian Antioch (11:19-26). Paradoxically, the *dispersion* of God's people advances *restoration* of the world under God's rule. Moreover, the former menace to the church, Saul, suddenly becomes a follower and witness of Christ, with special charge "to bring my [Christ's] name before Gentiles and kings and before the people of Israel" (9:15).
- **Expanding and Interpreting God's Mission (Acts 13–21)**. Under Saul/ Paul's leadership, the gospel makes its biggest leap in Acts, extending to both Diaspora Jews and Gentiles in populous urban centers throughout Asia Minor and Greece. The rapid influx of Gentiles—from both idol-worshiping and "God-fearing" backgrounds—particularly unsettles the early Christian movement and demands evaluation and explanation. Two "conferences" back in Jerusalem involving Paul and established church leaders tackle thorny matters surrounding the identity and interaction of God's "mixed" people, Jewish and Gentile (15:1-35; 21:17-26).
- **Defending God's Mission (Acts 21–28)**. Arrested by Roman soldiers for disturbing the peace and inciting mob violence in the temple, Paul undergoes, like Jesus, a series of judi-

cial trials before the Jewish Council and Roman governors of Judea. Unlike Jesus' shotgun trials, however, Paul's trials extend over a period of years, follow more formal legal procedure, and ultimately lead to Rome, awaiting an appeal before Caesar. Moreover, though Acts anticipates Paul's martyrdom in Rome, the narrative cuts off without recounting this tragic historical event (64 C.E.). The accent in the last quarter of Acts falls upon Paul's eloquent defenses of his faith and mission before various authorities and upon God's faithful protection of Paul throughout his Roman custody, including a protracted and hazardous voyage to Rome (27:1–28:15).[1]

In lieu of a step-by-step trek through Acts, this overview highlights one *main event* in each of the four mission stages, selected not only for the event's pivotal importance within a single section but also for its multiple *echo effects* across the larger Acts narrative. These reverberations signal major literary themes and theological aims discussed below. The action revolves around principal characters, Peter and Paul, who dominate the first (chs. 1–12) and second (chs. 13–28) halves of Acts, respectively, and both undergo major ideological changes. Geographically, the main events alternate between Jerusalem and Caesarea, that is, between the capitals of Jewish religious observance (Jerusalem) and Roman provincial government (Caesarea). Although God's mission in Acts radiates across the eastern Mediterranean world, it remains anchored in Judean-Roman religion and politics.

PENTECOSTAL CELEBRATION

1. Main Event: Outpouring of the Spirit in Jerusalem (2:1-42)
2. Echo Effects: "Pentecosts" in Samaria, Caesarea, and Ephesus (8:14-24; 10:44-48; 19:1-7)

In Jesus' day the pilgrimage festival of Pentecost, set fifty days after Passover in Jerusalem, celebrated both the ancient giving of the Law at Mt. Sinai and the annual spring harvest.[2] Adding to (not replacing) these elements, the earliest Christian (messianic) believers also associated Pentecost with God's abundant outpouring of the Holy Spirit in "the last days" (Acts 2:17). As through a resounding and fiery epiphany God graciously gave the Law to guide God's people (Exod 19:16-20), so through similar manifestations God graciously gave the Spirit to guide God's people and empower them to fulfill God's Law (Acts 2:1-4). God's glorious gifts of Law and Spirit thus complement rather than counterpoint each other.

Main Event: Outpouring of the Spirit in Jerusalem (2:1-42)

In fulfillment of Jesus' pre-ascension promise (1:4-5, 8), God mightily imbues the entire company of 120 believers (a multiple of twelve, like Israel's tribes and Jesus' apostles, symbolizing the restoration of God's people [1:15]) with the Holy Spirit. In addition to the sound like howling wind and the sight of holy fire, the assembly's sudden ability "to speak in other languages" (2:4) attends the Spirit's outpouring. This tongues speaking (*glōssolalia*) is somewhat distinct from the ecstatic utterances Paul discusses in 1 Corinthians 12–14. Both experiences involve supernatural out-bursts of "tongues" unknown to the speaker. But whereas the Corinthians worshiped God with some type of heavenly or angelic "tongue" also unknown to auditors (unless someone received divine "interpretation"), the community in Acts breaks out praising God in native dialects *known and understood* by the wider Pente-cost audience gathered from a variety of sectors across the Dias-pora. However we catalog the linguistic phenomena, the result is no less shocking or miraculous in Acts. The crowd is completely befuddled: "Are not all these who are speaking Galileans? And how is it that we hear, each of us, in our own native language?" (2:7-8). We know the "how" all right—"as the Spirit gave them ability" (2:4)—but the "what"—as in, *"What* does this mean?" (2:12, emphasis added)—which the audience also queries, is not so clear yet.

What indeed does this mean—socially, theologically? That is the interpretive crux of this event. And not surprisingly, the narrative answers its own question by appealing to Scripture. The disciples' chief spokesman, Peter, makes the key connection with the *prophet Joel*, who envisioned the day when God would pour out the Spirit upon "all flesh," equipping them for various tasks (Joel 2:28-32). That day has dawned here and now "in these last days," Peter announces, at 9:00 in the morning on Pentecost (Acts 2:14-17). Citing Joel, Peter highlights certain groups among "all flesh" that the Lord anoints with various Spirit-inspired gifts (2:17-18).

218

Character Groups	Spiritual Gifts
Sons/Daughters	Prophecy
Young Men/Old Men	Visions/Dreams
Male/Female Slaves	Prophecy

As an equal opportunity employer, the Spirit graces people across the social spectrum, cutting across typical discriminations of *age* (young/old), *gender* (male/female), and *class* (slave/free). Beyond the "all flesh" reference, the Joel reference places no particular emphasis on *ethnic* identity;[5] but the wider Pentecost story also suggests the outreach of God's Spirit to "every nation (*ethnos*) under heaven" (2:5) through the throng of pilgrims from numerous regions across the eastern Mediterranean world (2:8-11 lists *sixteen* areas). Although predominantly native Diaspora Jews sojourning in Jerusalem, these "devout" pilgrims (2:5) also include native Gentiles from Rome, no less, who had become Jewish "proselytes" (*prosylētoi*, 2:10-11). Some of these Jerusalem visitors are doubtless among the three thousand who accept Peter's messianic message, are baptized "in the name of Jesus Christ," and "receive the gift of the Holy Spirit" (2:37-41).

Echo Effects: "Pentecosts" in Samaria, Caesarea, and Ephesus (8:14-24; 10:44-48; 19:1-7)

The stage is set for extending God's Spirit-infused mission throughout the "world" among "all flesh" irrespective of age, gender, race, and ethnicity. Along with Jesus' original commissioned witnesses (1:8), we now have thousands of other potential agents of this "global" outreach that we expect to take off at any moment. But not so fast. Although the Spirit will indeed propel Christ's witnesses throughout various "nations," the earliest disciples are not in any rush to leave Jerusalem. Not until "a severe persecution" breaks out against it in Acts 8:1 does the Jerusalem church dispatch missionaries to other lands, and even then, curiously, "all *except the apostles* were scattered (*diesparēsan*)." Moreover, the anticipated explosion of spiritual activity across age, gender, and class lines does not fully materialize.

- Although a number of women, some socially prominent, participate in the early Christian movement, none has any significant speaking part. The "sons" of God have all the major speeches in Acts, prophetic or otherwise. Philip's four virgin daughters are credited with having "the gift of prophecy" (21:8-9), but they never use it in the narrative (oddly, a male prophet, Agabus, comes from Jerusalem to Philip's house in Caesarea to deliver a special prophecy to Philip's guest, Paul [21:10-11]: why not let one of the daughters do it?). Priscilla, though never designated a prophet, functions as a missionary and teacher, but always in tandem with husband Aquila and under Paul's supervision (18:1-3, 24-28). Overall the women of Acts remain safely contained in conventional boxes.[4]
- Although "elders" (*presbyteroi*) emerge as leaders in various churches (11:30; 14:23; 15:2, 4, 6, 22; 16:4; 20:17), none has any special dream or revelation (Simeon remains the only example of a Spirit-guided "elderly" man granted a messianic epiphany; see Luke 1:25-35).
- With one notable exception, the "young men" (*neaniskoi/ neanioi*) who appear in Acts do not distinguish themselves as a crack corps of spiritual visionaries. One, the very unlucky Eutychus (ironically meaning "Lucky") can't even stay awake during one of Paul's extended sermons and falls out an upper story window to his death (no sweet Spirit-dreams here). The one designated "young man" (*neanios*, 7:58) who eventually receives a life-changing vision of Christ is Saul/Paul (we don't know, however, if he's still "young" when this occurs; 9:1-19); after his "conversion," he continues to have periodic visionary experiences (16:6-10; 18:9-11; 22:17-21; 27:21-26).[5]
- A couple of slave-girls (*paidiskai*) speak out in Acts (and speak the truth!), but in one case a house-church mocks her (Rhoda) as a madwoman ("You are out of your mind," [12:15]), and in the other Paul exorcises a "fortune-telling" slave-girl for having a "spirit of divination" (16:16-18). Again, the prospects in Acts for prophetic women, or vocal women of any kind, are not bright.[6] As for other slaves or "lower"-class persons, Acts doesn't match Luke's interest in

such folk. Although large households, no doubt including servants, are "saved" in Acts (11:13-14; 16:15, 30-34), the spotlight falls more on believing householders and other prominent free citizens.

The Acts story does not perfectly live up to Joel's inclusive paradigm. It hints at the dynamic participation of women, young and old men, and slaves in God's household, but falls short of demonstrating "equal opportunity" for "all flesh" in God's mission. Sexism, ageism, and class hierarchy are nothing new in both church and society. Perhaps, in his second volume, Luke proceeds cautiously so as not to rock too many boats in the dominant Roman environment. Although happily trumpeting Joel's ideal, Luke leaves others to work out the details. Or maybe more accurately—and more hopefully—Luke leaves *God's Spirit* to work out the Pentecost vision. Where Luke shows restraint in depicting social revolution in Acts, he in no way restrains (as if he could) the explosive flood of the Spirit throughout the Roman Empire. The Pentecost experience reverberates several times in Acts with similar (but not identical) phenomena. A close connection between *water-baptism* (in Jesus' name) and *Spirit-baptism* (cf. 1:5) adds an *immersive* (along with the explosive) dimension to the Spirit's tidal wave.

	(Second) Jerusalem "Pentecost" (4:23-31)	**Samaritan "Pentecost" (8:4-25)**	**Caesarean Gentile "Pentecost" (10:1-48)**	**Ephesian "Baptist Pentecost" (19:1-7)**
Recipients	Jewish Christians in Jerusalem	Samaritan Christians among "the people (*ethnos*) of Samaria" (8:9)	God-fearing Gentile centurion, Cornelius, and his household in Caesarea	About twelve "disciples" of John the "Baptist" in Ephesus (19:1-3, 7)
Agents/ Means	Congregational prayer	Prayer and laying on of hands by Peter and John	Spontaneous, direct action by the Spirit	Laying on of hands by Paul

	(Second) Jerusalem "Pentecost" (4:23-31)	Samaritan "Pentecost" (8:4-25)	Caesarean Gentile "Pentecost" (10:1-48)	Ephesian "Baptist Pentecost" (19:1-7)
Contexts	Prayer for power and protection after Peter and John's release from prison	Philip's gospel-preaching and miracle-working mission to Samaria	Peter's proclamation of the gospel in Cornelius' house	Paul's "finding" (19:1) and instructing these "Baptist" disciples in Ephesus
Effects	Place "shaken"; all filled with the Spirit and proclaim God's word "with boldness" (4:31)	Unspecified manifestations that Simon Magus "saw," prompting him to offer money for Spirit-imparting "gift" (8:18-20)	"Speaking in tongues and extolling God" (10:46)	"They spoke in tongues and prophesied" (19:6)
Water- and Spirit-Baptism Sequence	Many previously baptized in water on Pentecost and presumably received Spirit soon thereafter (2:38-39, 41); 4:31 reports a renewal of that experience	Philip baptized believing Samaritans in water "in the name of Jesus Christ," but the Spirit did "*not* come upon any of them" until Peter and John arrived (8:12-17, emphasis added)	Spirit poured out upon Cornelius' house *before* they are "baptized in the name of Jesus Christ"; Spirit-baptism a catalyst for water-baptism (10:44-48)	(a) Baptized "into John's baptism" but with no knowledge "that there is a Holy Spirit" (19:2-3) (b) (Re-)baptized "in the name of the Lord Jesus" and then soon receive the Holy Spirit (19:4-6)

Two major convictions stand out among these various "Pentecosts." First, shared experience of God's Spirit through Jesus Messiah fosters religious unity amid ethnic diversity. The Spirit brings Jews (including Jewish "Baptists"), Samaritans, and God-fearing Gentiles together under God's rule. But, second, such Spirit-based unity is not uniformity. God's people draw from a common pool of spiritual practices—water baptism, gospel preaching, prayer, laying on of hands, speaking in tongues—but the Spirit's "flow" through these practices follows no rigid agenda. The Spirit is as likely to "fall" *interrupting* the sermon (Peter's) or *preceding* water-baptism (10:44-48) as *following* preaching or baptizing by one Spirit-led agent (Philip, cf. 6:5; 8:29, 39) *until* other agents arrive (Peter and John in Samaria, 8:14-17). The Holy Spirit is God's *dynamic, free gift* to God's people, not subject to control or manipulation by human hands (even those "laid" by apostles and evangelists), as the mercenary Simon Magus rudely discovered: "May your silver perish with you," Peter thunders at Simon, "because you thought you could obtain *God's gift* with money!" (8:20).[7]

PETER'S TRANSFORMATION

1. Main Event: Outreach to the Gentiles in Caesarea (10:1-48)
2. Echo Effects: Peter's Reminiscences (11:1-18; 15:7-11)

Jesus' prayer for the fickle Peter that his "faith may not fail" and that he nurture his fellow disciples "when once you have turned back" (from denying Jesus) (Luke 22:31-32) comes to fruition early in Acts. Remarkably, this weak denier emerges as a bold leader and chief witness for Christ in Jerusalem, even in the face of threats and seizures by Council authorities (see Acts 4:1-22; 5:17-41). Moreover, Peter becomes well known in the region for working wonders (in Jesus' name), including restoring the lame and raising the dead (3:1-16; 9:32-43); some think even his shadow generates healing power (5:15). But as we begin to assume Peter has come back all the way (and then some), God suddenly confronts him with another serious failing. At a strategic point in Acts and in the church's mission, Peter undergoes another major transformation.

Main Event: Outreach to the Gentiles in Caesarea (10:1-48)

As the persecuted early church branches out to new geographic areas, it also starts to establish new *ethnic* frontiers beyond its native Jewish (and proselyte) roots. Philip the evangelist launches the first large-scale mission to the Samaritans, a marginal group with deep roots in Israel's heritage but regarded as ethnically distinct from first-century Jews (8:4-13).[8] The next logical step leads to God-fearing Gentiles, who have not become proselytes, and here again Philip makes the first move—or more accurately, the Spirit directs Philip (8:29)—to an Ethiopian official "returning home" after worshiping in Jerusalem (8:27-28). But this is an isolated "desert/wilderness (*erēmos*)" (8:26) encounter with a figure from a remote territory; and after being baptized, he "went on his way [home] rejoicing," while the Spirit "snatched Philip away" to another mission site (8:39). It's a marvelous story, but if readers blink their eyes they may miss it.[9]

Acts gives more attention to Peter's outreach to the God-fearing Roman centurion, Cornelius, in Caesarea, which prompts the Spirit's outpouring on a Gentile household and provokes a stir among certain members of the Jerusalem church. But first God must change Peter's attitude. Cornelius grows in religious under-standing (about Jesus Messiah) and experience (receiving God's Spirit) but does not really undergo a "conversion" *from* anything. His reputation as a generous, Jewish sympathizing, prayerful, "devout man who feared God with all his household" is firmly estab-lished at the outset of the story (10:2), and we have no evidence that he ever opposed Jesus or his followers (cf. supportive centu-rions in Luke 7:1-10; 23:47). Further, his belief and baptism in Christ's name in no way demands any abandonment of his adopted Jewish faith and practices. It is not Cornelius, but *Peter*, who undergoes the most dramatic transformation *from* one position *to* another. For all his spiritual progress in Acts, he has not yet embraced the full scope of God's kingdom in these "last days." In particular, Peter retains a critical blind spot with respect to uncir-cumcised, non-kosher Gentiles outside (pagan idol-worshipers) or, at best, on the margins (non-proselyte "God-fearers") of God's household. He may have thought God would deal with the Gentiles one way or another—ultimately saving or destroying them (both views have biblical support)—but in any case, he (Peter) should have nothing to do with them. He even goes so far as to confess a highly rigid, sectarian view not held by most Jews in Greco-Roman antiquity, namely, that "it is unlawful for a Jew to associate with or to visit [or approach] a Gentile" (10:28).

God breaks through this parochial perspective with an epiphany during Peter's noontime devotions on a rooftop in Joppa. Three times God drops down "something like a large sheet" (canvas, screen) from heaven containing images of various non-kosher ("unclean") animals which God orders Peter to "kill and eat." And three times Peter refuses to comply (10:9-16). Although reminiscent of his threefold denial of Jesus, Peter has a better case this time: why should he, a loyal and devout Jew, violate standard dietary laws? As the story unfolds, however, the point is less about *what* Peter should eat than *whom* he should eat with. While Peter is "greatly puzzled [and] . . . still thinking about the vision," messengers from Cornelius (who also received a vision) arrive,[10] with instructions to bring Peter to their master's household (10:17-23). Finally, Peter follows the Spirit's lead, goes to Cornelius' house in Caesarea, stays several days (presumably eating non-kosher fare), and proclaims the good news of "peace by Jesus Christ" (10:23-48). He also confesses the touchstone of his "conversion": "I truly understand [now!] that God shows no partiality, but in every nation (*ethnos*) anyone who fears [God] and does what is right is acceptable to [God]" (10:34-35). If he has any lingering doubts about the Gentiles' partnership in God's kingdom, they are thoroughly quashed when the Spirit "baptizes" Cornelius and company in the middle of Peter's sermon!

Echo Effects: Peter's Reminiscences (11:1-18; 15:7-11)

Whereas Peter now affirms that Jews and God-fearing, *non*-proselyte Gentiles share full and open fellowship in God's family, some colleagues back in Jerusalem remain more skeptical. Although God's *gracious election* has always been the *means* of inclusion in the covenant community, since Abraham *ritual circumcision* has functioned as the principal *badge* of male membership (see Gen 17:1-27). How then can Peter justifiably "go to *uncircumcised* men" (11:3), lodge with them, and extend to them "the right hand of fellowship" (cf. Gal 2:9)? He has some serious explaining to do to the "circumcised believers" (Acts 11:2) in Jerusalem. And the narrative gives him time to do just that. On two occasions, Peter rehearses the circumstances leading up to and including his encounter with Cornelius. Amid expected "redundancies"[11] between these two reviews and the original story are telling distinctions, not least in narrative viewpoints: the primary account is conveyed in "omniscient" third-person, whereas the secondary reports emerge from Peter's more limited and self-interested character perspective.[12]

First, Peter gives a "step by step" (11:4) account that both adds and omits a few steps to the narrator's initial report. For example, he *adds* that the animal screen-vision "came *close* to me" (11:5, emphasis added)—intensifying the immediacy of the experience—and that "*six brothers* . . . accompanied me" to Cornelius' house (11:12, emphasis added)—quantifying the number of corroborating witnesses among "circumcised believers" (cf. 10:45) and embracing them as "brothers." On the other hand, he conveniently *omits* his great puzzlement and persisting thought "about what to make of the vision" (cf. 10:17-19), preferring to cut to the chase that "we entered the man's house" in obedience to the Spirit's command "not to make a distinction between them and us" (11:12). Peter also slides over the content of his message to Cornelius' household (cf. 10:34-43) and gets right to the climax: "And as I began to speak, the Holy Spirit fell upon them just as it had upon us at the beginning" (11:15). This statement seals the connection and blurs the distinction between "us" (circumcised Jews) and "them" (God-fearing Gentiles). "Their" experience of the Holy Spirit is "*just like*" "ours" at Pentecost. How can you argue with that? If you try, you'll find yourself bucking the very will and work of God: "If then *God gave them* the *same/equal gift* that [*God*] *gave us* when we believed in the Lord Jesus Christ, who was I [Peter] that I would hinder *God*?" (11:17, emphasis added). Who is anyone that would resist God? Not any faithful Jew, that's for sure, as Gamaliel voiced earlier in Acts (5:38-39) and as the Jerusalem church now affirms with Peter: "And they praised God, saying, "'Then God has given even to the Gentiles the repentance that leads to life'" (11:18). Theology trumps sociology.

But not once for all. Matters of intense religious debate are seldom settled once for all. After a period of great expansion in the Gentile mission, spearheaded by Paul and Barnabas under the auspices of the Syrian Antioch church (not by Peter from the Jerusalem church), the circumcision issue again raises its head. The "Gentile question" has become more complicated in that the Pauline mission has accepted not only God-fearing Gentiles affiliated in some way with the synagogue but also those "turn[ing] . . . to the living God" directly from the worship of idols ("worthless things," 14:15). In any case, some itinerant teachers from Judea arrive in Antioch, flatly asserting: "Unless you are circumcised according to the custom of Moses, you cannot be saved" (15:1).

Period. End of discussion. Actually it's just the beginning of "no small dissension and debate" between these visiting teachers and Paul and Barnabas (15:2). Soon the "talks" shift to Jerusalem. Although the church and its leaders "welcome" Paul and Barnabas, "some believers" (in Jesus Christ) among the Pharisees up the ante even more:[13] "It is necessary for them [the Gentiles] to be circumcised *and ordered to keep the law of Moses*" (15:5, emphasis added). Nothing short of becoming full proselytes will suffice.

The stage is set once again for Peter. He stands up and silences the contentious assembly with his story. They've heard it before but apparently forgotten its significance. It's not so much his story as *God's story*:

- "*God made a choice* . . . that I should be the one through whom the Gentiles would hear the message of the good news and become believers" (15:7, emphasis added).
- "*God*, who knows the human heart, *testified* to them by *giving* them the Holy Spirit, just as [*God*] *did* to us" (15:8, emphasis added).
- "And in *cleansing* their hearts by faith [*God*] *has made no distinction* between them and us" (15:9, emphasis added).

Pay close attention (again) to what *God has done* among the Gentiles, and beware hindering God's purpose, or as Peter now puts it more ominously, "Why are you *putting God to the test (peirazō)*" by requiring more from Gentiles than God does! Recalling the tragic case of Ananias and Sapphira, "testing" (*peirazō*) God or God's Spirit is futile and not a little frightening (5:1-11, especially v. 7, emphasis added).

ECUMENICAL CONVERSATION

1. Main Event: Unity Conference in Jerusalem (15:1-29)
2. Echo Effects: Proofs and Problems of Unity (15:30–16:5; 21:17-26)

Although the assembly's circumcision advocates do not refute Peter's testimony, the conference in Jerusalem is far from over. All sides need to be heard, not least that of Paul and Barnabas who have the most at stake here. Surprisingly, however, Acts' "minutes" of the proceedings report only a brief summary of their report: "they told of all the signs and wonders that God had done through them among the Gentiles" (15:12). Of course, readers can look back to Acts 13–14 for the details, but it's curious that the present context does not "echo" some of these wondrous deeds. The effect of such a quick glance at Paul and Barnabas places the main spotlight on the next speaker.

Main Event: Unity Conference in Jerusalem (15:1-29)

A man named *James* now offers the keynote address, offering a "judgment" (*krinō*, 15:19) that the entire assembly approves (15:13-29). This James clearly has tremendous influence in the Jerusalem church. Who is he? He's obviously not James, the brother of John and one of the twelve apostles (Luke 6:14; 9:54; Acts 1:13), whom Herod had "killed with the sword" (12:2). The only other prior reference to another James appears in Peter's passing comment to a prayer group gathered in Mary's home: "Tell this to James and to the believers [brothers]" (12:17). Luke never bothers to profile this James; apparently he is so well known as to need no introduction. This can only be James, the brother of Jesus, who quickly rose to a high position of leadership in the Jerusalem congregation after Jesus' resurrection (see 1 Cor 15:7; Gal 1:19; 2:9; James 1:1). In any case, when this James speaks in Acts, the "whole church"— including apostles and elders (15:22)—listens!

James begins his speech by endorsing Peter's[14] previous witness about God's gracious choice to call out among the Gentiles "a people (*laos*) for [God's] name" (15:4) and by connecting it with Amos' prophecy that God's restoration of Israel (reconstruction of "David's tent") *includes* the salvation of Gentiles (*ethnē*). What Joel's vision lacked in terms of *ethnic* outreach, Amos' clearly exclaims: "I will rebuild the dwelling of David . . . I will set it up, so that *all other peoples* (*anthrōpōn*) may seek the Lord—even *all the Gentiles* (*ethnē*) over whom my name has been called" (15:16-17; Amos 9:11-12).[15] But then James, with bold authority, issues a "decision" (Acts 15:19, emphasis added) that adds an important new element to the proceedings. Although concurring with the more "liberal" camp that circumcision and the full weight of the law should not be imposed on Gentile believers, James also grants notable concessions to more "conservative" interests. In order to maintain fellowship among God's people, Gentiles must shun certain "essential" (or "necessary," 15:28) taboos stipulated in Mosaic law. In particular, they must abstain from four things (15:20, 29):

- Things polluted by idols (*eidōla*)
- Fornication (*porneia*)
- Whatever has been strangled (*pniktos*)
- Blood (*haima*)

The last two items both ban partaking meat not fully drained of animal blood (butchering by strangling retains blood), a major tenet of kosher diet based on the fundamental principle that "the life of the flesh is in the blood" (Lev 17:11; cf. 17:10-16). The issue, however, is less about diet and nutrition (our modern preoccupation) than worship and theology. In the ancient world, meat processing typically occurred in conjunction with sacrificial offerings to the gods. The butcher block was the altar of sacrifice. Hence meat consumption signified an act of communion with the divine.[16] As Paul put it in 1 Corinthians 10:18, "Are not those who eat the sacrifices *partners in the altar*" (emphasis added). By eating meat sacrificed to God and slaughtered so as to sap the animal's blood, the Israelites affirmed their worship of and partnership with the Life-Giving God who atones for human failing through blood offerings (Lev 17:1-16). Conversely, by eating meat sacrificed to pagan gods that retains blood in the animal's flesh, Gentiles, from the perspective of Jewish law, participated in idolatrous and immoral practices. The first two taboos in James' list reinforce the point: "things polluted by idols" includes meat sacrificed to idols (cf. 1 Cor 8:1-13; 10:14-33) and "fornication" encompasses "sacred" sexual unions with pagan temple prostitutes (cf. 1 Cor 6:12-20).

Thus James' four prohibitions cohere around the problem of *idol worship* or, positively, around the *proper worship of the One True, Living God*.[17] Gentiles do not have to be circumcised or comply with Mosaic legislation in every respect. But they must keep the law at those critical points that demonstrate that they have truly "turn[ed] from these worthless things [idols] to the living God, who made the heaven and the earth and the sea and all that is in them" (Acts 14:15). God's covenant relationship with humanity is strong and resilient, rooted in deep love and forgiveness; but in Acts' view, solidly grounded in Scripture, humans—Jewish and Gentile— must beware that idolatry is the quintessential, nonnegotiable deal breaker.

All the Jerusalem conferees unanimously agree, so much so that they codify James' decision in a letter to be circulated throughout the Gentile congregations (15:23-29). This missive's common designation as the "Apostolic Decree" misleads: its stamp of approval derives not only from the apostles but also from the elders, "the consent of the whole church" (15:22), and most importantly, the Holy Spirit: "For it has seemed good to the Holy Spirit and to us . . ." (15:28). Moreover, although resembling something of an ecclesiastical "decree," the main thrust of the decision and letter is collegial and compromising. The Jerusalem believers are concerned not only about their own community but also about Gentiles in the Pauline churches "disturbed" and "unsettled" by misguided advocates of circumcision and proselytism (15:23-24). Though considerably more cumbersome, perhaps a better label for the conference's verdict would be: the "Great Spirit-Inspired, Ecumenical-Congregational Compromise."

Echo Effects: Proofs and Problems of Unity (15:30–16:5; 21:17-26)

As anyone who has hashed out a difficult issue in a committee meeting or denominational convention knows, the final resolution that passes, even by a wide margin, does not really end the discussion. The buzz continues long after the conference. The stunning report of the Jerusalem assembly's "unanimous" (*homothymadon*)[18] decision (15:25) leaves us wondering how the letter will be received and how the fellowship issue will play out among the churches? Is all this overwhelming consensus just a little too good to be true?

The church at Antioch supported and "rejoiced at the [letter's] exhortation"—that's promising (15:30-33). But then, Paul and Barnabas, of all people, break the spirit of unity by *severing their long and successful missionary partnership*. Ostensibly, their "sharp disagreement" (15:39) has nothing to do with the recent conference. The matter is personal, specifically over whether to take John Mark with them on their second mission. Mark had deserted them early in the first mission (13:13), and in Paul's mind, that disqualified him from itinerant service. Barnabas, on the other hand, wants to give Mark another chance. So they head off together in one direction, Paul takes another route with a new partner, and that is that (15:36-41)—the last we see of Barnabas and Mark in Acts. One suspects there is more behind this rift than a personality tiff (cf. Gal 2:1-14).[19] Barnabas and Mark have deeper roots than Paul in the Jerusalem church (cf. 4:36-37; 9:26-27; 11:22; 12:12). Perhaps Paul is less enthusiastic than they about the "compromise" letter to the Gentiles (it isn't *his* letter, after all). Acts never says as much, but Paul's volatility remains a concern.

The next scene, however, largely dispels any lingering doubts about Paul's commitment to the Jerusalem Conference. Along with his new partner, Silas, Paul recruits for his missionary team "a disciple named Timothy . . . well spoken of by the believers" (16:1-2). Timothy had a mixed heritage—Jewish mother/Greek father—and had not been circumcised (16:1-2). Of course, the recent decision did not require circumcision for Greek believers, but it in no way decreed or even considered an exemption for *Jewish* disciples and their families. Neither did it consider hybrids like Timothy. So what to do? Paul chooses to play it safe and give his fellow Jews no cause for offence: "he took [Timothy] and had him circumcised" (16:3). Further, in journeying "from town to town," the Pauline mission party "delivered to them for observance" the stipulations of the Jerusalem Conference, while the churches continued thriving (16:4-5).

Paul further demonstrates his personal endorsement of Jewish practices among Jews by cutting his hair in Cenchrea (in accordance with a vow of consecration) before entering the synagogue in Ephesus for a "discussion with the Jews" (18:18-19).[20] But for all his efforts at conciliating his Jewish compatriots, the polls are not encouraging. When Paul arrives in Jerusalem (following his extended mission around the Aegean coast) for a second meeting with "James . . . and all the elders," despite the "warm welcome" he receives, he's also hit with the shocking report that "many thousands" (*myriades*, 21:20) of fervent Jewish believers think that Paul has been "teach[ing] all the Jews living among the Gentiles to forsake Moses, and . . . tell[ing] them not to circumcise their children or observe the customs" (21:21). Paul has been doing nothing of the kind in Acts, but negative press is tough to overcome. It's hard not to believe that "myriad" smoke signals scream, "Fire!" In order to douse the spreading blaze of rumors, James and company advise Paul to display his loyalty publicly by participating in another consecration vow with four members of the Jerusalem church and paying for all their ritual expenses in the temple (21:23-26). All this Paul promptly does "the next day" (21:26).

Having addressed the "Jewish question"—Must faithful Jews who believe in Jesus Christ abandon venerable rites of circumcision and consecration? (No!)—James and the elders also briefly reprise the "Gentile question"—Must Gentile believers become circumcised and keep the whole Mosaic law? (No!) Curiously, however, they mention the letter and list the four concessions required of Gentiles *as if Paul were hearing about this for the first time* (21:25). Their statement sounds more like a fresh announcement than an echo of the first Jerusalem Conference (15:21-29), which it clearly is. So why this narrative glitch? Eschewing the flimsy explanation that Luke has done a sloppy job integrating his sources here, I sense some continued anxiety in the story about Paul's solidarity with James and the Jerusalem church. Yes, he attended the first conference, endorsed its proceedings, and circulated its decisions. But did he catch the full spirit of the matter? Did he make the letter his own? Does he now need reminding because he has let the issue slide? In any case, Luke's assessment of Paul is just beginning: defending Paul's mission dominates the final quarter of Acts.

PAUL'S VINDICATION

1. Main Event: Defense Testimony in Caesarea (26:1-23)
2. Echo Effects: Prior Reports of Paul's "Conversion" (9:1-9; 22:6-21)

Despite the best-laid plans, Paul's temple visit does not go well. Some immigrant "Jews from Asia" grab Paul and incite a mob ("the whole crowd") against him with the most damning charges: "This is the man who is teaching everyone everywhere against our people, our law, and this place; more than that, he has actually brought Greeks into the temple and has defiled this holy place" (21:27-28). In his Diaspora mission, Paul faced similar mobs (though hardly "everyone everywhere") and charges of opposing the Jewish people and law (18:12-13; cf. 17:5-9, 13). But the accusation that he "has defiled this holy place" raises the stakes considerably, as Stephen could attest *if he hadn't been stoned to death* for allegedly "saying things against this holy place" (6:12-14)![21] With Paul, the charge comes with a more specific allegation that he had ushered a Gentile from Ephesus named Trophimus into the temple precincts and across the "No Trespassing" zone—*on pain of death*—not only for Gentiles apparently but also for Jews, like Paul, who accompany them.[22]

Although Paul had brought Trophimus, among others, to Jerusalem (cf. "we"-party in 20:4-6; 21:15-17), he did not bring him into sacred temple space or otherwise violate Jewish law. These are patently *false* charges (cf. 6:13); recall that Paul was in the temple to complete *purification rites* with fellow Jews! But the facts of the case become muddled in the riot that erupts, prompting the Roman tribune stationed in Jerusalem to arrest and bind Paul (for his own safety as much as to quell the mob). From this point to the end of Acts, Paul remains in Roman custody. Over the lengthy course of these final chapters, Paul offers self-defenses before *five* different officials—one Jewish, one Herodian, and three Roman—starting in Jerusalem (first two) and then moving to Caesarea (Acts 21–26). From there he is transferred to Rome, awaiting a hearing before Caesar himself when the narrative breaks off (Acts 27–28).

As Paul remains a controversial figure among Jews and Romans alike, Luke gives him ample opportunity to explain himself. The following table summarizes the main elements of Paul's defenses before various officials.

	Claudius Lysias 21:37–22:30	Ananias 23:1-11	Antonius Felix 23:23–24:26	Porcius Festus 25:1-22	Herod Agrippa II 25:23–26:32
Official's Position	Roman tribune over military cohort in Jerusalem	Jewish High Priest in Jerusalem (c. 48–66 C.E.)	Roman Governor of Judea, based in Caesarea (c.52–59 C.E.)	Roman Governor of Judea, based in Caesarea (c. 59–61 C.E.)	Herodian "king" of parts of Palestine after 50 C.E., visiting Festus in Caesarea
Wider Audience	Temple crowds crying, "Away with him [Paul] (21:36; 22:22); "all the city" (21:30); violent mob	Roman tribune; entire Jewish Council, including members of Sadducees and Pharisees	Prosecutors Ananias the high priest and elders from Jerusalem, with "attorney" Tertullus (24:1); later, Felix's Jewish wife, Drusilla (24:24)	"Chief priests and the leaders of the Jews" who bring "serious charges against [Paul], which they could not prove" (25:2, 5-7)	Wife/sister Bernice, Governor Festus, Roman military officers, and "prominent men of the city" (25:23)

Paul's Defense	Testimony of "zealous" (22:3) Jewish background; persecution against the Christian "Way" (22:4); Damascus Road vision; commission "far away to the Gentiles" (22:21)	Challenges high priest's order to strike him as a "violation of the law" (23:3); divides Council by identifying with Pharisees and their belief in "resurrection of the dead" (23:6)	*Flat denial* of provoking any disturbance in the temple; *firm avowal* of hope and belief in "the God of our ancestors," the law and prophets, and the resurrection from the dead (24:12-15, 20)	Denial of any "offense against the law of the Jews, or against the temple, or against the emperor" (25:8); appeals to Caesar in Rome	Testimony of faithful Pharisaic background; persecution against Jesus movement; belief in God's promise to restore Israel and raise the dead; obedience to Damascus road vision; mission to Gentiles so they might "turn to God" (26:20); prophets' witness to Messiah's suffering; public witness to work "not done in a corner" (26:26)
Official's Decision	Arrests, binds, and places Paul in custody; prepares to flog Paul until learning he's a Roman citizen; finally releases him to Jewish Council	Beyond ordering Paul struck on the mouth, Ananias renders no judgment; tribune takes Paul back into protective custody	Postpones verdict; places Paul in custody with freedom to receive visitors; later hears Paul again, becomes "frightened" at his words, hopes for a bribe, and lets Paul languish in prison for two years	Grants Paul's appeal to be tried before the emperor; holds Paul until sending him to Rome	Affirms Paul's innocence; "could have been set free if he had not appealed to the emperor" (26:32)

Main Event: Defense Testimony in Caesarea (26:1-23)

I focus here on Paul's last and longest defense speech, which pulls together and expands upon most elements in the previous four. As with Jesus' final "trial," Paul's takes place before a member of Herod's dynasty. However, where Jesus "gave . . . no answer" to Herod (Antipas) in Jerusalem (Luke 23:9), Paul takes the floor, "stretch[es] out his hand" in good rhetorical posture (cf. 12:17; 13:16; 21:40), and offers a forensic oration appealing to five established emphases of persuasive testimony.[23]

- **Official's Honor**. What we might call "buttering up" the judge, the ancients called *captatio benevolentiae*, "capturing" the magistrate's good will by acknowledging his superior qualities to make a fair judgment. Paul opens with how "fortunate" he feels to be testifying before one so "familiar" with Jewish traditions and practices (26:2-3; cf. vv. 26-27).
- **Noble Heritage**. His affiliation with a new Jewish messianic sect was a big problem for Paul in an environment that valued long-standing religious tradition. Plus Paul was something of a "Johnny-come-lately" even within the Jesus movement. Although he may appear to lack solid religious roots, Paul in fact makes bold appeal to his fervent devotion to Judaism "from the beginning" of his life, maturing into faithful participation with the Pharisees, "the strictest sect of our religion" (26:4-5). Moreover, his belief in the restoration and resurrection of God's afflicted people stems from Pharisaic teaching (cf. 23:6) and the "promise made by God to our *ancestors*" (26:6, emphasis added). His present belief in Jesus Christ reinforces and in no way replaces his ancestral faith.
- **Heavenly Vision**. Although *not* undergoing a *conversion from Judaism* (Pharisaic or otherwise), Paul experienced a radical transformation in attitude toward Jesus' messianic movement. And in his anxious environment (again) that cherished religious stability, if he'd changed some substantial aspect of his faith and practice, he better have a good reason for it. Paul's particularly zealous brand of Pharisaism (not shared by all or even most Pharisees) led him to persecute Jesus' followers vigorously (pursuing them to "foreign

cities") and violently ("cast[ing] my vote" for the death penalty [26:9-11]).[24] What in the world, then, could suddenly turn such an ardent opponent of Jesus Christ into a leading proponent of the same, even to Gentiles? Nothing less than a personal, celestial ("brighter than the sun," 26:12), apocalyptic confrontation by the living Jesus himself on the Damascus highway. Hard to argue with that, as Paul candidly confesses: "After that, King Agrippa, I was not disobedient to the heavenly vision" (26:19).

- **Prophetic Authority**. Even though Paul may appear to some as a troublemaking upstart, he claims to carry on the same biblical-prophetic tradition venerated by his people and affirmed by Agrippa ("King Agrippa, do you believe the prophets? I know that you believe" [26:27]). However, though Paul's people honor the prophets in principle, they also have a long history of violently opposing particular prophets, even within the holy city and temple of Jerusalem. Thus Paul's recent attack and seizure by "the Jews" in the temple compound are of a piece with the hard experiences of Isaiah, Jeremiah, and the like. And they likewise follow in the bloody footsteps of Jesus Messiah, whose death, resurrection, and proclamation of "light both to our people [like Paul] and to the Gentiles [through Paul]" was precisely "what the prophets and Moses said would take place" (26:22-23). A few prophetic citations would have been nice, but Paul assumes Agrippa (and readers) know the chapters and verses.[25] In any case, Paul roundly contends he is "saying [and doing] *nothing but* what the prophets" prefigured (26:22, emphasis added).

- **Public Integrity**. When Governor Festus (who was hosting King Agrippa) rudely blurts out in the middle of Paul's defense, "You are out of your mind, Paul!" (26:24)—the kind of disruption that might throw lesser orators off their game—Paul doesn't skip a beat. He immediately negates the charge (26:25) and then shrewdly shifts the focus back to Agrippa. From his limited, provincial Roman perspective, Festus is not really competent to judge Paul's case; but the better informed Agrippa "*knows about these things*" (26:26). And indeed, Paul assures Agrippa, pretty much everyone else (but Festus) knows what Paul has truly done and not done.

236

Paul is not one to mince words or cover up his actions. He's all about "the sober truth," speaking honestly and "freely" and doing nothing "in a corner" (26:26). He and his mission are open books, as surely ("I am certain" [26:26]) Agrippa knows and appreciates.

Echo Effects: Prior Reports of Paul's "Conversion" (9:1-19; 22:6-21)

Paul's life-shattering encounter with the living Christ on the Damascus Road is the linchpin of his apologetic portrait in Acts, which gives this experience considerably more attention than Paul does in his letters (cf. Gal 1:11-12; 2 Cor 4:5-6). The testimony before Agrippa comes as the crowning *third report* of Paul's "heavenly vision." As with Peter, Acts presents three accounts of Paul's transformation: the first from a third-person narrative viewpoint (Acts 9:1-19) and the second two channeled through Paul's character voice (22:6-21; 26:1-29). In contrast with Peter, however, Paul delivers his pair of personal testimonies before large public audiences of Jews and Romans, first in Jerusalem and then Caesarea, whereas Peter moves in the opposite direction, from Caesarea to Jerusalem, and speaks to Jewish assemblies of the Jerusalem church. Paul's more open venues and outward movements (from Jerusalem) befit his chief role in advancing God's mission throughout the world.

Although Acts' triple accounts of Paul's Damascus Road Christophany repay careful analysis of differences as well as similarities, I highlight here the brief, but poignant, conversation between the luminescent risen Jesus and the shell-shocked Saul common to all three versions (9:4-6; 22:7-10; 26:14-16; I cite the first text below as the model; the brackets enclose material lacking in the final text).

Jesus: Saul, Saul, why do you persecute me?
Saul: Who are you, Lord?
Jesus: I am Jesus, whom you are persecuting. But get up [and enter the city, and you will be told what you are to do].

It would be hard to overestimate the potential of these words to comfort and challenge Luke's communities of readers, from his day to ours. For a people wondering in the difficult and anxious interim between Christ's death/resurrection and return—"Who are you, Lord? Where are you, Lord, when we need you? What should we do, Lord?"—these words are pure practical-theological gold.

- **Who is this Lord?**—A Lord named Jesus who knows what it is to suffer in this evil world and who *continues to suffer with and in his followers*: you hurt his disciples, you hurt *him*; he takes it very personally.
- **Where is this Lord when his people need him?**—Right here, dynamically present in and with God's people through God's Spirit—and if need be, through the occasional lightning bolt to check—and even change!—chief persecutors, like Saul.
- **What should the Lord's people do?**—Get up and do whatever the Lord wants, whenever and however he makes his will known. Although Saul's case is extraordinary in many respects, at the point of following the Lord's guidance—even blindly at times—he illustrates the most basic tenet of discipleship.

Of course, obedience is easier said than done. The way Paul couches his testimony to Agrippa—"I was *not disobedient* to the heavenly vision"—although rhetorically more persuasive than a simple positive statement, also conveys the distinct possibility that even dramatic visions can be and are *dis*obeyed. Further, Paul adds one telling maxim to Jesus' Damascus Road announcement that also stresses the struggle at hand: "Saul, Saul, why are you persecuting me? *It hurts you to kick against the goads*" (26:14, emphasis added). A popular proverb via Euripides (*Bacchae* 794-95), it acknowledges the common human experience of kicking back against a master's "goad" (think "cattle prod"). We don't like being told what to do and where to go, even by God. But the saying also makes clear that "resistance is futile" (to quote *Star Trek*), that ultimately *we* are the ones "hurt" by disobedience to God—not because God will zap us, but because we will fail to realize God's good purposes for our lives. God's hurting people need not *hurt themselves* further by kicking against God's goads. So says Euripides. So says Paul. So says Luke. And so say we all. Amen.

Notes

PREFACE TO PART ONE

1. I follow this convention in the present study; since Luke and Acts are anonymous narratives, however, we cannot be certain who wrote these volumes.

2. Luke 1:1; Acts 1:1. Henry J. Cadbury (*The Making of Luke-Acts* [London: SPCK, 1961], 11) suggests the designations *Ad Theophilum I* and *Ad Theophilum II*.

3. Some might wonder at the lack of a separate "historical" or "sociohistorical" focus. I take seriously Luke's first-century context and incorporate social and historical analysis into my treatments of Luke's literature and theology. But I am less interested in secondary issues of "historicity" (i.e., what "really" happened).

1. LITERARY FRAMEWORK: HOW WERE LUKE AND ACTS COMPOSED?

1. See Heidi J. Hornik and Mikeal C. Parsons, *Illuminating Luke: The Infancy Narrative in Italian Renaissance Painting* (Harrisburg, Pa.: Trinity Press International, 2003); *Illuminating Luke: The Public Ministry of Christ in Italian Renaissance and Baroque Painting* (London: T&T Clark, 2005).

2. See Dennis R. MacDonald, *Does the New Testament Imitate Homer?: Four Cases from the Acts of the Apostles* (New Haven, Conn.: Yale University Press, 2003); Marianne Palmer Bonz, *The Past as Legacy: Luke-Acts and Ancient Epic* (Minneapolis: Augsburg Fortress, 2000); Kathy Chambers, "'Knock, Knock—Who's There?': Acts 12:6-17 as a Comedy of Errors," in *A Feminist Companion to the Acts of the Apostles*, ed. Amy-Jill Levine (London: T&T Clark, 2004), 89-97.

3. Johannes P. Louw and Eugene A. Nida, eds., *Greek-English Lexicon of the New Testament Based on Semantic Domains*, Vol. 1 (New York: United Bible Societies, 1988), 612.

4. Henry J. Cadbury, *The Making of Luke-Acts* (London: SPCK, 1961), 11.

5. See Stephen D. Moore, *Literary Criticism and the Gospels: The Theoretical Challenge* (New Haven, Conn.: Yale University Press, 1989).

6. Mikeal C. Parsons and Richard I. Pervo, *Rethinking the Unity of Luke and Acts* (Minneapolis: Fortress Press, 1993), 61-63.

7. See William H. Shepherd, Jr., *The Narrative Function of the Holy Spirit as a Character in Luke-Acts*, Society of Biblical Literature Dissertation Series 147 (Atlanta: Scholars Press, 1993); Max Turner, *Power From On High: The Spirit in Israel's Restoration and Witness in Luke-Acts*, Journal of Pentecostal Theology Monograph Supplement Series 9 (Sheffield, England: Sheffield Academic Press, 1996).

8. The careers of Andrew, Philip, and Thomas, among other apostles, will be elaborated in later apocryphal Acts.

9. See John A. Darr, *On Character Building: The Reader and the Rhetoric of Characterization in Luke-Acts*, Literary Currents in Biblical Interpretation (Louisville: Westminster John Knox Press, 1992).

10. See Bart D. Ehrman, *Lost Christianities: The Battles for Scripture and the Faiths We Never Knew* (Oxford: Oxford University Press, 2003), 9-11, 29-32.

11. Jacob Jervell, *The Theology of the Acts of the Apostles* (Cambridge: Cambridge University Press, 1996), 61.

12. E.g., *Acts of Paul; Acts of Peter; Acts of John; Acts of Andrew; Acts of Thomas*. See Wilhelm Schneemelcher, ed., *New Testament Apocrypha*, Vol. 2, rev. ed., trans. Robert McL. Wilson (Louisville: Westminster John Knox Press, 1992), 75-86; Robert F. Stoops, Jr., ed., *The Apocryphal Acts of the Apostles in Intertextual Perspectives*, *Semeia* 80 (Atlanta: Scholars Press, 1997).

13. See Cadbury, *Making of Luke-Acts*, 76-97, 178-83 (comparing Mark 12:35-44 and Luke 20:41–21:4).

14. E.g., Burton H. Throckmorton, Jr., ed., *Gospel Parallels: A Comparison of the Synoptic Gospels*, 5th ed. (Nashville: Thomas Nelson, 1992); Kurt Aland, ed., *Synopsis of the Four Gospels*, 6th ed. (Stuttgart, Germany: United Bible Societies, 1983).

15. See Mark Goodacre, *The Case Against Q: Studies in Markan Priority and the Synoptic Problem* (Harrisburg, Pa.: Trinity Press International, 2002).

16. See the helpful analysis in Graham N. Stanton, *The Gospels and Jesus*, rev. ed., Oxford Bible Series (New York: Oxford University Press, 2002), 6-12.

17. See also Acts 2:46-47; 3:2; 16:5; 17:11; 19:9.

18. Cadbury, *Making of Luke-Acts*, 103, 216-17.

19. *On Writing History*, 58; cf. Thucydides, *History* 1.22; Cadbury, *Making of Luke-Acts*, 184-93.

20. See Marion L. Soards, *The Speeches in Acts: Their Content, Context, and Concerns* (Louisville: Westminster John Knox Press, 1994).

21. See William S. Kurz, *Reading Luke-Acts: Dynamics of Biblical Narrative* (Louisville: Westminster John Knox Press, 1993).

22. See Steve Walton, *Leadership and Lifestyle: The Portrait of Paul in the Miletus Speech and 1 Thessalonians*, Society for New Testament Studies Monograph Series 108 (Cambridge: Cambridge University Press, 2000); Richard I. Pervo, *Dating Acts: Between the Evangelists and the Apologists*

(Santa Rosa, Calif.: Polebridge Press, 2006), 111-35. Pervo argues at length (51-147) for Acts' *direct literary dependence* on the terminology and ideas of the Pauline letter-corpus, despite the lack of explicit citation.

23. On David and Solomon (son of David), see Luke 1:32, 69; 2:1-11; 6:1-5; 11:31; 18:38-39; 20:41-44; Acts 2:25-36; 4:24-26; 7:45-50. On Moses and Elijah, see below.

24. Luke 2:22; 5:14; 16:29, 31; 20:28, 37; 24:27, 44; Acts 3:22; 6:11, 14; 7:37; 13:39; 15:1, 5, 21; 21:21; 26:22; 28:23.

25. David P. Moessner, *Lord of the Banquet: The Literary and Theological Significance of the Lukan Travel Narrative* (Harrisburg, Pa.: Trinity Press International, 1989).

26. Ibid., 84.

27. Craig A. Evans, "Luke 16:1-18 and the Deuteronomy Hypothesis," in *Luke and Scripture: The Function of Sacred Tradition in Luke-Acts*, ed. C. A. Evans and J. A. Sanders (Minneapolis: Augsburg Fortress, 1993), 121-39.

28. Cf. James A. Sanders, "The Ethic of Election in Luke's Great Banquet Parable," in *Luke and Scripture*, ed. Evans and Sanders, 106-20.

29. Evans, "Luke 16:1-18 and the Deuteronomy Hypothesis," 133; cf. Robert W. Wall, " 'The Finger of God': Deuteronomy 9.10 and Luke 11.20," *New Testament Studies* 33 (1987): 144-50; "Martha and Mary (Luke 10:38-42) in the Context of a Christian Deuteronomy," *Journal for the Study of the New Testament* 35 (1989): 19-35.

30. Cf. Thomas L. Brodie, "Towards Unraveling Luke's Use of the Old Testament: Luke 7:11-17 as an Imitatio of 1 Kings 17:17-24," *New Testament Studies* 32 (1986): 247-67.

31. Brodie also argues that Luke models Jesus' heading toward Jerusalem in 9:51-56 after 2 Kgs 1:1–2:6, though Jesus declines to call down fire from heaven Elijah-style ("The Departure for Jerusalem [Luke 9:51-56] as a Rhetorical Imitation of Elijah's Departure for Jordan [2 Kgs 1:1–2:6]," *Biblica* 70 [1989]: 96-109).

32. MacDonald, *Does the New Testament Imitate Homer?*; "Luke's Eutychus and Homer's Elpenor: Acts 20:7-12 and *Odyssey* 10-12," *Journal of Higher Criticism* 1 (1994): 5-24; "The Ending of Luke and the Ending of the *Odyssey*," in *For a Later Generation: The Transformation of Tradition in Israel, Early Judaism, and Early Christianity*, eds. Randal A. Argal, Beverly A. Bow, and Rodney A. Werline (Harrisburg, Pa.: Trinity Press International, 2000), 161-68.

33. MacDonald, *The Homeric Epics and the Gospel of Mark* (New Haven, Conn.: Yale University Press, 2000), 189.

34. Ibid., 188; cf. 174-75.

35. See summary of these cases and criteria for "mimetic" analysis in MacDonald, *Does the New Testament Imitate Homer?*, 1-15, 146-51; cf. also MacDonald, "Paul's Farewell to the Ephesian Elders and Hector's Farewell to Andromache: A Strategic Imitation of Homer's *Iliad*," in *Contextualizing Acts: Lukan Narrative and Greco-Roman Discourse*, ed. Todd Penner and Caroline Vander Stichele (Atlanta: Society of Biblical Literature, 2003), 189-203.

36. MacDonald, *Homeric Epics and Mark*, 170 (emphasis added).

37. Karl Olav Sandnes, "*Imitatio Homeri?* An Appraisal of Dennis R. MacDonald's 'Mimesis Criticism'," *Journal of Biblical Literature* 124 (2005): 718.

38. MacDonald, *Homeric Epics and Mark*, 170.

39. Sandnes, "*Imitatio Homeri?*," 731.

40. Ibid., 732.

41. On "co-text," "inter-text," and "context" in interpreting Luke's narratives, see Joel B. Green, "Discourse Analysis and New Testament Interpretation," in *Hearing the New Testament: Strategies for Interpretation*, ed. J. B. Green (Grand Rapids, Mich.: Eerdmans, 1995), 183-95.

42. See the pioneering work by Charles H. Talbert, *Literary Patterns, Theological Themes, and the Genre of Luke-Acts*, Society of Biblical Literature Monograph Series 20 (Missoula, Mont.: Scholars Press, 1974). On Luke's penchant for parallel characters, see more recently Andrew C. Clark, *Parallel Lives: The Relation of Paul to the Apostles in Lucan Perspective*, Paternoster Biblical and Theological Monographs (Carlisle, England: Paternoster Press, 2001).

43. See Mary Rose D'Angelo, "Women in Luke-Acts: A Redactional View," *Journal of Biblical Literature* 109 (1990): 441-61; Turid Karlsen Seim, *The Double Message: Patterns of Gender in Luke-Acts* (Nashville: Abingdon Press, 1994).

44. See Barbara E. Reid, *Choosing the Better Part? Women in the Gospel of Luke* (Collegeville, Minn.: Liturgical Press, 1996); Spencer, *Dancing Girls, "Loose" Ladies, and Women of the "Cloth": Women in Jesus' Life* (New York: Continuum, 2004), 144-91.

45. Another possible married couple may be Dionysius and Damaris of Athens in Acts 17:34.

46. See Spencer, "Neglected Widows in Acts 6:1-7," *Catholic Biblical Quarterly* 56 (1994): 715-33.

47. Robert C. Tannehill, *The Narrative Unity of Luke-Acts: A Literary Interpretation*, 2 vols. (Philadelphia: Augsburg Fortress, 1986-90). A number of his essays are conveniently collected in *The Shape of Luke's Story: Essays on Luke-Acts* (Eugene, Ore.: Cascade Books, 2005).

48. Tannehill, *Shape of Luke's Story*, 185.

49. Ibid., 106-7; and *Narrative Unity*, vol. 1, 20-23.

50. Tannehill views Israel's story in Luke and Acts as ultimately tragic (*Shape of Luke's Story*, 105-44).

51. Spencer, *The Portrait of Philip in Acts: A Study of Roles and Relations*, Journal for the Study of the New Testament Supplement 67 (Sheffield, England: Sheffield Academic Press, 1992), 131-35.

52. See Spencer, "The Ethiopian Eunuch and His Bible: A Social-Science Analysis," *Biblical Theology Bulletin* 22 (1992): 155-65.

53. See Charles H. Talbert, *Reading Luke: A Literary and Theological Commentary*, rev. ed. (Macon, Ga.: Smyth & Helwys, 2002), 117-19; Craig L. Blomberg, "Midrash, Chiasmus, and the Outline of Luke's Central Section," in *Studies in Midrash and Historiography*, ed. R. T. France and D. Wenham, Gospel Perspectives 3 (Sheffield, England: Journal for the Study

of the Old Testament, 1983), 233-48; Kenneth E. Bailey, *Poet and Peasant* (Grand Rapids, Mich.: Eerdmans, 1976), 79-85; cf. discussion in Evans, "Luke 16:1-18," 124-27.

54. Richard Pervo, "Israel's Heritage and Claims upon the Genre(s) of Luke and Acts," in *Jesus and the Heritage of Israel: Luke's Narrative Claim on Israel's Legacy*, ed. David P. Moessner (Harrisburg, Pa.: Trinity Press International, 1999), 131, 136.

55. Cf. discussion in Stanley E. Porter, "The Genre of Acts and the Ethics of Discourse," in *Acts and Ethics*, ed. Thomas E. Phillips (Sheffield, England: Sheffield Phoenix Press, 2005), 1-15.

56. Talbert, *Literary Patterns*, ch. 8; *Reading Luke*, 2-6; *Reading Luke-Acts in Its Mediterranean Milieu*, Novum Testamentum Supplement 107 (Leiden, Netherlands: Brill, 2003), 19-55; "The Acts of the Apostles: Monograph or 'Bios'," in *History, Literature and Society in the Book of Acts*, ed. Ben Witherington III (Cambridge: Cambridge University Press, 1996), 58-72.

57. L. C. A. Alexander, "Acts and Ancient Intellectual Biography," in *The Book of Acts in Its First Century Setting. Vol 1: Ancient Literary Setting*, ed. Bruce W. Winter and Andrew D. Clarke (Grand Rapids, Mich: Eerdmans, 1993), 31-63.

58. Beverly Roberts Gaventa, *The Acts of the Apostles*, Abingdon New Testament Commentaries (Nashville: Abingdon Press, 2003), 27-44; cf. further discussion in chapter 2.

59. Miles's study focuses on the Hebrew Bible (*God: A Biography* [New York: Knopf, 1995]).

60. David E. Aune, *The New Testament in Its Literary Environment*, Library of Early Christianity (Philadelphia: Westminster Press, 1987), 116.

61. Darryl W. Palmer, "Acts and the Ancient Historical Monograph," in *Book of Acts in Its First Century Setting* vol. 1, ed. Winter and Clarke, 1-29.

62. Pervo, *Profit with Delight: The Literary Genre of the Acts of the Apostles* (Philadelphia: Fortress Press, 1987).

63. Robert Maddox, *The Purpose of Luke-Acts*, Studies of the New Testament and Its World (Edinburgh, Scotland: T&T Clark, 1982), 16; Brian S. Rosner, "Acts and Biblical History," in *Book of Acts in Its First Century Setting*. vol. 1, ed. Winter and Clarke, 80; cf. 65-82. In "Israel's Heritage," 130-31, Pervo also concedes the affinities of Luke's work with biblical historiography.

64. Gregory E. Sterling, *Historiography and Self-Definition: Josephos, Luke-Acts and Apologetic Historiography*, Novum Testamentum Supplement 64 (Leiden, Netherlands: Brill, 1992), 17.

65. Ibid., 297-310.

66. Ibid., 357-58.

67. Bonz, *Luke-Acts and Ancient Epic*, 56-60.

68. Ibid., 19.

69. Ibid., 25-29, 56-60.

70. Ibid., 26-27; cf. Sterling, *Historiography and Self-Definition*, 363.

71. Bonz, *Luke-Acts and Ancient Epic*, 26.

72. Sterling, *Historiography and Self-Definition*, 363.

2. THEOLOGICAL FOCUS: WHY WERE LUKE AND ACTS WRITTEN?

1. Mikhail M. Bakhtin, *The Dialogic Imagination,* ed. Michael Holquist (Austin: University of Texas Press, 1981), 276; cited in Patricia K. Tull, "Rhetorical Criticism and Intertextuality," in *To Each Its Own Meaning: An Introduction to Biblical Criticisms and Their Application,* rev. ed., eds. Steven L. McKenzie and Stephen R. Haynes (Louisville: Westminster John Knox Press, 1999), 167.

2. Tull, "Rhetorical Criticism," 167.

3. I use the "immersion" image in F. Scott Spencer, "Preparing the Way of the Lord: Introducing and Interpreting Luke's Narrative: A Response to David Wenham," in *Reading Luke: Interpretation, Reflection, Formation,* eds. Craig G. Bartholomew, Joel B. Green, and Anthony C. Thiselton, Scripture and Hermeneutics 6 (Grand Rapids, Mich.: Zondervan, 2005), 122. I have been a proponent of narrative-critical approaches to Luke and Acts and will continue to use them in the present study, while also engaging in more explicit theological analysis.

4. Cf. Spencer, "Acts and Modern Literary Approaches," in *The Book of Acts in Its First Century Setting.* Vol 1: *Ancient Literary Setting,* ed. Bruce W. Winter and Andrew D. Clarke (Grand Rapids, Mich.: Eerdmans, 1993), 381-414.

5. The classic study by Hans Conzelmann, *The Theology of St. Luke,* trans. Geoffrey Buswell (London: SCM, 1960), pins too much on Luke's preoccupation with the single issue of the delay in Christ's return. In "Preparing the Way," 118-21, I critique Wenham's emphasis on Claudius' expulsion of Jews from Rome (49 C.E.) as a principal event sparking Luke's work (cf. David Wenham, "The Purpose of Luke-Acts: Israel's Story in the Context of the Roman Empire," in *Reading Luke,* eds. Bartholomew, Green, and Thiselton, 95-102).

6. Jacob Jervell, *The Theology of Acts* (Cambridge: Cambridge University Press, 1996), 129. Jervell also concludes, "The very centre of Luke's theology is his notion about *God* as the God of Israel" (18; cf. 18-34).

7. Joel B. Green, *The Gospel of Luke,* New International Commentary on the New Testament (Grand Rapids, Mich: Eerdmans, 1997), 22.

8. Beverly Roberts Gaventa, *The Acts of the Apostles,* Abingdon New Testament Commentaries (Nashville: Abingdon Press, 2003), 26.

9. Jervell, "The Future of the Pasts: Luke's Vision of Salvation History and Its Bearing on His Writing of History," in *History, Literature and Society in the Book of Acts,* ed. Ben Witherington III (Cambridge: Cambridge University Press, 1996), 113.

10. Cf. also Cicero, *Nat. d.* 3.1.5–4.10; Louis H. Feldman, *Jew and Gentile in the Ancient World* (Princeton, N.J.: Princeton University Press, 1993), 177-78.

11. Feldman, *Jew and Gentile,* 177-200.

12. Ibid., 198.

13. See David W. Pao, *Acts and the Isaianic New Exodus* (Grand Rapids, Mich.: Baker Academic, 2002), 70-110.

14. See John B. F. Miller, *Convinced that God Had Called Us: Dreams, Visions, and the Perception of God's Will in Luke-Acts,* Biblical Interpretation 85 (Leiden, Netherlands: Brill, 2006); and John J. Pilch, *Visions and Healing in the Acts of the Apostles: How the Early Believers Experienced God* (Collegeville, Minn.: Liturgical Press, 2004).

15. Clinton E. Arnold, *Ephesians: Power and Magic* (Grand Rapids, Mich.: Baker, 1992), 18.

16. See Elaine Pagels, *The Origin of Satan* (New York: Random House, 1995).

17. See Howard Clark Kee, *Medicine, Miracle, and Magic in New Testament Times,* Society for New Testament Studies Monograph Series 55 (Cambridge: Cambridge University Press, 1986).

18. Susan R. Garrett, *The Demise of the Devil: Magic and the Demonic in Luke's Writings* (Minneapolis: Fortress Press, 1989), 4-5.

19. Ibid., 101.

20. Ibid., 61-109; Hans-Josef Klauck, *Magic and Paganism in Early Christianity: The World of the Acts of the Apostles,* trans. Brian McNeil (Edinburgh, Scotland: T&T Clark, 2000).

21. On these "macro-stories," see Marcus J. Borg, *Meeting Jesus for the First Time: The Historical Jesus and the Heart of Contemporary Faith* (New York: HarperSanFrancisco, 1994), 121-37.

22. Erich S. Gruen, *Diaspora: Jews Amidst Greeks and Romans* (Cambridge, Mass.: Harvard University Press, 2002), 2.

23. Robert C. Tannehill, *The Narrative Unity of Luke-Acts: A Literary Interpretation.* Vol 2: *The Acts of the Apostles* (Minneapolis: Augsburg Fortress, 1990), 93-94.

24. Wayne A. Meeks, *The First Urban Christians: The Social World of the Apostle Paul,* 2nd ed. (New Haven, Conn.: Yale University Press, 2003); Gerd Theissen, *The Social Setting of Pauline Christianity: Essays on Corinth,* ed. and trans. John H. Schütz (Philadelphia: Fortress Press, 1982).

25. Meeks, *First Urban Christians,* 51.

26. Meeks, *First Urban Christians,* 51-110, 117-31; Theissen, *Social Setting.*

27. See Spencer, *Dancing Girls, "Loose" Ladies, and Women of "the Cloth"* (New York: Continuum, 2004), 144-65.

28. Meeks, *First Urban Christians,* 55.

29. Spencer, *Dancing Girls,* 177-81.

30. Philip F. Esler, *Community and Gospel in Luke-Acts: The Social and Political Motivations of Lucan Theology,* Society for New Testament Studies Monograph Series 57 (Cambridge: Cambridge University Press, 1987), 221.

31. See Tannehill, *The Shape of Luke's Story* (Eugene, Ore.: Cascade Books, 2005), 286-97.

32. John Dominic Crossan and Jonathan L. Reed, *In Search of Paul: How Jesus's Apostle Opposed Rome's Empire with God's Kingdom* (New York: HarperCollins, 2004), 124-29, 167-77.

33. See J. M. Reynolds and R. Tannenbaum, *Jews and God-Fearers at Aphrodisias: Greek Inscriptions and Commentary,* Cambridge Philological

Society Supplement 12 (Cambridge: Cambridge Philological Society, 1987); Irina Levinskaya, *The Book of Acts in Its Diaspora Setting*, Vol. 5 of *The Book of Acts in Its First Century Setting*, ed. Bruce Winter (Grand Rapids, Mich.: Eerdmans, 1996), 51-82.

34. See Spencer, "Metaphor, Mystery, and the Salvation of Israel in Romans 9–11," *Review and Expositor* 103 (2006): 113-38.

35. See Warren Carter, *Matthew and Empire: Initial Explorations* (Harrisburg, Pa.: Trinity Press International, 2001); Richard A. Horsley, *Jesus and Empire: The Kingdom of God and the New World Disorder* (Minneapolis: Augsburg Fortress, 2003); Spencer, "'Follow Me': The Imperious Call of Jesus in the Synoptic Gospels," *Interpretation* 59 (2005): 142-53.

36. See Spencer, *What Did Jesus Do?: Gospel Profiles of Jesus' Personal Conduct* (Harrisburg, Pa.: Trinity Press International, 2003), 142-45.

37. Jack T. Sanders, *The Jews in Luke-Acts* (London: SCM, 1987); cf. Joseph B. Tyson, *Marcion and Luke-Acts: A Defining Struggle* (Columbia: University of South Carolina Press, 2006). Although appreciating that Luke-Acts highly values Old Testament law and prophecy as preludes to Christianity, Tyson argues (too sweepingly in my judgment) that Luke's work also "denigrates most ancient and contemporary Jews. For the most part, the Jewish people in Luke-Acts are cast in the role of opponents to Jesus and his followers" (128).

38. Jervell, *Theology of Acts*, 61.

39. Cf. 1 Pet 4:16; Pilch, *Visions*, 96.

40. Luke designates the Jesus movement "The Way" (*ho hodos*) in Acts 9:2; 18:25-26; 19:9, 23; 22:4; 24:14, 22; cf. 16:17.

41. Another example may be the Ethiopian eunuch, who "worshiped" (*proskyneō*) in Jerusalem (8:27); see discussion in Spencer, *The Portrait of Philip in Acts: A Study of Roles and Relations,* Journal for the Study of the New Testament Supplement 67 (Sheffield, England: Sheffield Academic Press, 1992), 158-72.

42. See Gaventa, *Acts*, 220-24, and further discussion in chapter 7.

PREFACE TO PART TWO

1. On Luke's theology of mission, see Eckhard J. Schnabel, *Early Christian Mission,* 2 vols. (Downers Grove, Ill.: InterVarsity, 2004), 1.729-35, 2.1497-1502; Robert L. Gallagher and Paul Hertig, eds., *Mission in Acts: Ancient Narratives in Contemporary Context,* American Society of Missiology Series 34 (Maryknoll, N.Y.: Orbis, 2004); David J. Bosch, *Transforming Mission: Paradigm Shifts in Theology of Mission,* American Society of Missiology Series 16 (Maryknoll, N.Y.: Orbis, 1991), 84-122; Donald Senior and Carroll Stuhlmueller, *The Biblical Foundations for Mission* (London: SCM, 1983), 255-79.

2. F. Scott Spencer, *Journeying Through Acts: A Literary-Cultural Guide* (Peabody, Mass.: Hendrickson, 2004).

3. PREPARING GOD'S MISSION IN JUDEA AND GALILEE

1. See Charles H. Talbert, *Reading Luke-Acts in Its Mediterranean Milieu,* Novum Testamentum Supplement 107 (Leiden, Netherlands: Brill, 2003), 65-77.

2. Cf. Frederick W. Danker, *Jesus and the New Age: A Commentary on St. Luke's Gospel,* rev. ed. (Philadelphia: Fortress Press, 1988), 31: "A cultured Greek might well have recalled the lament of the Greek poet Hesiod about the Age of Iron, that parent was unlike children and children unlike parent (*Works and Days* 182)."

3. See Joel B. Green, *The Gospel of Luke,* New International Commentary on the New Testament (Grand Rapids, Mich.: Eerdmans, 1997), 76-77; and discussion of "Displaced Exiles" and "Stratified Society" in chapter 2.

4. Isaiah 7:14, cited in Matthew 1:23, does not unambiguously predict a virginal conception. The Hebrew simply denotes that "a young woman (*'almah*) is with child and shall bear a son." Matthew follows the Greek version's (LXX), "Look, the virgin (*parthenos*) shall conceive and bear a son," which says nothing about the *means* of conception.

5. Cf. the restored lame man who "leaps" through the temple precincts in Acts 3:1-10. The summary statement—"For the man on whom this sign of healing had been performed was more than *forty years old*" (4:22, emphasis added)—provides a symbolic link with the ancient Israelites' *forty years* of wilderness wandering before reentering the promised land. See Spencer, *Journeying through Acts: A Literary-Cultural Reading* (Peabody, Mass.: Hendrickson, 2004), 55-57, 61-62.

6. Cf. Richard A. Horsley, *The Liberation of Christmas: The Infancy Narratives in Social Context* (New York: Crossroad, 1989).

7. Cf. David L. Tiede, "'Glory to Thy People Israel': Luke-Acts and the Jews," in *Luke-Acts and the Jewish People: Eight Critical Perspectives,* ed. Joseph B. Tyson (Minneapolis: Augsburg Fortress, 1988), 21-34.

8. My translation, reflecting the ellipsis: "I must be in/about the ... (*tois* [plural definite article]) of my Father." The traditional reading, "in my Father's *house*," in NRSV and other versions fills in the gap too specifically in my judgment.

9. On Luke's technique of "climactic parallelism," see Robert C. Tannehill, *The Narrative Unity of Luke-Acts: A Literary Interpretation.* Vol. 1: *The Gospel According to Luke* (Philadelphia: Augsburg Fortress, 1986), 216; Helmut Flender, *St. Luke: Theologian of Redemptive History* (London: SCM, 1967), 20-27.

10. See Spencer, *The Portrait of Philip in Acts: A Study of Roles and Relations,* Journal for the Study of the New Testament Supplement 67 (Sheffield, England: Sheffield Academic Press, 1992), 220-40.

11. Tiede, "The Gospel According to Luke," in *The HarperCollins Study Bible: New Revised Standard Version with the Apocryphal/Deuterocanonical Books,* rev. ed., gen. ed. Harold W. Attridge (New York: HarperCollins, 2006), 1767.

12. Jesus at prayer develops into a significant Lukan theme; cf. 5:16; 6:12; 9:18, 28; 11:1-2; 22:39-46; 23:34, 46; and discussion in chapter 4.

13. "I will tell of the decree of the LORD: He said to me, '*You are my son*; today I have begotten you'" (Ps 2:7, emphasis added); "Here is my servant, whom I uphold, *my chosen, in whom my soul delights*" (Isa 42:1, emphasis added).

14. Rom 5:12-21; 1 Cor 15:20-22, 45-49; Phil 2:5-8.

4. ESTABLISHING GOD'S MISSION IN GALILEE AND SURROUNDING AREAS

1. Around 19 C.E. Herod Antipas moved his principal residence from Sepphoris to Tiberias. On the two cities see John J. Rousseau and Rami Arav, *Jesus and His World: An Archaeological and Cultural Dictionary* (Minneapolis: Fortress Press, 1995), 248-51, 316-18.

2. On Bethsaida, see Rousseau and Arav, *Jesus and His World*, 19-24; on Herod Philip see Josephus, *Bib. Ant.*, 18.106-8; David C. Braund, "Philip," *Anchor Bible Dictionary* 5.310-11.

3. Not surprisingly, some early copyists altered the text to "the synagogues *of Galilee*." The more difficult reading of "Judea" is most likely the original; cf. Bruce M. Metzger, *A Textual Commentary on the Greek New Testament*, 2nd ed. (Stuttgart, Germany: German Bible Society, 1994), 114-15.

4. See Robert C. Tannehill, *The Shape of Luke's Story: Essays on Luke-Acts* (Eugene, Ore.: Cascade Books, 2005), 3-30; *Luke*, Abingdon New Testament Commentaries (Nashville: Abingdon Press, 1996), 90-95.

5. See Sharon H. Ringe, *Jesus, Liberation, and the Biblical Jubilee*, Overtures to Biblical Theology 19 (Philadelphia: Fortress Press, 1985).

6. The root *thrauō* denotes "literally *break in pieces*, as pottery," and may be used "figuratively . . . of persons broken in spirit by oppression" (Timothy and Barbara Friberg, *Analytical Lexicon to the Greek New Testament* [Grand Rapids, Mich.: Baker, 2000]). There is also a double emphasis on "sent" (*apostellō*) in Luke 4:18—the anointed figure in Isaiah is "sent" by the Spirit to "send" freedom to the broken/oppressed.

7. See F. Scott Spencer, *What Did Jesus Do? Gospel Profiles of Jesus' Personal Conduct* (Harrisburg, Pa.: Trinity Press International, 2003), 36-38.

8. According to Leviticus 13–14, lepers were numbered among "the unclean." By "cleansing" the leper, Luke's Jesus thus allows him to join God's people on the "Holy Way" through the wilderness.

9. On the distinction between "disease" and "illness" in medical anthropology, see John J. Pilch, "Sickness and Healing in Luke-Acts," in *The Social World of Luke-Acts: Models for Interpretation*, ed. Jerome H. Neyrey (Peabody, Mass.: Hendrickson, 1991), 190-200.

10. On the judicial role of the "Son of Man" figure, see Dan 7:9-14; Luke 21:27; 22:69; Acts 7:55-56.

11. Luke frequently uses "today" or "this day" (*sēmeron*) to mark God's significant work through Christ (see 2:11; 4:21; 5:26; 13:32-33; 19:5, 9; 23:43).

12. Some widows in the ancient world inherited substantial wealth, allowing them to live well after their husband's death. But many were not so fortunate. In Luke's writings, *chēra* (widow) usually identifies a poor, destitute widow. In the present scene, though we have no details about the bereaved widow's social status, the loss of her "only son" suggests a particularly desperate situation in "no-man's" land. See Spencer, "Neglected Widows in Acts 6:1-7," *Catholic Biblical Quarterly* 56 (1994): 715-33. But also see now the stimulating study stressing widows' potential "power" in Barbara E. Reid, "The Power of the Widows and How to Suppress It (Acts 6:1-7)," in *A Feminist Companion to the Acts of the Apostles*, ed. Amy-Jill Levine (London: T&T Clark International, 2004), 71-88.

13. David L. Tiede, "The Gospel According to Luke," in *The Harper-Collins Study Bible: New Revised Standard Version with the Apocryphal/ Deuterocanonical Books*, rev. ed., gen. ed. Harold W. Attridge (New York: HarperCollins, 2006), 1776.

14. For a trenchant critique of common misunderstandings regarding Jesus and "purity" issues, see Amy-Jill Levine, *The Misunderstood Jew: The Church and the Scandal of the Jewish Jesus* (New York: HarperSanFrancisco, 2006), 144-49, 172-77.

15. Barclay M. Newman, Jr., *A Concise Greek-English Dictionary of the New Testament* (Stuttgart, Germany: German Bible Society, 1993), 158-59.

16. Robert J. Karris, *Eating Your Way Through Luke's Gospel* (Collegeville, Minn.: Liturgical Press, 2006), 97-98.

17. See Karris, *Luke: Artist and Theologian* (New York: Paulist Press, 1985), 47-78; David B. Gowler, *Host, Guest, Enemy, and Friend: Portraits of the Pharisees in Luke and Acts*, Emory Studies in Early Christianity (New York: Peter Lang, 1991); Dennis E. Smith, "Table-Fellowship as a Literary Motif in the Gospel of Luke," *Journal of Biblical Literature* 106 (1987): 613-38.

18. See Spencer, "'Follow Me': The Imperious Call of Jesus in the Synoptic Gospels," *Interpretation* 59 (2005): 142-53.

19. On Herodian economics in Jesus' day, see K. C. Hanson and Douglas E. Oakman, *Palestine in the Time of Jesus: Social Structures and Social Conflicts* (Minneapolis, Minn.: Fortress, 1998), 99-129; Marianne Sawicki, *Crossing Galilee: Architectures of Contact in the Occupied Land of Jesus* (Harrisburg, Pa.: Trinity Press International, 2000), 27-30, 133-53; Sean Freyne, "Herodian Economics in Galilee: Searching for a Suitable Model," in *Modelling Early Christianity: Social-Scientific Studies of the New Testament in Its Context*, ed. Philip F. Esler (London: Routledge, 1995), 23-46.

20. See Guy D. Nave, Jr., *The Role and Function of Repentance in Luke-Acts*, Academia Biblica 4 (Atlanta: Society of Biblical Literature, 2002).

21. Cf. Acts 9:36-42 (Tabitha); 12:12-16 (Rhoda); 16:14-18 (Lydia; fortune-telling slave-girl); 18:1-3 (Priscilla).

22. See Spencer, *Dancing Girls, "Loose" Ladies, and Women of "the Cloth"* (London: Continuum, 2004), 108-43.

23. Matthew's Gospel identifies this figure as "Matthew the tax collector" (one of the Twelve; 9:9; 10:3), not Levi. Mark calls him "Levi son of Alphaeus" (2:14; the Twelve include a "son of Alphaeus" named James, 3:18). Luke's "Levi" has no direct tie with the Twelve.

24. Cf. Spencer, "'Follow Me'," 143-46.

25. Cf. Petr Pokorný, *Theologie der lukanischen Schriften*, Forschungen zur Religion und Literatur des AT und NT 174 (Göttingen, Germany: Vandenhoeck & Ruprecht, 1998), 182-85.

26. Cf. Richard B. Hays, *The Moral Vision of the New Testament: Community, Cross, New Creation. A Contemporary Introduction to New Testament Ethics* (New York: HarperCollins, 1996), 196-97; Spencer, *What Did Jesus Do?*, 253-56.

5. EXPANDING AND INTERPRETING GOD'S MISSION ON THE WAY TO JERUSALEM

1. David B. Gowler, *What Are They Saying About the Parables?* (New York: Paulist Press, 2000), 102. For a detailed analysis of specific parables, see John R. Donahue, *The Gospel in Parable* (Minneapolis: Fortress Press, 1988); Bernard Brandon Scott, *Hear Then the Parable: A Commentary on the Parables of Jesus* (Minneapolis: Fortress Press, 1989); Arland J. Hultgren, *The Parables of Jesus: A Commentary* (Grand Rapids, Mich.: Eerdmans, 2000); William R. Herzog II, *Parables as Subversive Speech: Jesus as Pedagogue of the Oppressed* (Louisville: Westminster John Knox Press, 1994); Kenneth E. Bailey, *Poet & Peasant and Through Peasant Eyes: A Literary-Cultural Approach to the Parables of Luke*, combined ed. (Grand Rapids, Mich.: Eerdmans, 1990).

2. Jesus refers to Sodom, Chorazin, Bethsaida, Capernaum, Tyre, and Sidon in 10:13-15 in denouncing unrepentant cities; but he does not visit these places on this journey.

3. Barclay M. Newman, *A Concise Greek-English Dictionary of the New Testament* (Stuttgart, Germany: German Bible Society, 1993), 147.

4. Cf. the Isaianic servant's determination: "I have set my face like flint" (Isa 50:7); David L. Tiede, "The Gospel According to Luke," in *The Harper-Collins Study Bible: New Revised Standard Version with the Apocryphal/Deuterocanonical Books*, rev. ed., gen. ed. Harold W. Attridge (New York: HarperCollins, 2006), 1783.

5. Cf. Josephus, *J. W.* 2.232-45; *Ant.* 15.118-36; 18.29-30.

6. Modern English versions vary in reading "seventy" or "seventy-two" messengers in Luke 10:1, 17, reflecting the uncertainty among textual critics. Cf. Roger L. Omanson, *A Textual Guide to the Greek New Testament* (Stuttgart, Germany: German Bible Society, 2006), 127-28: "The external [manuscript] evidence is almost evenly divided," and "the factors that are significant for evaluating the internal evidence are ambiguous."

7. Some Jewish groups, like the Sadducees and perhaps these "lawyers," considered only the Torah (Genesis-Deuteronomy) as authoritative Scripture, relegating the prophetic books to secondary status.

8. On this woman's physical disability and other aspects of her characterization, see Mikeal C. Parsons, *Body and Character in Luke and Acts: The Subversion of Physiognomy in Early Christianity* (Grand Rapids, Mich: Baker Academic, 2006), 83-95; Frances Taylor Gench, *Back to the Well:*

Women's Encounters with Jesus in the Gospels (Louisville: Westminster John Knox Press, 2004), 84-108.

9. Cf. Jacob Jervell, "The Divided People of God: The Restoration of Israel and Salvation for the Gentiles," in *Luke and the People of God: A New Look at Luke-Acts* (Minneapolis: Augsburg, 1972), 41-74.

10. Charles H. Cosgrove, "The Divine *Dei* in Luke-Acts: Investigations into the Lukan Understanding of God's Providence," *Novum Testamentum* 26 (1984): 168-90.

11. This story of the man with dropsy in 14:1-6 parallels that of the bent-over woman in 13:10-17. In both cases, Jesus heals on the Sabbath and defends himself by appealing to the common practice of tending to one's ox on the Sabbath (leading it to water [13:15], rescuing it from a well [14:5]).

12. On the consummation of God's kingdom envisioned as a wedding/marriage feast, see Isa 62:1-9; Matt 9:14-15; 22:1-10; 25:1-13; Luke 5:33-35; John 2:1-11; Rev 19:6-9; 22:17.

13. See Richard L. Rohrbaugh, "The Pre-Industrial City in Luke-Acts: Urban Social Relations," in *The Social World of Luke-Acts: Models for Interpretation*, ed. Jerome H. Neyrey (Peabody, Mass.: Hendrickson, 1991), 125-49.

14. See Kenneth E. Bailey, *Poet & Peasant* (Grand Rapids, Mich.: Eerdmans, 1976), 161-69.

15. On "limited goods," see the following in *Social World of Luke-Acts* (ed. Neyrey): Bruce J. Malina and Neyrey, "Honor and Shame in Luke-Acts: Pivotal Values of the Mediterranean World," 28-32; Douglas E. Oakman, "The Countryside in Luke-Acts," 159.

16. See Halvor Moxnes, "Patron-Client Relations and the New Community in Luke-Acts," in *Social World of Luke-Acts*, ed. Neyrey, 241-68.

17. In some extracanonical "gospels," Jesus says something similar to his disciples about God's kingdom being within/among them; see *Oxyrhyncus Papyrus* 654.2 and *Gospel of Thomas* 3, 113; Burton H. Throckmorton, Jr., *Gospel Parallels: A Comparison of the Synoptic Gospels*, 5th ed. (Nashville: Thomas Nelson, 1992), 140.

18. Warren Carter renders *basileia theou* as "empire of God" and interprets Matthew's story of God's empire (kingdom) revealed in Christ as a "counternarrative" to Roman imperial theology. See *Matthew and Empire: Initial Explorations* (Harrisburg, Pa.: Trinity Press International, 2001); *Matthew and the Margins: A Sociopolitical and Religious Reading*, Bible and Liberation Series (Maryknoll, N.Y.: Orbis, 2000).

19. See F. Scott Spencer, "Neglected Widows in Acts 6:1-7," *Catholic Biblical Quarterly* (1994): 718-21, 724-26.

20. See Walter Bauer, William F. Arndt, F. Wilbur Gingrich, and Frederick W. Danker, *A Greek-English Lexicon of the New Testament and Other Early Christian Literature*, 2nd ed. (Chicago: University of Chicago Press, 1979), 848.

21. See John Dominic Crossan, *The Historical Jesus: The Life of a Mediterranean Jewish Peasant* (New York: HarperCollins, 1991), 266-69.

22. The term *perilypos* connotes deep struggle and distress. Mark uses it of Jesus' anguish in Gethsemane regarding his imminent death: "He

. . . began to be distressed and agitated. And he said to [his disciples], 'I am deeply grieved [*perilypos*], even to death'" (Mark 14:33-34; cf. 6:26; Matt 26:38).

23. Some manuscripts stress that Jesus especially considered the man's distress (*perilypos*): "Jesus looked at (*idōn*) him, *who had become sad/ distressed* (*perilypon*), and said . . ." (18:24). Cf. 7:13 where Jesus "looked at" (*idōn*) a grieving widow and "had compassion for her."

24. Cf. Parsons, *Body and Character*, 97-108.

25. In an earlier parable, Jesus placed the "lost" son in a "distant country (*chōran makran*)," in Gentile territory (with pig farming, 15:13-15). The identical location in the present parable may thus hint at the Gentile mission as well as the protracted period of delay before Christ's return.

26. Securing a never-ridden mount suggests Jesus' unique role as Israel's Messiah and perhaps his total consecration to God (cf. Num 19:2; Deut 21:3; 1 Sam 6:7).

27. Cf. Spencer, *Dancing Girls, "Loose" Ladies, and Women of "the Cloth"* (London: Continuum, 2004), 129-35.

6. DEFENDING GOD'S MISSION IN JERUSALEM AND JUDEA

1. Cf. also 20:39 where "some of the scribes" tell Jesus he "has spoken well." Typically, however, the scribes in Luke resist Jesus.

2. Cf. N. T. Wright, *Jesus and the Victory of God* (Minneapolis: Augsburg Fortress, 1996), 502-7.

3. In this parable of the wicked tenants, Jesus represents the vineyard owner's (God's) "beloved son" and "heir" whom the tenants reject and kill (20:13-15).

4. For a counterview arguing that Luke does envision "the death of Jesus as an atoning event," see David P. Moessner, "The 'Script' of the Scriptures in Acts: Suffering as God's 'Plan' (*boulē*) for the World for the 'Release of Sins'," in *History, Literature and Society in the Book of Acts,* ed. Ben Witherington III (Cambridge: Cambridge University Press, 1996), 218-50.

5. Tacitus, *Ann.* 15.44; Josephus, *Ant.* 18.63.

6. Some early manuscripts lack this statement. For a detailed discussion supporting its authenticity and analyzing its meaning, see Raymond E. Brown, *The Death of the Messiah from Gethsemane to the Grave: A Commentary on the Passion Narratives in the Four Gospels,* 2 vols., Anchor Bible Reference Library (New York: Doubleday, 1994), 1.179-90.

7. At first blush, Jesus' reproof of his disciples' swordplay during his arrest (22:49-51) seems at odds with his recent advice that "the one who has no sword must sell his cloak and buy one" (22:36). It is doubtful, however, that Jesus urges his followers literally to purchase swords. For when they pipe up like schoolchildren—"Lord, look, here are two swords"— Jesus promptly dismisses their enthusiasm. "It is enough," he says (22:38), with stinging irony: how could a single pair of swords possibly fend off Roman military attack? Jesus' point seems simply to alert his disciples of

their need to prepare for persecution that looms ominously on the horizon. See F. Scott Spencer, *What Did Jesus Do?: Gospel Profiles of Jesus' Personal Conduct* (Harrisburg, Pa.: Trinity Press International, 2003), 233-34.

8. Acts 4:1-22; 7:2-53; 21:40–22:21; 22:30–23:10; 24:10-21; 25:8-12; 26:1-29. See discussion of Paul's forensic defense speeches in chapter 7.

9. Cf. John Dominic Crossan, *Who Killed Jesus? Exploring the Roots of Anti-Semitism in the Gospel Story of the Death of Jesus* (New York: Harper-Collins, 1995), 160-69.

10. On burial customs in Jesus' environment, see Byron R. McCane, *Roll Back the Stone: Death and Burial in the World of Jesus* (Harrisburg, Pa.: Trinity Press International, 2003).

11. "Minor" characters, in terms of the relatively small amount of space devoted to them, can still carry "major" significance in the story. Cf. Elizabeth Struthers Malbon, *In the Company of Jesus: Characters in Mark's Gospel* (Louisville: Westminster John Knox Press, 2000), 189-225.

12. The passive "was torn" with an unspecified subject/agent implies the providential action of God (the "divine passive").

13. On *boulē tou theou* (purpose/plan of God) in Luke and Acts, see Robert C. Tannehill, *The Narrative Unity of Luke-Acts: A Literary Interpretation*. Vol. 1: *The Gospel According to Luke* (Philadelphia: Augsburg Fortress, 1986), 1-3; John T. Squires, *The Plan of God in Luke-Acts*, Society for New Testament Studies Monograph Series 76 (Cambridge: Cambridge University Press, 1993).

14. Some early manuscripts lack this statement. For a thorough discussion supporting its authenticity and expounding its meaning, see Brown, *Death of the Messiah*, 2.971-81.

7. HIGHLIGHTING GOD'S MISSION FROM JERUSALEM TO THE "ENDS OF THE EARTH"

1. On Paul's imprisonment in Acts 21–28, see Matthew L. Skinner, *Locating Paul: Places of Custody as Narrative Settings in Acts 21-28*, Academia Biblica 13 (Atlanta: Society of Biblical Literature, 2003); Brian Rapske, *The Book of Acts and Paul in Roman Custody*. Vol. 3 of *The Book of Acts in Its First Century Setting*, ed. Bruce Winter (Grand Rapids, Mich.: Eerdmans, 1994).

2. See Lev 23:15-21; Deut 16:9-12; Tob 2:1; 2 Macc 12:31-32; *Jub.* 6.17-22; Philo, *Decal.* 46-49.

3. Luke's citation strategically cuts off at Joel 2:32, just before the prophet proceeds to pronounce *judgment* against the foreign nations for scattering God's people (3:2-12).

4. On women in Acts see F. Scott Spencer, *Dancing Girls, "Loose" Ladies and Women of "the Cloth": Women in Jesus' Life* (London: Continuum, 2004), 144-91; Ivoni Richter Reimer, *Women in the Acts of the Apostles: A Feminist Liberation Perspective*, trans. Linda M. Maloney (Minneapolis: Fortress Press, 1995). Priscilla is, however, cited before her husband Aquila in 18:18, 26, perhaps suggesting her greater prominence and authority.

5. Cf. Spencer, "Wise Up, Young Man: The Moral Vision of Saul and Other *neaniskoi* in Acts," in *Acts and Ethics,* ed. Thomas E. Phillips, New Testament Monographs 9 (Sheffield, England: Sheffield Phoenix Press, 2005), 34-48.

6. Cf. Spencer, *Dancing Girls,* 144-65.

7. See C. K. Barrett, "Light on the Holy Spirit from Simon Magus (Acts 8.4-25)," in *Les Actes des Apôtres: Traditions, Rédaction, Théologie,* ed. J. Kremer; Bibliotheca Ephemeridum Theologicarum Lovaniensium 48 (Paris-Gembloux: Duculot, 1979), 281-95.

8. See Spencer, *The Portrait of Philip in Acts: A Study of Roles and Relations,* Journal for the Study of the New Testament Supplement 67 (Sheffield, England: Sheffield Academic Press, 1992), 26-87.

9. Ibid., 128-87; Spencer, "The Ethiopian Eunuch and His Bible: A Social-Science Analysis," *Biblical Theology Bulletin* 22 (1992), 155-65; Mikeal C. Parsons, *Body and Character in Luke and Acts: The Subversion of Physiognomy in Early Christianity* (Grand Rapids, Mich.: Baker Academic, 2006), 123-41.

10. On the concurrent "double vision" technique linking two figures together in Acts, see 9:1-18; 10:1-23, 30-33; 11:4-14; Robert C. Tannehill, *The Narrative Unity of Luke-Acts: A Literary Interpretation.* Vol. 2: *The Acts of the Apostles* (Minneapolis: Augsburg Fortress, 1990), 116.

11. Cf. studies by Ronald D. Witherup, "'Functional Redundancy' in the Acts of the Apostles: A Case Study," *Journal for the Study of the New Testament* 48 (1992): 67-86; "Cornelius Over and Over Again: 'Functional Redundancy' in the Acts of the Apostles," *Journal for the Study of the New Testament* 49 (1993): 45-66.

12. On narrative viewpoint in Luke's writings, see William S. Kurz, *Reading Luke-Acts: Dynamics of Biblical Narrative* (Louisville: Westminster John Knox Press, 1993), 39-131.

13. Cf. Beverly Roberts Gaventa, "The Acts of the Apostles," in *The HarperCollins Study Bible: New Revised Standard Version with the Apocryphal and Deuterocanonical Books,* rev. ed., ed. Harold W. Attridge (New York: HarperCollins, 2006), 1883-84.

14. Strangely, James identifies Peter as "Simeon" in Acts 15:14. Although "Simeon" approximates Peter's given Jewish name ("Simon"), this form is not applied to Peter anywhere else in Luke's writings. On a literary level, it may suggest some symbolic link with the "Simeon," who prophesied in Luke's birth narrative about God's providing "a light for revelation to the Gentiles" through the Christ child (2:32).

15. On the strategic importance of this Amos citation in Acts' narrative, see Robert Wall, "Israel and the Gentile Mission in Acts and Paul: A Canonical Approach," in *Witness to the Gospel: The Theology of Acts,* ed. I. Howard Marshall and David Peterson (Grand Rapids, Mich.: Eerdmans, 1998), 449-52.

16. Since meat was much less affordable and available in the ancient world than in modern Western societies, many would only have it during special religious festivals. "The poor in fact rarely ate meat; the occasions when they did tended to be cultic, whether public or private" (Wayne A.

Meeks, *The First Urban Christians: The Social World of the Apostle Paul*, 2nd ed. (New Haven, Conn.: Yale University Press, 2003), 69.

17. See the trenchant discussion in Gaventa, *The Acts of the Apostles*, Abingdon New Testament Commentaries (Nashville: Abingdon, 2003), 220-25.

18. A common term in Acts emphasizing unity and harmony among God's people (1:14; 2:46; 4:24; 5:12; 8:6; 15:25). At times it also refers to united *opposition* against God's work (7:57; 18:12; 19:29). Outside these several uses in Acts, *homothymadon* appears only once elsewhere in the New Testament (Rom 15:6).

19. See especially Gal 2:13. On the distinct accounts of the Jerusalem Conference in Galatians 2 and Acts 15 and questions of historicity and intertextuality , see Paul J. Achtemeier, *The Quest for Unity in the New Testament Church: A Study in Paul and Acts* (Philadelphia, Pa.: Fortress Press, 1987); C. K. Barrett, "Paul: Councils and Controversies," in Martin Hengel and C. K. Barrett, *Conflicts and Challenges in Early Christianity*, ed. Donald A. Hagner (Harrisburg, Pa.: Trinity Press International, 1999), 42-74; Richard I. Pervo, *Dating Acts: Between the Evangelists and the Apologists* (Santa Rosa, Calif.: Polebridge Press, 2006), 79-96.

20. Perhaps related to a Nazirite vow of dedication (Num 6:1-21), involving abstinence from drinking wine and from cutting one's hair (cf. Judg 13:4-5; 1 Sam 1:11; Luke 1:15).

21. Ironically, Paul recalls in the present defense speech his earlier witness and approval of Stephen's execution (Acts 20:20). Paul now eerily finds himself in a precarious situation much like Stephen's.

22. The mob cry against Paul—"Away with such a fellow from the earth! For he should not be allowed to live" (Acts 22:22)—evokes memory of the crowd's shouts against Jesus—"Away with this fellow . . . Crucify, crucify him" (Luke 23:18-21). On the temple inscription warning of death for Gentile trespassers into the inner courts, see Josephus, *J. W.* 5.193-94; 6:124-26; *Ant.* 15.417; Philo, *Embassy* 212.

23. On the rhetorical dimension of Paul's forensic defense speeches in Acts, see Alexandru Neagoe, *The Trial of the Gospel: An Apologetic Reading of Luke's Trial Narratives*, Society for New Testament Monograph Series 166 (Cambridge: Cambridge University Press, 2002), 175-218; Jerome H. Neyrey, "The Forensic Defence Speech and Paul's Trial Speeches in Acts 22–26: Form and Function," in *Luke-Acts: New Perspectives from the Society of Biblical Literature Seminar*, ed. Charles H. Talbert (New York: Crossroad, 1984), 210-24.

24. Curiously neither Acts nor Paul's letters spell out the precise motives for Saul/Paul's persecution of the early church or his major bones of contention with Jesus and his gospel. It's likely, however, that before his "revelation" of Jesus Christ (Gal 1:12-16) he regarded belief in a "crucified Messiah" as particularly offensive and scandalous (cf. 1 Cor 1:18-25).

25. Although Paul mentions no specific Old Testament text here, his testimony that the risen Christ "would proclaim light both to our people and to the Gentiles" echoes his citation of Isa 49:6 in Acts 13:47: "For so the Lord has commanded us, saying, 'I have set you to be a light for the Gentiles, so that you may bring salvation to the ends of the earth.'"

SELECTED BIBLIOGRAPHY

Barrett, C. K. *A Critical and Exegetical Commentary on the Acts of the Apostles.* 2 vols. ICC. London: T&T Clark International, 1994-98.

Bartholomew, Craig G., Joel B. Green, and Anthony C. Thiselton, eds. *Reading Luke: Interpretation, Reflection, Formation.* Scripture and Hermeneutics 6. Grand Rapids, Mich.: Zondervan, 2005.

Bovon, François. *Luke the Theologian: Fifty-five Years of Research (1950-2005).* 2nd rev. ed. Waco, Tex.: Baylor University Press, 2006.

Cadbury, Henry J. *The Making of Luke-Acts.* London: SPCK, 1961.

Clark, Andrew C. *Parallel Lives: The Relation of Paul to the Apostles in the Lucan Perspective.* Paternoster Biblical and Theological Monographs. Carlisle, England: Paternoster Press, 2001.

Culpepper, R. Alan. "The Gospel of Luke." In *The New Interpreter's Bible.* Vol. 9. Nashville: Abingdon Press, 1995: 1-490.

Danker, Frederick W. *Jesus and the New Age: A Commentary on St. Luke's Gospel.* Rev. ed. Philadelphia: Fortress, 1988.

Darr, John A. *On Character Building: The Reader and the Rhetoric of Characterization in Luke-Acts.* Literary Currents in Biblical Interpretation. Louisville: Westminster John Knox Press, 1992.

Esler, Philip F. *Community and Gospel in Luke-Acts: The Social and Political Motivations of Lucan Theology.* Society for New Testament Studies Monograph Series 57. Cambridge: Cambridge University Press, 1987.

Evans, Craig A. and James A. Sanders. *Luke and Scripture: The Function of Sacred Tradition in Luke-Acts.* Minneapolis: Fortress Press, 1993.

Fitzmyer, Joseph A. *The Gospel According to Luke I-IX: A New Translation with Introduction and Commentary.* Anchor Bible 28. Garden City, N.Y.: Doubleday, 1981.

———. *The Gospel According to Luke X-XXIV: A New Translation with Introduction and Commentary*. Anchor Bible 28A. Garden City, N.Y.: Doubleday, 1985.

Garrett, Susan R. *The Demise of the Devil: Magic and the Demonic in Luke's Writings*. Minneapolis: Fortress, 1989.

Gaventa, Beverly Roberts. *The Acts of the Apostles*. Abingdon New Testament Commentaries. Nashville: Abingdon Press, 2003.

Green, Joel B. *The Gospel of Luke*. New International Commentary on the New Testament. Grand Rapids, Mich.: Eerdmans, 1997.

———. *The Theology of the Gospel of Luke*. Cambridge: Cambridge University Press, 1995.

Jervell, Jacob. *Luke and the People of God. A New Look at Luke-Acts*. Minneapolis: Augsburg, 1972.

———. *The Theology of the Acts of the Apostles*. Cambridge: Cambridge University Press, 1996: 61.

Johnson, Luke Timothy. *The Acts of the Apostles*. Sacra Pagina 5. Collegeville, Minn.: Liturgical Press, 1992.

———. *The Gospel of Luke*. Sacra Pagina 3. Collegeville, Minn: Liturgical Press, 1991.

Karlsen Seim, Turid. *The Double Message: Patterns of Gender in Luke-Acts*. Nashville: Abingdon Press, 1994.

Keck, Leander E., and J. Louis Martyn. *Studies in Luke-Acts: Essays Presented in Honor of Paul Schubert*. Nashville: Abingdon Press, 1966.

Kurz, William S. *Reading Luke-Acts: Dynamics of Biblical Narrative*. Louisville: Westminster John Knox Press, 1993.

Levine, Amy-Jill, ed., with Marianne Blickenstaff. *A Feminist Companion to the Acts of the Apostles*. Feminist Companion to the New Testament and Early Christian Writings 5. London: T&T Clark, 2004.

———. *A Feminist Companion to Luke*. Feminist Companion to the New Testament and Early Christian Writings 3. London: Sheffield Academic Press, 2002.

Marshall, I. Howard, and David Peterson, eds. *Witness to the Gospel: The Theology of Acts*. Grand Rapids, Mich.: Eerdmans, 1998.

Moessner, David P., ed. *Jesus and Israel's Heritage: Luke's Narrative Claim on Israel's Legacy*. Harrisburg, Pa.: Trinity Press International, 1999.

————. *Lord of the Banquet: The Literary and Theological Significance of the Lukan Travel Narrative*. Harrisburg, Pa.: Trinity Press International, 1989.

Neagoe, Alexandru. *The Trial of the Gospel: An Apologetic Reading of Luke's Trial Narratives*. Society for New Testament Studies Monograph Series 166. Cambridge: Cambridge University Press, 2002.

Neyrey, Jerome H., ed. *The Social World of Luke-Acts: Models for Interpretation*. Peabody, Mass.: Hendrickson, 1991.

Parsons, Mikeal C. *Body and Character in Luke and Acts: The Subversion of Physiognomy in Early Christianity*. Grand Rapids, Mich.: Baker Academic, 2006.

Parsons, Mikeal C., and Richard I. Pervo. *Rethinking the Unity of Luke and Acts*. Minneapolis: Fortress Press, 1993.

Penner, Todd, and Caroline Vander Stichele, eds. *Contextualizing Acts: Lukan Narrative and Greco-Roman Discourse*. Atlanta: Society of Biblical Literature, 2003.

Pervo, Richard I. *Dating Acts: Between the Evangelists and the Apologists*. Santa Rosa, Calif.: Polebridge Press, 2006.

Phillips, Thomas E., ed. *Acts and Ethics*. New Testament Monographs 9. Sheffield, England: Sheffield Phoenix Press, 2005.

Reid, Barbara E. *Choosing the Better Part? Women in the Gospel of Luke*. Collegeville, Minn.: Liturgical Press, 1996.

Reimer, Ivoni Richter. *Women in the Acts of the Apostles: A Feminist Liberation Perspective*. Trans. Linda M. Maloney. Minneapolis: Fortress Press, 1995.

Richard, Earl, ed. *New Views on Luke and Acts*. Collegeville, Minn.: Liturgical Press, 1990.

Robinson, Anthony B., and Robert W. Wall. *Called to Be Church: The Book of Acts for a New Day*. Grand Rapids, Mich.: Eerdmans, 2006.

Shepherd, William H., Jr. *The Narrative Function of the Holy Spirit as a Character in Luke-Acts*. Society of Biblical Literature Dissertation Series 147. Atlanta: Scholars Press, 1993.

Soards, Marion L. *The Speeches in Acts: Their Content, Context, and Concerns*. Louisville: Westminster John Knox Press, 1994.

Spencer, F. Scott. "Acts and Modern Literary Approaches." In *The Book of Acts in Its First Century Setting*. Vol. 1: *Ancient Literary Setting*. eds. Bruce W. Winter and Andrew D. Clarke. Grand Rapids, Mich.: Eerdmans, 1993: 381-414.

———. *Journeying through Acts: A Literary-Cultural Reading.* Peabody, Mass.: Hendrickson, 2004.

Talbert, Charles H. *Literary Patterns, Theological Themes, and the Genre of Luke-Acts.* Society of Biblical Literature Monograph Series 20. Missoula, Mont.: Scholars Press, 1974.

———, ed. *Luke-Acts: New Perspectives from the Society of Biblical Literature.* New York: Crossroad, 1984.

———. *Reading Luke-Acts in Its Mediterranean Milieu.* Novum Testamentum Supplement 107. Leiden, Netherlands: Brill, 2003.

Tannehill, Robert C. *Luke.* Abingdon New Testament Commentaries. Nashville: Abingdon Press, 1996.

———. *The Narrative Unity of Luke-Acts: A Literary Interpretation.* 2 vols. Minneapolis: Augsburg Fortress, 1986–1990.

———. *The Shape of Luke's Story.* Eugene, Ore.: Cascade Books, 2005.

Tuckett, C. M., ed. *Luke's Literary Achievement: Collected Essays.* Journal for the Study of the New Testament Supplement 116. Sheffield, England: Sheffield Academic Press, 1995.

Turner, Max. *Power From On High: The Spirit in Israel's Restoration and Witness in Luke-Acts.* Journal of Pentecostal Theology Monograph Series 9. Sheffield, England: Sheffield Academic Press, 1996.

Tyson, Joseph B. *The Death of Jesus in Luke-Acts.* Columbia: University of South Carolina Press, 1986.

———, ed. *Luke-Acts and the Jewish People: Eight Critical Perspectives.* Minneapolis: Augsburg Fortress, 1988.

———. *Marcion and Luke-Acts: A Defining Struggle.* Columbia: University of South Carolina Press, 2006.

Wall, Robert W. "The Acts of the Apostles." In *The New Interpreter's Bible.* Vol. 12. Nashville: Abingdon Press, 2002: 1-368.

Witherington, Ben, III, ed. *History, Literature and Society in the Book of Acts.* Cambridge: Cambridge University Press, 1996.